hip hop america

hip hop america

Stereo

87138-9

by nelson george

for my family

VIKING
Published by the Penguin Group
Penguin Putnam Inc., 375 Hudson Street, New York, New York 10014, U.S.A.
Penguin Books Ltd, 27 Wrights Lane, London W8 5TZ, England
Penguin Books Australia Ltd, Ringwood, Victoria, Australia
Penguin Books Canada Ltd, 10 Alcorn Avenue, Toronto, Ontario, Canada M4V 3B2
Penguin Books (N.Z.) Ltd, 182–190 Wairau Road, Auckland 10, New Zealand
Penguin India, 210 Chiranjiv Tower, 43 Nehru Place, New Delhi 11009, India

Penguin Books Ltd. Registered Offices:
Harmondsworth, Middlesex, England

First published in 1998 by Viking Penguin,
a member of Penguin Putnam Inc.

10 9 8 7 6 5 4 3 2 1

LIBRARY OF CONGRESS CATALOGING IN PUBLICATION DATA
George, Nelson.
Hip hop America / by Nelson George.
p.   cm.
Includes bibliographic references (p.   ) and index
ISBN 0 670 87153 2 (alk. paper)
1. Rap (Music)—History and criticism.   2. Hip-hop—United States.   3. Popular culture—
United States.   4. Music and society—United States.   I. Title.
ML3531.G46   1998
782.421649—dc21   98–23414

This book is printed on acid-free paper.

Printed in the United States of America
Set in Centaur
Designed by Mark Melnick

contents

introduction

IN THE '30S, ON ANY BALMY SUMMER EVENING THROUGHOUT THE rural South, the evening's entertainment—boxing—would usually begin with a battle royal. This regal name hardly describes the nature of the event. A gang of "colored" youngsters—ranging from adolescent to college age—gathered in a boxing ring for a blindfolded, no-holds-barred brawl. There were no weapons except fists, but the physical damage that ensued in the frenzy was monumental. The last man standing won a nominal prize that hardly compensated for the broken teeth and fractured bones resulting from these gang bangs.

To the (white) audiences who witnessed these battles royal, it was an appetizer for an entire night of manly action. Ernest Hemingway, that definer of all things American and masculine, used to organize battles royal for boxing events he hosted in his beloved Key West, Florida.

For the young black men who pummeled each other in the quest for a bit of spare change, it was a chance to prove their toughness to friends, rivals, and themselves. For the biggest and most brutal participants, it was a way to get paid and, in a weird way, flaunt the physical power that the white viewers otherwise feared in everyday life. For white audiences, the heated bout allowed them to see the blacks as comical figures whose most aggressive urges were neutered for their amusement.

At certain moments, when hip hop is at its most tragically comic, I can imagine it as a '90s battle royal, where young African-Americans step into an arena to verbally, emotionally, and, yes, physically bash each other for the pleasure of predominantly white spectators worldwide. Ralph

Ellison's description of a battle royal in *Invisible Man* could be a contemporary rap lyric: "I played one group against the other, slipping in and throwing a punch then stepping out of range while pushing the others into the melee to take the blows blindly aimed at me. The smoke was agonizing and there were no rounds, no bells at three minute intervals to relieve our exhaustion. The room spun round me, a swirl of lights, smoke, sweating bodies surrounded by tense white faces."

But most of the time I know, and I'm grateful, that this is the '90s, not the '30s. Battling may be essential to hip hop's evolution and the energy that keeps it dynamic, but its manifestations and effects are too complex and often contradictory for a single metaphor, no matter how resonant, to capture its essence. There is the will to battle, but other threads in its fabric involve fun, dance, literature, crime, sex, and politics—too many to simply say that hip hop means any one or even two things.

Think about this post-soul moment: One New York afternoon you're checking out that funky pop-jazz standard from 1975, "Mr. Magic" by Grover Washington, Jr., on the black oldies station KISS-FM. Then you move a few spots down the dial to the hip hop–oriented Hot 97 and hear the music from "Mr. Magic" sampled to create the backing track on "Candy Rain," a 1995 techno-R&B hit by a teenage vocal group named Soul for Real, most of whose members weren't born when "Mr. Magic" first appeared. In the post-soul era, shards of the black past exist in the present at odd and often uncomfortable angles to each other.

At its most elemental level hip hop is a product of post–civil rights era America, a set of cultural forms originally nurtured by African-American, Caribbean-American, and Latin American youth in and around New York in the '70s. Its most popular vehicle for expression has been music, though dance, painting, fashion, video, crime, and commerce are also its playing fields. It's a postmodern art in that it shamelessly raids older forms of pop culture—kung fu movies, chitlin' circuit comedy, '70s funk, and other equally disparate sources—and reshapes the material to fit the personality of an individual artist and the taste of the times.

In 1987, I wrote a book titled *The Death of Rhythm and Blues*, which looked at the transformation of black music within the white-dominated music industry from the '30s to the '80s. It was about music, but also business, the media, integration, politics, and the intersection of race and economics in contemporary America. It was a different way of telling the story of civil rights and the generation who fought for them on both sides of the color line. I ended that book with some pretty gloomy predictions about the diluting effects of assimilation, but I was able to point to some artists and producers who seemed to be following a different agenda, one more centered around the survival of a black culture. Now we know that rap music, and hip hop style as a whole, has utterly broken through from its ghetto roots to assert a lasting influence on American clothing, magazine publishing, television, language, sexuality, and social policy as well as its obvious presence in records and movies.

Hip Hop America looks at how hip hop's aesthetic was created, mutated, and affected America (and the world) in the three last decades of the twentieth century. The story goes way beyond the A&R offices of the music industry. It is about the society-altering collision that has taken place during the last two decades between black youth culture and the mass media, about the discovery (and maybe hijacking) of black youths as creators and consumers. It looks explicitly at how advertisers, magazines, MTV, fashion companies, beer and soft drink manufacturers, and multimedia conglomerates like Time-Warner have embraced hip hop as a way to reach not just black young people but *all* young people. It is an extension of the mid-'70s record biz concept of crossover, which itself was a by-product of Motown's '60s success; at some point Run-D.M.C. became the Supremes. But in the '90s, with more sophisticated marketing techniques and more complicated motions across old racial boundaries, the payoffs are bigger than Berry Gordy could cash in on. Soul music in the '60s, which is so heavily sampled by rap, is literally the foundation that the post-soul generation stands on yet, at the same time, subverts and even ridicules. And like soul, in many ways, it no longer belongs to its very creators. How did that happen—again?

I'm offering no single organizing theory for understanding hip hop because I think its use, and therefore its meaning, has evolved too rapidly since it first appeared on the national radar screen back in 1979. However, I do hope to communicate a sense of its multifaceted, interactive nature. It might be that to truly understand hip hop you need a masters degree in sociology, a stint in the joint, *and* an intimate understanding of African rhythm. Whenever I think I know enough, there's another twist in the saga, another way to see this culture and the country that spawned it.

Hip Hop America is a kind of love-hate story, both between hip hop and America and between hip hop and me. I was in college when I first wrote about hip hop, a skinny kid who wanted to be a rock critic because it seemed like fun. Now there is gray in my beard and I write about music not because it still obsesses me but because I can't escape it. Every time I read a piece attacking hip hop, its makers, and its audience, no matter how much truth it may contain, I get upset. The attacks, quite often from black people my age, are often indictments full of legitimate and well-articulated anger but no love. It's as if attacking hip hop is a way to unleash an often despicable racial and generational hatred.

Thinking generationally, it becomes increasingly clear to me why hip hop occupies such contested ground. Born in 1957, I am a late-cycle baby boomer. I missed the civil rights movement except as a elementary school observer, so those momentous events were as much a TV show for me as *McHale's Navy*. I was too young for the marches and too old for the demographic construction known as Generation X. Although I share many of hip hop's interests and have reported on its cultural frontiers for twenty years, it has always been as an affectionate older observer, not quite a peer. Motown 45s and rap 12-inches are *both* prized parts of my vinyl record collection. Standing in the psychic space between Berry Gordy and Russell Simmons is often a difficult place to be; at times I've felt trapped between the two very different visions of African-American self-expression that their companies, Motown and Def Jam, epitomize.

So while I love hip hop's spirit and rhythmic intensity, I often find myself at odds with some of its values and how those values are expressed. Because I did not grow up with hip hop as the dominating pop music of my childhood, I don't have the unvarnished devotion to it that younger writers do. Not only do I see its warts, I see how it could end as well. The Brits once boasted that the sun never set on the British Empire, but now they live under a perpetual cloud cover. At its peak, every powerful cultural movement feels unassailable, undeniable, and indestructible. And then one day it's a piece of nostalgia on AM radio.

In its third decade of existence, hip hop's influence is pervasive. While there are signs of weakness—its overwhelming dependence on major corporations for funding, its occasionally gleeful celebration of anti-social tendencies—it shows no signs of heading for the respirator anytime soon. Hip hop has outlived all its detractors and even surprised most ardent early supporters by always changing, and with each change, expanding its audience. It has outgunned punk, post-punk, New Wave, Rave, House, techno, and every other much-hyped musical form of the age. In 1986, I contributed to a book called *Fresh, Hip Hop Don't Stop*. And I don't see it stopping anytime soon.

Hip Hop America starts "back in the day"—the late '70s—when hip hop sprang off the uptown streets of New York City via block parties and jams in public parks, sparked by the innovative moves of a handful of pioneering men. Working under wild monikers, they called themselves "DJs," but they left in the dust any traces of the AM radio jocks who first popularized that term. On their wheels of steel Kool Herc, Afrika Bambaataa, and Grandmaster Flash staked out a loud, scratchy, in-your-face aesethetic that, to this day, still informs the culture. But it didn't come out of nowhere—no spontaneous generation of this deadly virus. The b-boys—the dancers, graffiti writers, the kids just hanging out—who carried the hip hop attitude forth were reacting to disco, to funk, and the chaotic world of New York City in the '70s. These b-boys (and girls) were mostly black and Hispanic. They were hip hop's first generation. They were America's first post-soul kids.

By that I mean they came of age in the aftermath of an era when many of the obvious barriers to the American Dream had fallen. Black people now voted wherever and whenever they wanted and attended integrated schools. They moved into new neighborhoods, took new career paths, hurried toward a future with a different set of assumptions from any minority kids in American history. Yeah, the old barriers were down—but new, more subtle ones were waiting in that much-heralded rainbow future.

Post-soul kids grew up with the Vietnam War. Their fathers came back with drugs and bad dreams—if they came back at all. As they grew up, both the black middle class and the black lower class expanded; they grew up with Wall Street greed, neo-con ideology, Atari Gameboys, crack, AIDS, Afrocentricity, and Malcom X as movie hero, political icon, and marketing vehicle. They saw Nelson Mandela walk out of jail and Mike Tyson walk in. Some say this is the first generation of black Americans to experience nostalgia. And it all showed up in the music.

B-boys were not the only products of the post-soul era. Buppies, those upwardly mobile enough to get into the newly opened doors at major white universities and corporate white collar gigs, were products of this new landscape too. Their interaction with hip hop is part of this story, as is the role of Caucasians in hip hop history. White America has been a big part of hip hop since the early '80s in a number of ways: as audience, creators, and financiers. In fact, many of the most important figures in its growth—Fab Five Freddie, Russell Simmons, Eazy-E—succeeded by making strong connections with white supporters of the music. Is this just a replay of the same coalition that doomed soul in the '60s? If it was, then the title of this book would be *The Death of Rhythm and Rap*. But, for important reasons it isn't.

There are two non-music driven threads that I think play crucial roles in the story of hip hop, by both affecting and reflecting it: drugs and basketball. It's no coincidence that hip hop germinated in the economics of Ronald Reagan's America and that rap seemed to draw on the same strength and vitality that crack sapped. On any given inner-city day, drug dealers—who commit crimes, make money, and influence street wardrobes—ply their destructive trade within feet of basketball courts where dreams of public glory, mad loot, and innovative, idiosyncratic style are dearly held. Sometimes the dealers and the players are the same people, men (and now women) torn between hoop dreams and immediate green. Sometimes they are friends, both stars in their local 'hood. We'll look at how the history of drugs and basketball travels a similar trajectory to hip hop.

Technology is also integral to this story. Trawling for new ways to apply technology, to hijack it, has taken place on small and large scales. Drug dealers were the first people outside the medical community to discover beepers; think where this useful, if invasive, communications tool has taken us today. At the opposite end of the scale, sampling technology changed *everything* about making records, creating a generation of producers for whom previous recordings are their primary tools of composition. Naturally, this raises questions about the nature of creativity and originality (to say nothing of the subtleties of copyright infringement), and it changes the relationship of the past to the present in ways that conventional historians might take notice. What is the past now?

Rap itself was also shaped by old forms and new modes of communication. Just as hip hop reinvented the role of sampling, music videos have altered hip hop. Once an underground music based on beats and rhymes, in the '90s hip hop is the most image-driven part of pop music. Videos sprang out of the era of the disco—and now rap stars have found the visual opportunity of a lifetime. Stylists and cinematographers now play an essential role.

Still, the music remains its core. *Hip Hop America* is actually the biography of two overlapping generations—"old school" hip hop people, who gravitated to the music right out of disco and funk (1977 to 1987), and the newer generation who have grown up with Run-D.M.C., Kurtis Blow, among others as the root of their musical culture. I focus on the crucial producers (Rick Rubin, Teddy Riley, Dr. Dre, Puff Daddy) and on the true stories of where they come from and what they went through to make it. I'm interested in the nature of rapping as art, both as an extension of African-American maleness and as a showcase for the art of verbal dexterity and storytelling.

It is also essential to understand that the values that underpin so much hip hop—materialism, brand consciousness, gun iconography, antiintellectualism—are very much by-products of the larger American culture. Despite the "dangerous" edge of so much hip hop culture, all of its most disturbing themes are rooted in this country's dysfunctional values. Anti-Semitism, racism, violence, and sexism are hardly unique to rap stars but are the most sinister aspects of the national character.

As in *The Death of Rhythm and Blues, Hip Hop America* does not offer a chronological account that tells you, in order, who cut what record, made what clothing deal, moved to what label, bought or sold what creation. Instead, I tell the stories of individuals who either perfectly reflect a particular trend, for better or for ill, or who contributed something special to the culture's growth. It's been said that African-American culture is the most marketable pathology in the world, but I hope this world is not that simpleminded or one-dimensional. Hip hop has brought America a new language of rhythm, speech, and movement that has inspired a generation to take to verse to say what was too long unspoken about this nation. If rap went away tomorrow, would the discussion disappear too? Or would it just come coded in an alternative form?

Hip Hop America is not the story of an embittered minority breaking out of the ghetto, or of a marginal culture, or of a passing fad. It chronicles a generation coming of age at a moment of extreme racial confusion—in these years since official apartheid was legislated out of existence and de facto segregation grew—who have been grappling with what equality means during the worst economic conditions for the under-class since the Depression. Hip hop is, as we'll see, the spawn of many things. But, most profoundly, it is a product of schizophrenic, post–civil rights movement America.

chapter 1
post-soul

I GOT SO MUCH TROUBLE ON MY MIND
(ON MY MIND)
I REFUSE TO LOSE
HERE'S YOUR TICKET
HEAR THE DRUMMER GET WICKED

>   —CHUCK D,
>   "WELCOME TO THE TERRORDOME"

THIS STORY BEGINS AS ANOTHER IS ENDING. THE FIRST STORY IS FULL OF
optimism and exalted ideas about humanity's ability to change through
political action and moral argument. The next story, the plot we're living
right now, is defined by cynicism, sarcasm, and self-involvement raised to
art. The turning point was the early '70s. Dashikis, platform shoes, and
Richard Nixon were still in vogue. The phase of the civil rights movement led by Dr. King, with its philosophy of nonviolence, its marchers in
starched white shirts and narrow ties, was already literally long dead. The
succeeding phase of angry, burn-baby-burn rhetoric was itself receding
as heroin's vicious grip, the mercenary diligence of FBI informants, and a
philosophy of benign neglect replaced liberal guilt as the engine of our
government's policy toward the poor. Street agitation for social change
was over. Now African-Americans could sit at the front of the bus and
downstairs at movie theaters. Now we could vote all over these United
States. Now black politicians set their sights on controlling City Hall in
big cities and small towns. Now ambitious black graduates of white colleges began slipping into corporate America's awkward, monied embrace.
    Dr. Martin Luther King's dream of civil rights as a way to open doors
of opportunity was working—for some. The '70s would spawn the first
graduating class of affirmative action babies. They weren't called buppies

(black urban professionals) yet—there weren't even yuppies yet—but these pioneers blazed trails for them. They walked through doors cracked open by dog-bitten marchers in the South and radical nationalists in the North. They were not smarter or more worthy than their parents; they were just better trained in the ways of white mainstream protocol, proud of their new clout and poised for frustrations more nuanced than African-Americans had ever confronted.

Starting in the '70s, the new black professionals had an opportunity to pursue their ambitions with a freedom previously unknown to African-Americans. But they were faced with a new conflict between maintaining loyalty to their generally white employers—protect that job!—and espousing a problack agenda that could endanger their jobs. Just because you're in doesn't mean you *fit* in. It's no wonder that the business magazine *Black Enterprise*'s July 1974 issue focused on hypertension, noting that six of the nation's twenty-three million victims were black, making it the number-one health risk for African-Americans.

This new black middle class—products of tokenism, affirmative action, and their own hard work—lived as most middle class Americans of the '70s. They moved to the suburbs, often to predominantly black enclaves like Teaneck, New Jersey; Baldwin Hills, California; and Silver Springs, Maryland. They dabbled in cocaine, seeking the slick rush and status its ingestion implied. The Cadillac, historic symbol of big money among African-Americans, slowly gave way to less ostentatious European luxury cars.

Corporations were, at last, looking at the black community with an eye to more than narrow recruitment. Along with the growth of black professionals came an acknowledgment by America's CEOs that there was money to be made in catering directly to the black masses. So the '70s saw the proliferation of "special markets" (i.e., black), divisions aimed at tapping the once ignored black consumer. In *Black Enterprise* during the '70s, one encounters the special markets euphemism used for hawking goods by General Foods, Johnson & Johnson, and sundry other American manufacturers. For the first wave of black corporate employees, special markets were often a velvet trap that guaranteed its employees the perks of mainstream American life (suburban living, credit cards, ski weekends) yet kept them segregated from their businesses' major profit centers and from any real shot at company-wide power. Becoming a vice president of special markets usually meant you had limited opportunity to shift to areas of distribution or production central to the core of whatever business or product you were hawking. The black executives too often found their most prominent role was to be trotted out in front of stockholders and noted in Equal Employment Opportunity Commission compliance reports.

Until the '70s, the recording industry wasn't really viewed as part of corporate America. During the rebellious '60s it had opened its doors to dopehead guitarists and bands advocating free love and left-wing ideology, which scared the mainstream to death. Ironically, the profits from the rock revolution music, and the expanded market it created, made small labels bigger and led to a consolidation of power within the business. Fueled by revenue generated by the Doors, the Rolling Stones, Jimi Hendrix, and sundry other counterculture musicians, the record industry became fat with cash and had to grow to keep up with demand, particularly in the areas of merchandising and distribution. The merger joining Warner-Reprise, Elektra-Asylum, and Atlantic in 1970 to form the WEA distribution system was symptomatic of the time.

The '60s rock stars imagined a better world to go along with the rhetoric, yet like most other aspects of our public life in the '70s, they lost their utopian vision and became fragmented into subgenres that lent themselves to highly targeted marketing. However, black music—which independent labels like Motown, Stax, and Chess had dominated since World War II—seemed an area of untapped growth for the corporate labels. What had been proven in the '60s, particularly by Motown, was that R&B-based music by black singers could easily be sold in massive quantities to white teens, creating a lucrative commercial-cultural crossover.

Just like General Motors and General Foods, CBS Records in 1971 (followed by Warner Bros., Polydor, RCA, ABC-Dunhill, and the other significant American record labels) opened special markets divisions. A few even had the guts to call themselves R&B divisions or, more boldly, "black music" divisions. In essence they were established to employ African-Americans to sell black popular music within their community and identify performers with "crossover" appeal. In terms of employment opportunities, salaries, and advances paid to artists, this was an important development worth celebrating. Black vice presidents abounded.

Lavish parties ensued. Soul singers, traditionally underpaid by the feisty labels that had nurtured R&B since World War II, enjoyed increases in contracts, recording budgets, and royalty rates. In the overall schemes of CBS, WEA, or RCA, these black music divisions were the farm teams, from which crossover stars, such as the O'Jays, Earth, Wind & Fire, and Michael Jackson, would be developed.

Of course this transition wasn't always smooth or without complications. Many older established soul stars couldn't adapt to the demands of the black music divisions, since the desire to reach pop consumers was always ever present. Many performers who had thrived in the old environment (including Tyrone Davis, Bobby Womack, and Candi Staton) floundered within these larger systems.

In addition, the black executives at these departments, like their counterparts at General Motors and Johnson & Johnson, were not given latitude to work on selling the "product" (as records are called in the industry) when it crossed over. With rare execptions, any ambitious black executive soon slammed into the high, thick ceiling that cut off his or her ability to grow and gain power. While the music wasn't as boxed in by race, the staff developing the music absolutely was.

The sad irony of these divisions was that they were on their way to becoming corporate fixtures at exactly the same moment that one of African-American pop music's least creative periods began—roughly between 1976 and 1981. Two factors contributed mightily to this malaise. The first was that, hoping for crossover, producers artifically reshaped and usually diluted the sound of the records recorded and released. In many instances, singles were released only with potential crossover paramount in the label's mind. The arc of a performer's career, the taste of black consumers, and the record's quality were often secondary. While the records were initially marketed by black music departments, their long-range success was decided by the white executives who worked the record at pop (i.e., white) radio. Often the artist got lost in the translation. The second factor was the rise of disco. Not that the disco movement was, per say, bad for black music—it was not. What hurt was the perception of disco inside record companies and the subsequent attitudes of many white music fans.

DISCO TO GO

For those too young to remember, there were once vinyl records. New. Unscratched. Smooth. You tore open the plastic wrapping, pulled it out of the white paper inner sleeve and the sturdy cardboard jacket cover and in your hand was a black vinyl circle with a hole in the middle. Around the hole was paper with a design and words printed upon it. You placed it on your turntable and through stereo speakers the music played just like a CD. Forgive my nostalgia—I still love vinyl.

Discotheque is a French word coined in the '50s to describe clubs where people went to enjoy recorded, not live, music. In America, people had always danced at bars and malt shops to music from jukeboxes. But paying a cover charge for this privilege was rare. At the dawn of rock 'n' roll popularity, radio disc jockeys like Alan Freed and Murray the K hosted "teeny bopper" parties where kids paid to see the jock, see an act lip-synch to their hit, and dance to records. TV stations then began recruiting local DJs to host televised versions of their parties, which is how Dick Clark's *American Bandstand* got started in Philly before its two-decade-long national run. In the following decade, dance crazes (the Twist, the Frug, the Mashed Potato, the Hully Gully) established dancing to records at clubs—then often refered to as "go-gos"—as regular features of big city nightlife. Still, outside the New York–Los Angeles axis most bars and clubs featured live "cover" bands that played faithful renditions of current hits and oldies.

Up until this point technology was simple—recorded music in clubs came from either 7-inch singles played at 45 revolutions per minute or 12-inch albums played at 33 rpm on a single turntable. But the transitional decade of the '70s brought a change here too.

What happened was that a small bit of technology labeled a "mixer" was developed. The mixer allowed club DJs to shift the sound fluidly from one turntable to another, so that the party continued in a seamless flow of sound. The entire American disco experience, which flowered underground before its mainstream discovery circa 1976, was predicated on this simple technological breakthrough.

The ripple effect was profound. The continuous-sound environment created an atmosphere that was more conducive to dancing, drinking, and generally expanding the aural horizons of the customers. Live bands lost work, which meant less experience and exposure for them, which led to fewer live bands in dance music, which, along with the synthesizer, would ultimately change the nature of dance music from the arrangement of musical instruments to the manipulation of synthetic or prerecorded sound.

The advent of the mixer also inaugurated the cult of the club DJ. The record spinners behind the mixes became increasingly creative and idiosyncratic in their use of music. The more ambitious jocks began asking record labels for longer versions of their favorite cuts. Salsoul, West End, Wing & a Prayer, and other small dance-oriented independent companies began catering to DJs and their audiences by manufacturing extended 12-inch singles with vocal and instrumental versions for club use only. As certain DJs and their approach to mixing records at their clubs became known, the dance labels (and later the majors) began recording their mixes and selling them. A Larry Levan, Tom Moulton, or other star disco DJ enhanced the appeal of a record in the way a Puff Daddy mix does in the '90s, but for a smaller, more select audience.

By 1974, the phrase "disco" had become accepted as an overall description for both the clubs and the music they popularized. In New York City, discos were defined by money, sex, and race: There were gay discos in the West Village; Studio 54, Zenon, and other glitzy midtown spots for the monied; black discos for middle-class blacks, including Leviticus and Othello's; grittier black spots such as Harlem's Charles's Gallery; and white workng class clubs dominated by Italian DJs in Brooklyn, Queens, and New Jersey. By 1975, *Rolling Stone* estimated that 2,000 discos were operating in America, with 200 to 300 in the New York area. On any given weekend in the Big Apple, 200,000 people were said to be partying at discos.

Very significant, but little appreciated outside the New York's Caribbean community at the time, was the introduction of the Jamaican "sound system" style to the city's party-going mix. Using their own versions of mixing boards, since the '60s DJs around Jamaica had given "back-a-yard" parties where the bass and drum pounded like jackhammers. The "dub" style of these mobile DJs stripped away melody to give reggae's deep, dark grooves throbbing prominence. In ganja-filled gatherings, pioneering sound-system DJs such as King Tubby, Prince Buster, and Duke Reid created massive, rumbling sounds that elevated them to a star status rivaling the club DJs in the States.

If the bass beat orientation wasn't enough of a signature, over time DJs began to "toast" or talk about their prowess as lovers or DJs on microphones during their performances. One toasting DJ, U Roy, enjoyed large sales in Jamaica and even enjoyed a number-one hit on the island with "Wear You to the Ball." However, at the time the magic art of mixing smoothly—which drove disco—and the subterranean assault of the reggae sound system were not viewed in the same light. Disco was a pop culture phenomenon. Dub was an ethnic music lauded outside its community by rock critics and few others. Yet a synergy between disco mixing, dub sounds, and toasting would ultimately provide the techniques and sensibilities that allowed the birth of "hip hop."

DISCO SUCKS

The road that disco traveled—from underground style to regional scene to national and international trend—is a cultural migration pattern at the heart of popular culture. How the cultural artifact itself is transformed by the journey can not be predicted. In the case of disco, from 1973 to 1976, the music identified with the clubs would morph into a distinct and, depending on the taste of the club DJ, rigid formula of rhythms and instrumentation. Initially, music played in discos was dominated by high-quality black dance music, with Kenny Gamble and Leon Huff's elegantly funky Philly Sound productions and the lush sounds surrounding Barry White's bass voice the artistic benchmarks. Unfortunately, the most distinctive elements of the Philly Sound and White's hits gave way to a redundant blend of hi-hat drum patterns, swirling string arrangements, Latin percussion breaks, and moronic lyrics that crystalized negatively in the public consciousness as "disco."

Mainstream culture discovered this music around 1975 with the sudden appearance of disco records on the pop charts. Seeing how this music was escaping—or crossing over from—the dance underground ignited a feeding frenzy among the major labels. Black artists, most of whom were to some degree dance-floor friendly, were either pushed toward disco by producers and label executives or went on their own in pursuit of the disco dollar. This resulted in some major hits (Johnnie Taylor's "Disco Lady," Peaches & Herb's "Shake Your Groove Thing," Diana Ross's "Love Hangover"). More typical were records in which great voices and bands were sublimated to big, unwieldy orchestra arrangements and lousy rhythms. Among the disco era's noteworthy abominations were Aretha Franklin's awful "La Diva"; the Ohio Players' equally putrid "Everybody Up," produced by disco star Van McCoy, showing an exciting funk band pitifully selling out; and the Spinners' goofy "Dancin' and Lovin'," supervised by hack disco producer Michael Zager. Aside from wasting precious vinyl, these kinds of records (and other equally worthless novelties such as Meco's "Theme from *Star Wars*" and the Ritchie Family's "Brazil") sparked an antidisco backlash that tainted all black pop.

All this horrible music inspired the phrase "Disco sucks" and, sadly, it was often used in ignorant attacks against black artists in general. Despite optimistic talk inside the recording industry that disco would help black performers reach broader audiences and more lucrative careers, a glance at the charts from the period reveals just the opposite.

The willingness of pop radio to play black artists, and in the process reach a wider audience, actually decreased during disco's peak years. Look at the number of recordings by black artists to make *Billboard*'s list of top 10 singles from 1973 to 1978: In 1973, thirty-six records moved from the black singles chart to the top 100 on the year-end pop chart. In the next two years, as disco began to enter the popular consciousness and crossover thinking gripped the music business, the numbers fell to twenty-seven in 1974 and twenty-eight in 1975. The bicentennial year saw a rise up to thirty, which suggested the pendulum was swinging back. But in 1977, which can be considered disco's peak year, the crossover number was a disastrous twenty-three, including a few black radio-driven disco cuts.

Another reflection of the criminal disrespect then granted black pop was the outcome of the R&B song category in the 1977 Grammy Awards. Of the five slots for nominations two each went to the nondisco compositions of two great African-American bands: Earth, Wind & Fire and the Commodores. Yet all four of their songs were passed over in favor of white Englishman Leo Sayer's lightweight disco ditty, "You make

Me Feel Like Dancing." In the uninformed minds of Grammy voters, who at the time were almost uniformly white record industry employees, disco and R&B had become interchangeable. The corporate crossover agenda and the confusion over disco's impact on black music led to a profound musical identity crisis that—with notable exceptions like George Clinton's Parliament-Funkadelic, Marvin Gaye, and Stevie Wonder—very few African-American stars could avoid.

Calculated crossover, the obsession with disco, and the increasing corporate control of American music spoke to its insularity and narrow-mindedness. This corporate reality was mirrored by simple geography. In the mid-'70s, most of the major labels were clustered together in Manhattan on Sixth Avenue or a block or two east or west. All were in walking distance from each other and from the decade's posh discos—Regine's, Zenon, and the immortal Studio 54. The city's hippest black disco, Leviticus, was farther down Sixth, just off Herald Square and two blocks from Madison Square Garden. It was a place where suits were required, cognac was the favored drink, and all the newly minted special market executives of corporate America did the hustle while trying not to sweat.

The group mindset that grew out of this concentration of record companies, and the tendency of its executives to make professional judgments while doing blow in restroom stalls, is one reason the most important musical-cultural phenomenon of the last twenty years took so long to go mainstream. And, in retrospect, that was very fortunate.

THE BOOGIE DOWN

YOU GOTTA GO OUT AND PAINT AND BE CALLED AN OUTLAW AT THE SAME TIME.

—LEE QUINONES, GRAFFITI ARTIST,
IN THE FILM *WILD STYLE*

In 1976, after two hundred years of American history, the country gave itself a big party. Even neurotic New York, then in the depths of a frightening economic crisis, was laced with patriotic bunting and speeches full of high-minded boilerplate about democracy. In the great harbor, vintage tall ships sailed in tribute to a warm, loving America that existed only in a history that ignored Native American genocide, black lynchings, and the hypocrisy that begins with the words "All men are created equal."

America's dark side is comprised of those who don't fit neatly into the official history—unneeded workers and uneducated youth whose contact with American government is usually limited to mean-spirited policing, their filthy, abandoned neighborhoods covered up by graffiti. The suburban revolution, the one supported by the government and celebrated by major industry (auto, oil, rubber, real estate), along with prejudice against blacks and Hispanics, had left large chunks of our big cities economic dead zones that mocked the bicentennial's celebration of America as the promised land.

In the mid-'70s, when we did allow for some brief flickers of retrospection followed by judgmental finger-pointing, no place in America was held up more consistently as a symbol of our pitiful urban priorities than the Bronx, particularly its southernmost section. Despite the presence of the newly renovated Yankee Stadium and a pennant-winning team, images of burned-out buildings that left scores of blocks lifeless dominated the media. On *The Tonight Show* Johnny Carson and countless comedians, whenever in need of a cheap laugh, invoked the borough's name for sad isn't-New-York-pathetic chuckles. The borough had a gang problem, a heroin problem, and, like the other outlying boroughs, no industrial base on which to rebuild.

Hollywood capitalized on the South-Bronx-as-hell image in a number of exploitive films: *The Warriors* played the area as home base for highly stylized gang warfare and in *Fort Apache: The Bronx* Paul Newman revived his sagging career by playing a cop with a heart of gold languishing in the savage South Bronx. A few years later in his best-seller *Bonfire of the Vanities* Tom Wolfe caricatured and wallowed in white New York's worst fear—getting lost in the Bronx.

Yet, in 1976, the real Bronx was far from a cultural wasteland. Behind the decay and neglect the place was a cauldron of vibrant, unnoticed, and quite visionary creativity born of its racial mix and its relative isolation. It was within its boundaries that the expressions we associate with hip hop—graffiti art, break dancing, MCing, and mixing—all have roots.

TAGS

Graffiti has been around since man encountered his first stone wall. Much of what we know of the world's early history comes from pictures and symbols scrawled centuries ago. As humans grew more sophisticated and paper became the primary tool of communication, walls became sacrosanct and defiling them with words was viewed as a throwback to primitive times, which is surely why what we call graffiti has endured. As a way to pass on unconventional views, mark turf, or just make a brightly colored mess, graffiti will never disappear. It's too useful and way too much fun.

After World War II, when the country was putting a squeaky clean face on its history and architecture, contemporary graffiti began its career as a formal civic nuisance, yet it remained a modest urban irritant until a Bronx-inspired explosion in the '70s allowed graffitists to refine themselves as artists. Early in the decade, a community of graffiti artists began gathering in and around Dewitt Clinton High in the Bronx. Clinton is located just blocks from a Transit Authority yard where out-of-service subway cars are stored. Scribbling obscenities and doggerel on and inside subway cars has always been a pastime of the young and idle, but armed with Krylon, Rustoleum, Red Devil spray paint, Flowmaster Ink—and a relatively new bit of technology, the felt-tipped pen— Clinton students and their peers used the tools of the painter, art student and teacher, not to defile but to create guerilla art.

Since this activity was as illegal as it was fun, these teens gave themselves flamboyant new names, called "tags," that protected them from discovery and gave their work an air of mystery. Phase 2, the tag of Clinton student Lonny Wood, became one of the first to gain citywide renown as it appeared on subway cars up and down the IRT line. The lanky, light brown Wood is African-American but many of the key early graffiti writers were Puerto Rican and white. The display of a distinctive personal approach quickly outstripped racial background as an delineator of style. Not that the racial identity of graffiti's makers mattered to the average New Yorker. Most presumed it was the work of idle, and likely dangerous, youths. In fact, for many residents the surge of graffiti in the city's public life crystalized their fears about New York's decline. It made them feel things were out of control and proved to be a very strong argument for moving to Jersey, Florida, and elsewhere.

As the decade continued, the Big Apple's subway cars and stations became as much canvases as transportation. With creativity and a total contempt for the peace of mind of their fellow citizens, graffiti artists from every borough marked, defaced, and tagged (their prefered verb) public transports with large, elaborate murals that splashed the writer's slang name in colorful, cartoony letters across the length of a car. During graffiti's heyday there didn't seem to be a single car in the system that went unscathed.

To those young or observant enough to see beyond the nuisance caused to travelers, graffiti was the voice of kids using spray paint and Magic Markers to scream for attention and make art. For Mayors John Lindsay and Abe Beame, graffiti was a public policy nightmare. For those looking for manifestations of rebellion, for some last grasp for public defiance before the '60s spirit completely died, graffiti fit the bill—which was why by 1973 a gallery exhibit of twenty giant canvases won tremendous media attention, though many of the reviews were condescending and some downright contemptuous of claims that graffiti was art.

Interest in graffiti as "high" art quickly burned out. A 1975 gallery exhibit in SoHo, with prices ranging from $1,000 to $3,000, was deemed a disappointment and the trend spotters, once hot on turning this public nuisance into a saleable commodity, turned their appraising eye elsewhere.

Hip hop is nothing, however, if not resilient. While snubbed by highbrow critics, graffiti art found new followers in cutting-edge circles. This was partly the doing of several art-savvy promoters, including a young entrepreneur-artist born Fred Braithwaite, but better known to the world as Freddie Love and eventually as Fab Five Freddie, who started organizing graffiti artists and promoting them on the downtown art scene then blossoming in tandem with the punk rock club scene. His point was that this living, aggressive art was a perfect fit with the same antiestablishment attitudes that ruled at punk landmarks like CBGBs. If punk was rebel music, this was just as truly rebel art.

This revival of interest owed much to several charismatic personalities, the most prominent of which was Samo, a thin, curiously dreaded Brooklyn renegade who became the art world's primitive savant under his real name, Jean-Michel Basquiat. Sort of Jimi Hendrix with a paint can, Basquiat lived an intense twenty-seven years in which he moved from aerosol cans to canvas to three-dimensional forms. No matter his materials, Basquiat retained the passion of his Brooklyn background, a color palate that suggested his family's Haitian roots, and an offkilter perspective that was pure bohemian.

Sadly, his career, a trajectory of rise and fall worthy a pop star and later mythologized in a film, not only mirrored Hendrix's embrace by London's rock scene in the '60s but foreshadowed the suffocating success rappers would later experience when they were loved too well by those their art was intended to make uncomfortable. Basquiat died of a heroin overdose in 1988. Eight years later a wonderfully comprehensive retrospective at New York's Whitney Museum confirmed his status as an enduring artist.

At the dawn of the '80s, writers and hipsters in Greenwich Village, SoHo, and lower Manhattan began making the connection between the visuals produced by graffiti artists such as Phase 2, Dondi White, and Lee Quinones and the music and dance styles filtering through New York's streets. In 1982, a young white underground filmmaker named Charlie Ahearn scraped together the money to shoot *Wild Style*, a vibrant little film that used Quinones, Braithwaite, and other street artists to connect the dots between Bronx street culture and the downtown folks who embraced it as rebel art. Because of its uptown-downtown synergy *Wild Style* remains one of the best feature-length film documents of hip hop.

We know now that graffiti's spray can aesthetics and street roots combined to have an impact on artists worldwide. As a sales tool, early hip hop party promoters always used graffiti artists to design their flyers and posters. Later, as the music soared into the public consciousness, there was a period in the '80s when nothing related to selling the culture or, often more precisely, pimping hip hop didn't use some clichéd version of graffiti art. It still influences protest art wherever Magic Markers and spray paint are handy—for example, the angry scrawls of revolutionaries in Mexico and the bored paint jobs of restless teens in rich Zurich. In the gang-ridden cities of America today, warnings about turf and threats of violence are communicated via graffiti.

Unfortunately, in this country the overuse of graffiti style in advertising has drained the expression of its immediacy. Graffiti's wonderful subway-car-long pieces can now look as dated as unlaced Adidas. Yet there is a youthful integrity and humor to them that reminds us in the jaded '90s that hip hop didn't start as a career move but as a way of announcing one's existence to the world.

BREAKING

In 1997, the GhettOriginals, an all-star break-dancing crew that included the seminal b-boys K-Swift (Kenny Gabbert) and Crazy Legs (Richie Colon), did an international tour sponsored by Calvin Klein. Whether appearing on concert stages, in malls near the C.K. section, or at schools, these very adult men (and a few women) amazed audiences with moves they'd developed in the bygone era of shell-toed Adidas and straight-legged Lee riders.

I saw them at P.S. 122 in the East Village. I saw them at City College in Harlem. I saw them in Los Angeles at the Beverly Center mall. And everytime they performed I relived that time when breakers moonwalked for quarters in Times Square and no club was cool if it didn't have some kid in the corner spinning on his head. Breaking's story, however, is not one that fits easily into anyone's nostalgic memory.

This is because breakers are both hip hop's truest believers and its bitterest commentators. Their expression was spawned, celebrated, exploited, and spit out by the pop culture trend machine in a few overheated years. Breaking was not the only way to dance to hip hop in the '80s. You could turn out a party doing the Freak, the Smurf, the Patty Duke, or even the Wop. They were all fun, relatively simple social dances. Breaking, in contrast, was spectacular, dangerous, and, in its heart, grounded in a committment to competition. While rappers with record deals verbalize their dedication to hip hop, there are dancers who have been spinning on their heads and groovin' to "It's Just Begun" for twenty years earning only infrequent clothing deals, scant exposure, and small compensation.

Breaking, like graffiti, has two different phases to its history. The first came in the early '70s and coincided with the disco era. What came to be labeled "breaking" was actually a medley of moves adapting a number of sources—the shuffling, sliding steps of James Brown; the dynamic, plat-formed dancers on Don Cornelius's syndicated *Soul Train* television show; Michael Jackson's robotic moves that accompanied the 1974 hit "Dancin' Machine"; the athletic leg whips and spins of kung fu movies—all of which were funneled through the imagination of black New Yorkers.

The first break dancers were, according to old schoolers (I'll explain about the old and new schools of rap historians later), street gang members who danced upright, had names like El Dorado, Sasa, Mr. Rock, and Nigger Twins, and were overwhelmingly African-American. For them, breaking was just a way to dance at the time, not a lifestyle expression. Within the African-American community it came and went. Perhaps breaking would have been forgotten altogether if it hadn't been for the almost religious zeal of Puerto Rican teenagers.

Trac 2 of the seminal breaking crew Starchild La Rock remembered breaking's two lives this way in *Rap Pages*:

> "See, the jams back then were still close to 90 percent Afro-American, as were most of the earliest B-boys, but they took breaking more like a phase, a fad. I say this because I had to see the reactions on their faces when we started doing it. They were like 'Yo, breaking is played out' whenever the Hispanics would do it. For them, the 'Fad' was over by the mid-'70s and most of them got into something else—writing, graffiti, DJing. But we were still pulling crowds regardless. Hispanic kids were always in the circles dancing. When [Puerto Rican] Charles Chase came out DJing, it was a big boost for us 'cause now we had a Latino representing. It didn't matter what the black kids would say—we had a Puerto Rican DJ and we were gonna dance our Puerto Rican way."

Hispanics made breaking competitive. Breaking crews, in the long tradition of urban gang culture, challenged other dancers to meet them at a specific playground, street corner, or subway platform. Armed with large pieces of cardboard or linoleum, not guns or knives, they formed a circle where, two at a time, breakers dueled each other, move matching move, until one of the crews was acknowledged victorious. Like basketball, it was a team sport but it relied on the skill of individuals within each crew. It was a highly stylized form of combat that echoed the kung fu moves of

Bruce Lee and the rituals of martial arts. The hat-to-the-back look, while practical for spinning dancers, also suggested a confrontational attitude that still flows through the culture. Grandmaster Flash once recalled, "When dancers actually started making contact, like doing jump kicks and kicking people on the floor, that's when the hat started going sideways. It was like, 'I ain't dancing with you, I'm gonna try to hurt you.' "

The fascination with breaking crested in 1984 with a PBS documentary, *Style Wars*, and three quickie Hollywood flicks: *Beat Street*, *Breakin'*, and *Breakin' 2: Electric Boogaloo*. In addition, breakers turned up in sundry music videos of the period, ranging from R&B diva Gladys Knight's "Save the Overtime (For Me)" and the arty funk band Talking Heads' "Once in a Lifetime."

The durable contribution of breaking, however, is how primarily Hispanic dancers made an impact on hip hop's musical development. Records such as Jimmy Castor's "It's Just Begun," the Incredible Bongo Band's "Apache," and Herman Kelly's "Dance to the Drummer's Beat" didn't become hip hop classics in a vacuum. DJs played them, and often unearthed them, but it was the dancers who certified them. It was their taste, their affirmation of certain tracks as good for breaking, and their demand to hear them at parties that influenced the DJ's and MCs who pioneered hip hop's early sound.

MAKING MUSIC

In the fall of 1992, I sat down with Afrika Bambaataa (Afrika Bambaataa Aasim), Kool Herc (Clive Campbell), and Grandmaster Flash (Joseph Saddler) for a *Source* cover story. Bambaataa came to the interview with a small posse of Zulu Nation disciples, some of whom came to provide moral support, others to interrupt the interview and irritate the hell out of me. Bambaataa is a large man with a brooding, authoritative presence; he rarely smiled during the interview and gave up very little personal detail on or off the record. Bambaataa is so guarded on these matters that his birth name is as hard to uncover as the digits on a Swiss bank account. Yet on subjects he cared about (break beat records, the Zulu Nation, world peace), Bambaataa waxed eloquent.

Kool Herc came with his sister, who'd convinced the reluctant DJ to participate. Herc is more a myth than a man for even the truest hip hop fan. Tapes of his performances are rare and, since the '80s, he has performed only sporadically. Up until that 1992 *Source* interview, Herc's last major public exposure had been limited to a small role in the 1984 movie *Beat Street* and some speaking on Terminator X's 1994 solo album. If Bambaataa was selectively guarded, Herc spoke freely about "back-in-the-day" but didn't say much about the contemporary scene other than communicate his dismay with gangsta rap.

Grandmaster Flash came alone and was the most open and affable of the trio, perhaps because he's had the most successful career. Occasionally Herc and Bambaataa ganged up on him. For example, the question of who created "scratching" caused a bit of tension at the table. Though many initially credited Flash with its invention, it is now generally acknowledged that Grand Wizard Theodore (for a time Flash's helper) was the first to scratch but that Flash refined and popularized it. As the three legends got more comfortable, whatever tension that existed between them subsided and the conversation flowed. The hard edge of personality differences softened because this trio had so much in common. Sometime during the administrations of Gerald Ford and Jimmy Carter, Herc, Bambaataa, and Flash had created hip hop's sonic side.

Born in Jamaica and familiar with his native land's sound systems, Kool Herc is the man who, instead of just playing hits in parks and discos, sought out obscure records and played the instrumental breaks, extending them until they sounded like new records. Instead of disco spinning, Herc was doing what he called "break" spinning. Playing at the Bronx's Club Hevalo and Executive Playhouse clubs or in parks, Herc used the breaks and bridges from the Incredible Bongo Band's "Apache" and "Bongo Rock," Jimmy Castor's "It's Just Begun," James Brown's "Sex Machine" and "Give It Up or Turn It Loose," Baby Huey and the Babysitters' "Listen to Me," Mandrill's "Fencewalk," the Average White Band's "Pick Up the Pieces," and other records to create hip hop's original sound and build his rep.

It was equally important that Herc enhanced his presentation by employing a pal named Coke La Rock as his master of ceremonies (or MC) to introduce and comment on the selection. La Rock didn't rap as we'd recognize it now but was more in the style of the Jamaican sound system toasters or black radio announcers hyping a record. Still, several of his pet party motivating slogans ("Ya rock and ya don't stop!" "Rock on my mellow!" "To the beat y'all!") would become rap staples. Some old schoolers assert that La Rock was the first hip hop rapper. I'm not sure, but certainly La Rock's claim is as strong as anyone's.

While Herc's contributions were essentially musical, Bambaataa's most important contribution to developing hip hop may have been sociological. As a teenage record collector, Bambaataa attended some of Herc's parties and realized he owned many of the same records. Though he started from the same musical base as Herc, Bambaataa would range wider and include bits of African, Caribbean, soca, and D.C. go-go music in his mixes, giving his work an electric, multiethnic quality. As a result, Bambaataa was labeled "the master of records" by his many acolytes. Ralph McDonald's "Jam on the Groove" and "Calypso Breakdown," Herman Kelly's "Dance to the Drummer's Beat," the Mohawks' "Champ," and Kraftwerk's "Trans-Europe Express" are among the cuts he discovered, featured, and added to the hip hop canon.

Bambaataa is as important for the myth he embodies as for his eclectic taste. Growing up in the Bronx River Projects, Bambaataa became a member of one of the city's biggest youth gangs, the Black Spades. The standard issue story is that in the mid-'70s gangs like the Black Spades faded out (which did happen) and that the various hip hop expressions (graffiti, breaking, Djing, rapping) filled the gap, effectively killing the gang culture of New York. But when asked if he thought hip hop killed New York's gangs, Bambaataa didn't subscribe to that theory: "The women got tired of the gang shit," he replied. "So brothers eventually started sliding out of that 'cause they had people that got killed." From a '90s perspective there is something almost quaint about the idea that gangs could be ended in a major city by the love of the members' women.

In 1974, Bambaataa founded the Zulu Nation, a collective of DJs, breakers, graffiti artists, and homeboys that filled the fraternal role gangs play in urban culture while deemphasizing crime and fighting. Many crucial figures of the period were early members of the Zulu Nation (the Rock Steady Crew, DJ-producer Afrika Islam); twenty-five plus years later, the organization survives, serving as a anchor for its members and a safety valve for the culture. Over the years many hip hop beefs have been squashed after Bambaataa and the Zulu Nation came in to mediate.

Grandmaster Flash is now best known as a recording artist, but there are several purely technical DJ breakthroughs that owe their existence to his hand-and-eye coordination. As I noted earlier, Grand Wizard Theodore may have introduced scratching but Flash is certainly the man who made it matter. "Punch phrasing"—playing a quick burst from a record on one turntable while it continues on the other—and "break spinning"—alternately spinning both records backward to repeat the same phrase over and over—are credited to Flash. Moreover, Flash was a showman. Unlike Herc, who primarily hovered over his turntables and didn't say much to the crowd, Flash mixed and entertained. Crowd-pleasing tricks associated with hip hop, such as spinning with his back to the turntables and using his feet to mix, first flowed from Flash's imagination.

Flash, who at one point trained to be an electrician, was always exploring and refining his equipment. Out of his curiosity came the "clock theory" of mixing where Flash was able to "read" records by using the spinning logo to find the break. He converted a Vox drum machine into what he labeled the "beat box," a device that allowed him to add additional percussion to a musical mix and anticipated the use of drum machines in making rap records.

Just as Herc had Coke La Rock as MC, Flash had an on and off relationship with a group of young MCs who would come to be known as the Furious Five. Between 1976 and 1980, in the years before they began recording, Flash often performed alongside some combination of Cowboy (Keith Wiggins), Melle Mel (Melvin Glover), Kidd Creole (Nathanial Glover), Rahiem (Guy Williams), and Mr. Ness aka Scorpio (Ed Morris). Because money was short for playing at a gig at 116th Street's Harlem World Disco or Times Square's Diplomat Hotel, there were often disputes over money and professionalism: sometimes all five MCs showed, sometimes none. At other times, another young MC, Kurtis Blow (Curtis Walker), worked the mike with Flash.

With Flash and without him, the members of what would become the Furious Five came up with some of the culture's benchmark phrases. "Cowboy came up with a lot of phrases," Flash recalled, "and had a powerful voice that just commanded attention." Cowboy is credited with inaugurating "Throw your hands in the air and wave them like you just don't care!" and "Clap your hands to the beat!" and "Somebody scream!"—three essential clichés of hip hop performance.

Kidd Creole and his brother Melle Mel were, according to Flash, "the first rhyme technicians. They were the first to toss a sentence back and forth. Kidd would say 'I,' Mel would say 'was,' Kidd would say 'walking,' Mel would say 'down.' They just tossed sentences like that all day. It was incredible to watch, it was incredible to hear."

I've mentioned that we now think of "old" and "new" schools of rappers and rap enthusiasts. What today is called "the old school" are the founding fathers, so to speak—a loose community of energetic, creative, and rather naive young people from the Bronx and upper Manhattan who reached adolescence in the '70s. Naive is the key and perhaps unexpected adjective in describing this crew, yet I think it is essential. I'm not simply saying they were naive about money. That's a trait they shared with nearly every young musician I've ever met (and no amount of much touted "street knowledge" ever protects them from rip-offs).

By naive, I mean the spirit of openhearted innocence that created hip hop culture. The idea of parties in parks and community centers, which is celebrated nostalgically as the true essence of hip hop, means that money was not a goal. None of the three original DJs—Herc, Flash, Bambaataa—expected anything from the music but local fame, respect in the neighborhood, and the modest fees from the parties given at uptown clubs or the odd midtown ballroom. They may have pocketed a couple hundred bucks here or there but none thought these gigs would make them millionaires. Like the graffiti writers and the break dancers, the old-school DJs, and those that quickly followed their lead, did it because it felt good and because they could.

For the graffiti artists, tagging walls wasn't about mimicking art school technique or being self-consciously postmodern. For the Hispanic breakers, it wasn't about simply departing from the traditions of Latin social dancing with its rigorous turns and upright posture. For DJs, break spinning wasn't some departure from the norms of soul music. For all these old schoolers it was an accidental, offhand discovery of a way to distinguish themselves in a very direct, self-contained, and totally controllable way. They needed simple tools to make their art and they made their own decisions about what made it good. Hip Hop was not a mass market concept. It was not a career move.

No one from the old school knew where hip hop would go and all were surprised, pleasantly and otherwise, by how it evolved. When I first experienced hip hop I was living out in a drug-scarred, working-class part of Brooklyn and, believe me, I had no idea I'd still care about it decades later.

chapter 2

hip hop wasn't just another date

LOTS OF TIMES, WE'D GIVE SHOWS WITH RAPPERS AND GET BIGGER CROWDS THAN IF WE HAD A GUY WITH JUST RECORDS. THE MORE FLYERS AND STICKERS AND POSTERS THAT YOU COULD GET YOUR NAME ON, THE MORE POPULAR YOU'D BECOME AS A RAPPER.

—RUSSELL SIMMONS, 1985

HIP HOP IS NOT MY LIFE BUT IT HAS BEEN A LARGE PART OF IT. THERE have been times I've loved it more than any woman. There have been times I hated it with the viciousness usually reserved for a cheating lover. Today, just past forty, I have affection for it but my love wavers sometimes, as if the culture was a woman I loved long ago, now can barely remember why, yet still can't forget.

When I was a teenager my family lived in Brooklyn's East New York neighborhood, a mix of extremely modest two-story homes, tenements, and rapidly decaying public housing. It was the mid-'70s and my mother, sister, and I lived on a narrow street across from an elementary school and, crucial to the romance, a schoolyard. It was the era of the mobile disc jockey, when guys with crates of records and big speakers would roll into a public park and, for nothing but the pleasure of publicly rocking two turntables, play for hours.

One hot summer night in about 1977 a mobile jock with gigantic speakers and an ego to match introduced me to two records that were not simply fly, progressive things to play but that twenty years later still help define hip hop. Kraftwerk's "Trans-Europe Express" and MFSB's "Love Is the Message" are musically as different as night and day, yet they spoke to something special and, perhaps, new in urban youth. "Trans-Europe Express" is a dense, hypnotic synthesizer extravaganza created by a quartet of rather robotic looking Germans; "Love Is the Message" is a lush, funky product of the strong, racially integrated, very human team of musicians behind the Sound of Philadelphia.

At the time I didn't know all these details and nuances. I wasn't a critic then, just a bespectacled kid who enjoying reading the credits on records. All I truly knew was that "Trans-Europe Express" and "Love Is the Message" was the music outside my window; the music of girls in culottes; the music of ballplayers with sweat bands on their wrist and tight shorts on their behinds; the music of people who voted for Jimmy Carter and feared Ronald Reagan. It was the music of people who did the hustle on asphalt in the summer wearing Converse and espadrilles; it was the music of a city that was nearly bankrupt yet found millions to remodel Yankee Stadium for an ungrateful George Steinbrenner; it was the music of an aesthetic in transition. What gave these records kinship then would have been called "disco," but what I didn't know in Brooklyn was that these records were clearing a path to another musical place altogether.

My true entry into hip hop happened in 1978 when I was an intern at the *Amsterdam News*, New York's largest black weekly. After college classes in Queens I'd take the subway up to the paper's Harlem headquarters and do whatever was asked of me—open mail, rewrite press releases, write listings of church activities. Eventually I graduated to reviewing bad movies, doing the occasional baseball profile, and a few hard-news reports. At lunchtime I'd grab a sandwich at the 125th Street Blimpie a few doors down from the Apollo. When it was warm, as it was on this particular day, I'd stand outside to watch Harlem stroll by.

I was ordering lunch when a teenager came strutting by with his ghetto blaster cranked to ten. It was a fairly typical urban experience at the time. Portable radio–cassette players had been laying waste to the sanctity of public spaces for years by then. However, my man wasn't playing urban contemporary powerhouse WBLS or jazzy RVR or disco 92. He was jamming a tape with a man talking very fast in rhyme over, I believe, "Love Is the Message."

For years I'd heard radio jocks like WBLS's Frankie Crocker and WWRL's Gary Byrd talk over the beat. I'd heard Isaac Hayes and Barry

White "rap" (talk slowly and seductively) on records. But never had I heard anything this fast with this cadence. It was music from another planet and I'd just been transported there. "Yo, yo!" I asked, "who's that?"

"Hollywood," he said over his shoulder, with a tone that clearly communicated *How stupid could a guy get?* So I went on the prowl, and after a little investigative reporting I found out that homemade tapes like his were floating around the five boroughs, forming an underground musical economy way before the music found its way onto vinyl.

The next time I heard DJ Hollywood's name was a few weeks later at a concert held at the City College gym. On the bill were R&B oldsters Harold Melvin & the Blue Notes (Teddy Pendergrass was already gone), a fine self-contained band titled Brainstorm, and Evelyn "Champagne" King, who I'd done my first freelance piece on in *Billboard*. What caught my eye was the line that said Hollywood and a guy named Lovebug Starski would be hosting the evening. Somehow—perhaps through the young black promoter Jerry Roebuck (who'd later make a mint organizing Black Expos around the country)—I scammed two tickets.

On that very evening in 1978, I saw the passing of the torch from live R&B singers and bands to DJs, MCs, and a crate full of records. The veteran R&B groups were adequate, and King, then a teenager who sang with more grit than technique, was actually quite entertaining. But, just like me, most of the several thousand teens filling this basketball gym hadn't come to hear King but Hollywood. With Lovebug Starski cutting up break beats on the wheels of steel (i.e., turntables), Hollywood performed between R&B sets, and every time he did, he cold rocked the party, inciting the black and Latino kids in the audience to dance with great intensity. Hollywood didn't just lead the crowd to chant, he flowed into elaborate rhymes full of slang and syncopation like "dip dip dap, so socialize, open up your ears and wiggle your behind." From my seat across the gym I could see Hollywood was a rotund young man with a beard, close-cut hair, and bountiful good-time energy. His voice was a large, commanding baritone—sort of a happy-go-lucky version of the strident, booming delivery we now associate with Public Enemy's Chuck D.

Equally impressive was Starski's mixing style. He played some of the same records I'd heard in my Brooklyn schoolyard but the effect was entirely different. Starski used smaller bits, blending them into bite-sized chunks of funk. The best example I recall is Earth, Wind & Fire's "Brazilian Rhyme (Interlude)" from the album *All 'n All*. The original lasted only one minute and thirty seconds, its chief feature a melodic, wordless Philip Bailey vocal and a funky beat that came in about halfway through. The cut was so sweet I'd always wished it went on longer. Starski satisfied my desire by mixing "Brazilian Rhyme" over and over so that it rarely petered out to its anticlimatic recorded ending. Every time Starski cut up the track the CCNY crowd went wild and nothing Harold Melvin, King, or Brainstorm did could compete.

That night I also saw, as I would countless times afterward, that where there was hip hop there was battling. Twice during that concert brawls broke out down among the portable plastic seats on the gym-level floor. I was sitting up in the bleachers above the action, so I had a great view of the flailing fists, angry faces, and occasional flying chair. I marveled that night at how easily the crowd handled each outburst. Whenever a skirmish broke out the kids scattered quickly away from the conflict. And just as soon as the beef ended the crowd moved back into its seats, back to the job of having fun as quickly as they'd scattered. The violence neither intimidated nor surprised them—it was the price of the ticket. This unwillingness to be scared away from a good time would be characteristic of the hip hop crowd, be it the threat of violence within a concert crowd or the imagery of violence coming from the stage.

My next crucial hip hop moment occured later in that same summer of 1978, when I accompanied my mentor, *Billboard* correspondent Robert "Rocky" Ford, on an expedition to the Bronx. He'd been tipped that Kool Herc would be spinning in the Robert Taft High schoolyard. Ford had been turned on to the incipient hip hop scene by the staff at Times Square's Downstairs Records. Young black DJs had been searching through their stalls for obscure records with vibrant, percussive breaks. One particular record, "Bongo Rock" by the Incredible Bongo Band, couldn't be kept in stock.

When we reached the South Bronx school a crowd of Hispanic and black kids was already loitering around. At dusk a van rolled up with Kool Herc and his crew. His boys dragged a couple of portable tables into the schoolyard through a hole in the fence, while Herc unscrewed a plate in the base of the light pole and hooked a heavy industrial extension cord to an outlet inside. Soon crates of records, large speaker cabinets, and DJ equipment were set up and Herc started getting busy.

According to Bambaataa, Flash, and others, Herc's Herculoid speakers were supposedly so powerful no one dared challenge him in a schoolyard contest. But I don't recall them being any louder than any other mobile jock's. What was striking was how attentive many in the crowd were. There were groups of young males just standing around Herc's turntables, studying his style, mentally detailing his moves and what records he played—recognizing, absorbing, and preparing to rip off his masterful style.

I wrote about what I saw that evening for the *Amsterdam News*. It was one of my first professional pieces, definitely my first hip hop article and surely one of the first published pieces on a scene still a year away from vinyl. It was headlined "DJ Herc and his 'B-beats.' "

It's a warm Friday evening in the Bronx, and at the Taft High School field people have come from all around to hear DJ Herc jam. He's tall, 26 and quietly calm in a manner that makes adolescent girls giggle. His reputation as a party master is unsurpassed in the South Bronx.

But unlike many of his DJ counterparts, Herc (real name Clive Campbell) isn't a rapid rapper who keeps your head spinning with patter. No, Herc is a musical innovator of the turntables. Not satisfied with simply playing the latest sides, Herc began excavating in record bins for cut outs—the older records that sell for $2.99 and less. His DJ experience told him that the young dancers of the Bronx loved "breaks" in records, sections that deviate from the melody to showcase energetic Latin percussion work.

So by interjecting into the middle of a current hit the percussive sections of old hits like Dennis Coffrey's "Scorpio" or a section from the obscure *Willie Dynamite* soundtrack album, Herc creates a lengthened and more exciting dance experience. The DJ's greatest discovery was "Bongo Rock" by the Incredible Bongo Band, which featured nothing but conga and bongo playing. That record has become so popular that the tag "B-beat" was hung on Herc's technique in its honor. "B-beat" was developed about four years ago and is now being used in various forms by other inner city DJs.

Herc and his Herculoids (the nickname of his helpers) now regularly appear at high school dances, proms and at Herc's own disco, the Sparkle at 1590 Jerome Avenue.

A major reason for Herc's use of old records is that "the kids don't like music that sounds processed" as much of the music aimed at discos unfortunately does. Another factor is that much contemporary dance music is styled to accommodate the slick twist and turns of the hustle. But today, as a young lady called "Shortstuff" commented, "the hustle is out and the freak is in." The freak is a loose, funky dance which, at its most aggressive, resembles a fast grind. The dance's movements are best accompanied by a heavy rhythm track that B-beats provide.

As Herc begins playing at Taft High several folks in the crowd begin to freak. The music gets better, and the number of dancers increases while Herc and his Herculoids monitor sophisticated Star Trek looking electronic equipment. Many people may not appreciate disco music, but it's interesting to realize that a whole generation of young males have been turned on to electronics through working DJ equipment. The black electricians of the future may be playing disco music in the park tonight.

Leaving aside how elderly reading the piece makes me feel, it is fascinating to note how the culture has evolved from that point. Somehow B-beats became hip hip. I reported that B-beats were "developed about four years ago," a fact Herc gave me, which meant that he'd been doing this kind of mixing as early as 1974. Finally my last point, about "black electricians" proved to be way too narrow. In fact, an interest in technology led many African-American teens from park parties to record engineering and, once they had the cash, to learning how to set up home studios and later to embracing sampling. This molding of technology to fit a black aesthetic became a hallmark of hip hop.

Later that summer I ran into Willie Gums, a young party promoter doing teen dance parties at the Renaissance Ballroom, a crumbling dance hall on Seventh Avenue near 130th Street. Back in the '30s the "Renny" was the site of big band dances and the home games of the first black-owned basketball team, the Harlem Rens.

By the '70s Gums's Rolls Royce Movement and other small promoters were using the antique ballroom to cash in on the disco craze, which, because of the presence and participation of the young DJs, MCs, and breakers, was quietly evolving into an uptown hip hop central. The Renny was a block or so away from Small's Paradise, another venerable Harlem nightspot (basketball legend Wilt Chamberlain once owned it). That old jazz showcase was also the site of early hip hop parties MCed by Hollywood, Kurtis Blow, and others.

Unfortunately for Gums, the Renny was also right around the corner from the Abyssinian Baptist Church, a pillar of middle-class Harlem since the '20s, the place where Reverend and Congressman Adam Clayton Powell, Jr. built a power base by mixing politics, God, and agitation. Powell had been dead for years when Gums started promoting his throwdowns, but an aggressive young minister made the Rolls Royce Movement his business.

Reverend Calvin Butts, an intense young man with the stern overbearing manner of a man twenty years his senior, saw Gums's parties as a catalyst for drug taking, teen fornication, and general licentiousness just a few steps away from the Abyssinian's august doors. Butts, with the blessing of the church's parishioners, campaigned to shut down the Rolls Royce Movement.

I met Gums at the *Amsterdam News* offices where he came to tell his story. I, of course, was sympathetic. The paper, of course, was not. Championing the rights of young black people to party versus the wishes of the most prestigious church in Harlem was a no-brainer for the *Amsterdam's* management. Not long after I met Gums, his Rolls Royce Movement was bounced from the Renny.

More important historically, Butts was now on record as an implacable foe of this new, young culture. Years later Butts would crush rap records in front of the Abyssinian to protest their negative messages and engage in heated verbal sparring with Ice-T and other hip hop heads. Over the years Butts would be an insistent spokesman of a damning view of the music and the culture that supported it. For Butts the Rolls Royce Movement was just round one.

Throughout 1979 black and Hispanic audiences attended hip hop functions at uptown clubs (Small's Paradise, Broadway International, Charles's Gallery) and Times Square venues (the Diplomat Hotel ballroom, Nell Gwyn's disco). I went along with Rocky Ford who, with *Billboard* coworker J. B. Moore, was contemplating recording an uptown MC.

They had their eye on Eddie Cheeba, a fixture in Harlem and the Bronx, although they'd also had conversations with Kurtis Blow (Curtis Walker), a handsome Harlem native who had done a lot of shows in Queens because of a City College classmate turned promoter named Russell "Rush" Simmons.

It turned out my friends weren't alone in monitoring hip hop's development. In October 1979, the first copies of the Sugar Hill Gang's "Rapper's Delight" appeared. Initially they were in white 12-inch sleeves with orange labels. No blue Sugar Hill label. No elaborate multicolored art design. It didn't matter that the package lacked glitz—they couldn't keep it in stores. At Birdel's record store on Nostrand Avenue in Bedford-Stuyvesant, a small, cluttered, classic R&B record store, copies were flying out the door. Joe Long, a friend of my mother's since I was a child, raved about how hot "Rapper's Delight" was. The same excitement swept the country and eventually the world.

For the record, the Fatback Band's "King Tim III (Personality Jock)," a rap record featuring King Tim (Tim Christopher), actually predated the Sugar Hill Gang's but, like a lot of R&B people at the time, its makers underestimated the genre's potential. Spring Records fumbled the ball by putting "King Tim III" on the B-side of a single called "You're My Candy Sweet." By the time Spring realized its mistake, it was too late.

Although the appearance of "Kim Tim III" certainly caused a ripple in hip hop circles, "Rapper's Delight" was a tidal wave. The song's title gave the uptown MCs the title "rappers," which has stuck, though many old schoolers disdain the rap label to this day and continue to favor MC.

Many of those same old schoolers, people who hadn't imagined there was commercial viability in what they did, began waking up to a sudden opportunity. It was in the wake of "Rapper's Delight" that Mercury Records agreed to release a record made by my friends Ford and Moore. The holiday novelty was called "Christmas Rappin' " and it began the recording career of MC Kurtis Blow.

While hip hop was being noticed outside uptown, I wasn't, uptown or anywhere else. Layoffs at the *Amsterdam News* meant no regular gig for me after college. Even worse, the editor-in-chief at *Billboard*, where I'd been doing freelance interviews, wrote a memo accusing me of writing "black English" and banned me from the periodical. So my two chief sources of income disappeared within months of each other.

What saved me was that Ford, who'd been writing a record industry news column for *Musician* magazine before making "Christmas Rappin'," passed the gig to me. I was also scribbling furiously for fanzines like *Rock & Soul* for $100 apiece. I made a cameo appearance as a background chanter on Kurtis Blow's gold single, "The Breaks (Part I)," which was fun, but for most of 1980 money was too tight to mention.

In December, Peter Keepnews, the editor of *Record World* magazine, then *Billboard*'s chief competitor, remembered my *Billboard* work and offered me the job of black music editor. With solvency now within reach, I joined *Record World* in January 1981 and immediately began integrating the emerging hip hop scene into our black music coverage—something *Billboard* wasn't doing. My enthusiasm for the culture led me to suggest that *Record World* reach out to Sugar Hill Records, the makers of "Rapper's Delight," about a "special"—essentially an advertorial in which industry figures got friends to place ads to celebrate their largeness. For a couple of weeks in the spring of 1981 I found myself shuttling out to Englewood, New Jersey, to put this package together.

The Sugar Hill "complex" was a two-story structure with all the charm of a suburban strip mall. Outside it was completely nondescript. Inside it was lined with basement-grade wood paneling and had office furniture of equivalent grace. The lighting was uneven and the carpet thin. Still, if the physical plant was worn, the building was alive. A couple of years before, its owners, Joe and Sylvia Robinson, had run an independent R&B label, All-Platinum, out of the same location. Unfortunately, the operation had gone bankrupt, a victim of the growth of black music departments and their corporate resources that I described earlier. The competition in the R&B marketplace of the '70s crushed All-Platinum and saw their biggest act, the Moments, end up with the PolyGram Records family under the name Ray, Goodman & Brown. Sylvia herself had a long history as a recording artist, hitting it with "Love Is Strange" as Mickey & Sylvia in 1957 and as a solo artist with "Pillow Talk" in 1973.

So, when she saw some rappers perform at a birthday party held at the Harlem World Disco on 116th Street, Sylvia seized upon it as a way to get back in business. The Robinsons, particularly Sylvia, understood that rap could not only sell but could also create real careers. Using the same studios where All-Platinum once recorded the Moments, Shirley & Company, and her own solo efforts, the Robinsons built the first hip hop empire—Sugar Hill Records. The company put together a great house band, national tours that featured only its acts, and the first rap albums built around artists and not 12-inch compilations. Over the next four years, following the success of "Rapper's Delight," Sugar Hill released a slew of the most important hip hop records ever made, including "The Message" and "The Adventures of Grandmaster Flash on the Wheels of Steel." From 1979 to 1983, Sugar Hill would be the biggest, most visible record industry institution supporting hip hop. Rap records had given the Robinsons a new lease on their old house but left them with no time to refurbish it.

In the wake of "Rapper's Delight" other black-owned indies released 12-inch singles, but because of their head start the Robinsons eventually accumulated the capital and clout that allowed them to buy out the contracts of headlining acts signed to their rivals. During 1980 and 1981 Sugar Hill picked up Spoonie Gee from Winley, Grandmaster Flash & the Furious Five, the Funky Four + 1, and the Treacherous Three from Enjoy. They also signed the female rapping-singing trio Sequence. Even Sylvia's dormant vocal career got a boost when she cut "It's Good to be the Queen," an answer record to Mel Brooks's humorous "It's Good to be the King" from the *History of the World—Part I* soundtrack.

The couple behind this success made quite a team. Joe had a tough guy rep, and outwardly he fit the part. He had a ruddy, pockmarked complexion and a gruff, impatient voice. There was a large pale chip on his shoulder placed there by every white man who had ever messed with him. In his wood-paneled office Joe often went on long angry riffs against the status quo that would've made Al Sharpton blush. Yet, while Joe was straightforward and rough, Sylvia was transparently smooth. She had the honeyed ways and fake sincerity of someone so used to charming people she'd actually stopped working hard at it. Her words about the rappers she'd met were maternal yet sly. It was as if she was just adopting these nice people and not grossing millions in the process.

The racially integrated staff spoke about Joe and Sylvia with all due professional respect. Some artists, people like Melle Mel and the members of Sequence, went out of their way to praise Sylvia for her musical input, while others offered more lip service than enthusiasm. The most off-putting aspect of my time in Englewood was meeting a portly European gent who served in some hard-to-define financial capacity. The

Robinsons reentry into the business with Sugar Hill had been refinanced by Morris Levy, a legendary record business operator whose indie distribution network had handled All-Platinum. I fantasized that the European gent was around to protect Levy's investment, though he didn't say that and I didn't ask.

At the end of the day the Sugar Hill special was a minor disaster for *Record World*. Joe gave me a juicy but inflammatory attack on the record biz for the editorial portion of the package. When Sylvia finally read the Q&A she went ballistic and made us pull the piece until she'd rewritten it. That last minute switch caused a major production nightmare. Compounding that problem, Sugar Hill, which took out most of the ads in the advertorial, didn't pay their bills. It was never entirely clear to me what went down, but it didn't matter—*Record World* was left holding the bag for the production costs.

The Sugar Hill special was just one of many financial miscalculations that led *Record World* to shut down in spring 1982. Luckily for me, my year-plus stint at *Record World* jump-started my career. Aside from doing the Sugar Hill advertorial, I did major interviews with many of the era's classic crossover icons (Lionel Richie, Chic's Bernard Edwards and Nile Rodgers, Prince, Morris Day) and began a relationship with the *Village Voice*'s music editor Bob Christgau, who understood early on that hip hop was important.

The first pieces I sold to the *Voice* were short takes on Lovebug Starski & the Harlem World Crew's "Positive Life" on Harlem World Records and "The Adventures of Grandmaster Flash on the Wheels of Steel." In spring 1982 I was named black music editor at *Billboard* magazine, the industry's prestigious trade journal—and the one from which I'd been preemptively dismissed two years before. I gained the position because I'd been a college intern there (then-editor Adam White remembered me) and because of my passion for the newest trends in black pop—Prince's Minneapolis Sound and rap.

Luckily for me, I was in synch with the times. I moved into the industry mainstream just as hip hop began to get noticed outside of black 'hoods in New York—specifically those very midtown offices that had been touting disco as the record business's savior. It would take time for those executives, black and white, to truly get it. And, looking back, I'd have to say I played a part in delivering that wake-up call.

My first column at *Billboard* was about rap producers moving into R&B, specifically citing Larry Smith, a bassist, songwriter, and member of the Kurtis Blow production team, who by 1982 had graduated to producing the veteran group Con Funk Shun. In retrospect, my column was either prophetic or premature, as it would be another five years before hip hop–bred producers would truly begin to reinvent the sound of R&B.

Still, there was no doubt in my mind that hip hop was a coming cultural force. In 1982 this was far from conventional wisdom. At the time, graffiti and break dancing were still hotter on the nation's cultural radar screen than the music. It wouldn't be long, however, before hip hop's musical component reached its full potential and my love affair blossomed into a long-term relationship.

gangsters—real and unreal

PEOPLE ARE USUALLY THE PRODUCT OF WHERE THEY COME FROM. THE BONDS THAT YOU MADE, THE CODES THAT WERE THERE, ALL HAVE AN INFLUENCE ON YOU LATER IN LIFE. YOU CAN REJECT THEM. YOU CAN SAY "OKAY, THOSE CODES DON'T EXIST FOR ME, BE-CAUSE I'M NOT OF THAT WORLD ANYMORE." BUT THE REASON FOR THOSE CODES—WHY PEOPLE LIVE THAT WAY—ARE VERY STRONG LESSONS. THE MOST IMPORTANT REASON IS SURVIVAL. IT COMES DOWN TO THAT. THAT STRUGGLE OF THE HUMAN FORM, THE CORPO-RAL, THE FLESH, TO SURVIVE—ANYTHING TO SURVIVE. I THINK THOSE THINGS YOU CARRY WITH YOU THE REST OF YOUR LIFE.

—MARTIN SCORSESE, *ROLLING STONE,* 1990

IN THE WAKE OF THE CIVIL RIGHTS MOVEMENT BLACK MIDDLE-CLASS families, and many working-class families, finally had the freedom to live wherever they could afford. Of course racism still kept them out of cer-tain areas, but a lot of people up and down the economic ladder got enough capital—and guts—to finally get out of the old, embattled neighborhoods. Not just doctors and lawyers moved out of these black neighborhoods. So did bus drivers, teachers, and government bureaucrats with new gigs in municipal governments. Ironically, the enhanced mo-bility of black wage earners left the old neighborhoods wide open to in-creased crime, which led to an increase in white flight. White merchants, vilified as exploiters by many of their African-American customers, were either burned out by urban riots or chased out by crime.

And the majority of that crime was instigated by drugs. As was tellingly illustrated by Allen and Albert Hughes in *Dead Presidents,* the change happened with a lethal quickness. In their film, a black GI leaves for Vietnam from a tough, yet still hopeful neighborhood and returns to a meaner, more desperate and heroin-saturated ghetto. In fact, GIs con-tributed to this tragic change both as victims and predators.

In 1971, the U.S. Army estimated that 10 percent of our soldiers used heroin while in 'Nam and that 5 percent were hard-core junkies. Some black GIs, returning home to an uncertain future, brought heroin back with them as a hedge against unemployment. In so doing they participated in inaugurating a new wave of black criminal entrepreneurship—a street-corner response to President Nixon's rhetoric encouraging black capitalism in lieu of government aid.

The heroin invasion, while partially orchestrated by the Mafia and other established crime syndicates, brought new forces into American crime (Asian and South American traffickers) and empowered a new, vicious kind of black gangster. Heroin emboldened the black criminal class, which had been clustered in numbers running, prostitution, fencing, and robbery, to expand and become more predatory.

Prior to heroin's mass marketing in the late '60s, the prototypical black criminal was the numbers runner, a creature of the northern ghettos with a pedigree that went back to the '30s. Numbers runners were viewed as a necessary evil who, in the best case scenario, acted as community bankers, processing daily investments from their customers. Less romantically, numbers runners were also unreliable liars who skimmed profits from winners and conveniently disappeared when someone hit big, though too much inconsistency in payment endangered his or her livlihood (and life). As drug dealers would later, the numbers runner profited off the community's poorest. They sold dreams and, in dribs and drabs, drained money out of black America.

Of course running numbers wasn't selling an inherently lethal product—just elusive big money dreams, the same as horse racing and other games of chance. Numbers running employed people in a network of criminal activity that was condoned by the community and the police because it provided hope and, on occasion, large sums of money to its customers. Numbers were, in fact, part of the glue that held together many poor African-American neighborhoods, a shared enthusiasm that sustained daily life at the same time it undercut it.

Alongside the numbers runner in the pantheon of preheroin black criminality were the pimp and the wino. While obviously an exploiter of women and male sexual desire, the pimp has been, in the mind of many men and more women than would admit it, a figure of fascination, a certain awe, and supressed respect. At the core of this interest is the pimp's ability to control others. Any man who can, through business savvy, sexual prowess, understanding of human psychology, and yes, violence get others to perform the most intimate sexual acts and give him the money titillates many at some undeniably base level.

In a warped and unhealthy way the pimp's ability to control his environment (i.e., his stable of women) has always been viewed as a rare example of black male authority over his domain. Despite decades of moral censure from church leaders and those incensed by his exploitation of women, the pimp endures as an anithero among young black males. The pimp's garb, slang, and persona influences the culture to this day and shows no signs of abating.

In contrast to the potent, romanticized pimp, the wino was the precursor to the heroin addict as the embodiment of urban tragedy. Heroin junkies weren't new to the black community in the '60s. It's just that, in the rarified world of jazz and music, they were more isolated while the victims of cheap wine and alcohol had haunted street corners since African-Americans moved North. The sale of Ripple, Wild Irish Rose, and other juice-flavored poisons in poor and black neighborhoods foreshadowed the target marketing of malt liquor in the '80s and '90s.

Through black pop culture of the '60s and '70s one can experience the evolution in black criminal culture. In Richard Pryor's classic routine "The Wino and the Junkie," from his *That Nigger's Crazy* album, the great comedian depicts the wino as a city-living country wit and the junkie as a wasted young urban zombie. The split is significant in that Pryor, an artist/cocaine addict himself, provided nuance to the difference between addiction to heroin and alcohol and to how it would eventually affect the entire black community.

The Holloway House novels of Iceberg Slim and Donald Goines, published throughout the '60s and '70s, memorably documented the transition in black crime from pimping, numbers running, and grifting to selling smack. Slim (Robert Beck), a fair-skinned con man who often passed for white, wrote lovingly of country-bred hustlers who traveled to the big cities employing various psychological gambits to get women to prostitute themselves (as in *Pimp: The Story of My Life*) and to swindle men out of their hard-earned cash (as in *Trick Baby*). Goines, who succeeded Slim as essential black barbershop reading, was a longtime heroin addict gunned down in 1974, along with his wife, apparently while at his typewriter. During his tortured thirty-nine years on earth, Goines ground out sixteen novels about lost, mentally diseased people existing in squalid conditions in blunt, brutal prose that, early in his career, possessed the ugly poetry of bracing pulp fiction.

In the real world, African-American heroin empires grew during the '70s around the country: in Chicago under the rule of the violent El Rukins gang; in the District of Columbia run by Rayfield Edmonds, Sr.; in New York City, first by Frank Matthews and later by "Mr. Untouchable"—Leroy "Nicky" Barnes. They all established large distribution networks and, in the case of Barnes, made international contacts for importation that superceded traditional white ethnic control. Just as many blaxploitation movie scenarios revolved around struggles to control crime in black neighborhoods, these real-life black kingpins found themselves in high-pitched short-term battles with the fading Italian and Irish syndicates—in the long run new forces would come to replace the Italians. The long stable hierarchy of American crime crumbled when new drugs, such as angel dust and cocaine, became popular in the streets.

Heroin's growth as a mass market commodity ended the drug's romantic association with black musicians. The idea of Charlie Parker and other musicians as "beautiful losers" rather than as what they were— gifted people with a debilitating addiction—largely collapsed as the squalid junkie lifestyle became clear on America's streets. There was little inspiration in grown men begging for quarters, stealing car radios, and sleeping curled up in doorways.

Heroin couldn't have run wild in the streets without widespread police and political corruption aiding its dissemination. Hand in hand with this moral failure, the federal government under President Nixon cut back on Democratic antipoverty programs and systematically ignored the economic development pleas of America's urbanites, whose jobs were fleeing to the suburbs.

There are all kinds of conspiracy theories about why heroin flowed so intensely into black neighborhoods. There is evidence that the CIA was involved in the Asian "golden triangle," purchasing and helping distribute heroin as a way to fund assassinations and other covert operations. This fact has evolved into the theory that heroin was imported into black communities by government forces (including the virulent, racist Federal Bureau of Investigation honcho J. Edgar Hoover) to undermine the civil rights movement. This theory of government conspiracy provided the premise to Melvin Van Peebles's screenplay for son Mario's 1995 film

Panther. Sure, there's an edge of paranoia there, but the more you learn about the counterintelligence program (COINTELPRO) that the FBI and Justice Department targeted at black leaders, it isn't hard to give these theories some credence.

It is a fact that in the '70s agent provocateurs infiltrated Black Panther chapters around the nation, often rising to positions of authority where they helped sabotage an already high-strung organization. The police shooting of Chicago's Fred Hampton in 1969, instigated by a government informer in that Panther chapter, is just one of many documented episodes of internal espionage aimed at the period's black activists.

In August 1996, the Sacramento *Mercury News*, a California daily, ran a series called "Dark Alliance" that connected the CIA with the importation of crack into Southern California during the '80s. African-American activists like Dick Gregory and Congresswoman Maxine Waters of South Central Los Angeles embraced the report and stuck by its conclusions even after the CIA aggressively debunked the story and the *Mercury News* itself finally backed off most its original conclusions.

African-American belief in government duplicity toward them is deep-seated and even sometimes overly paranoid, yet there is an evil history that gives these conspiracies real credibility. From the Tuskegee syphilis experiment that poisoned the bodies of poor Alabama men with a venereal disease for over forty years at U.S. expense to the FBI putting microphones under Dr. Martin Luther King's bed to record his sex life and COINTELPROs subversion of black radical organizing, elements of this country's law enforcement branches have been performing nefarious deeds on its African-American citizens for decades. While the crack-CIA connection seems a dead end now, who knows what information will come to light in the next century?

Whether a covert government conspiracy or just the product of everyday law enforcement corruption and neglect, the growth of the urban drug culture stifled the civil rights movement around the country. It wore down white goodwill toward blacks' noble striving, particularly among big city Jews and liberals. By the early '70s it was crime, not equality, that became the focus of discussion between blacks and Jews, ultimately driving a wedge between these longtime allies that may never be smoothed over.

Heroin use declined in the early '80s due to a slackening of the supply, but the illegal drug industry, which has proven to be one of the most adaptable enterprises in our country, aimed a new product line at the nation's drug aficionados—angel dust aka PCP (phencyclidine). This man-made psychoactive drug produces hallucinations that can cause severe psychological trauma. Usually sprinkled on a regular or marijuana cigarette, angel dust can drive its users to uncontrollable violent reactions. Someone "dusty" is always dangerous, because you never know what the next puff can lead to. Local news broadcasts of the early '80s regularly led off the six o'clock news with footage of cops and hospital personnel struggling to subdue someone "beaming up to Scotty." Angel dust is, in effect, a lethal form of ghetto LSD, which many kids experimented with to enter a vibrant, animated dream world. In my experience, angel dust was particularly popular with people with rich fantasy lives who ignored the danger in exchange for high-intensity pleasure. I remember one dusty homie was always seeing space ships hovering over Harlem.

During the early days of hip hop, angel dust was the drug of choice at parties. It was cheap, fast, and readily available. Many rap stars and their fans attended hip hop events extremely dusty and, as a result, angel dust became a creative stimulant in hip hop culture. But while angel dust ruled the streets, a more potent form of cocaine was quietly trickling down from the Wall Street elite.

CRACK

In the "Superfly" '70s, coke was sniffed or snorted (choose your verb) in powder form from tabletops, album covers, and parts of other folks' bodies. In inner-city neighborhoods, coke users wishing to socialize with those of similar appetites gathered at after-hours clubs to separate themselves from marijuana smokers and heroin junkies. Back in 1979, I interviewed a dealer who said that "coke sniffers were Kings and Queens and heads of state"—as opposed to "the low rent people" he sold marijuana to.

By the early '80s, cocaine consumption turned toward smoking free-base, which is cocaine at its basic alkaloid level. Like many folks, I'd never heard of freebasing until Richard Pryor ran in a fiery ball out of his California home on June 9, 1980. Coke had always been an expensive drug and this "cooking" to create a smokable version just seemed another oc-cupation of the bored rich.

In freebasing, the cocaine is boiled in water and the residue is placed in cold water where it forms "base" or "freebase." The chipped-off pieces are called "crack" because it often makes a crackling sound as it burns. The popularity of this form of cocaine coincided with a dramatic in-crease in the growth of coca leaves in Bolivia, Peru, and Colombia that drove down the price of manufactured cocaine.

According to sociologist Terry Williams's insightful 1992 book about the crack lifestyle, *Crackhouse: Notes from the End of the Line*, the price dropped from $50,000 a kilo in 1980 to $35,000 in 1984 to $12,000 in 1992. Crack took cocaine away from high rollers and put it within reach of poorer addicts. For as little as $2, crack became available in plastic vials with red, blue, yellow, or green caps that denoted a particular dealer's ter-ritory or a particular dealer's product line. Often dealers named their brands after some pop culture artifact such as the movie *Lethal Weapon* or the band P-Funk.

The first references to mass market freebase came in two rap records—"White Lines" by Grandmaster Flash & the Furious Five, fea-turing Melle Mel, in 1983 and "Batterram" by Toddy Tee in 1985, which described a mini-tank the LAPD were using to break "rock houses." Soon the American media landscape would be littered with ref-erences to and discussions of crack. From those initial street reports, hip hop would chronicle, celebrate, and be blamed for the next level of drug culture development.

The crack industry became able employers of teenagers, filling the economic vacuum created by the ongoing loss of working-class jobs to the suburbs and then to poor Third World countries. Teenagers and ado-lescents were zealously recruited to provide the unskilled labor needed for manufacturing, packaging, and selling illegal drugs. By 1992 it was estimated that as many as 150,000 people were employed in New York City's drug trade. Similarly large numbers could be found in most major cities. MC Guru was not joking when he termed dealing "a daily opera-tion," since the financial life of significant portions of the American economy suddenly became driven not by the stock market but by the crack industry.

Drug addiction has always been an equal opportunity exploiter. It strikes old, rich, white, and black. Yet there was something profoundly disheartening about crack's impact on young women. Williams estimated that 40 percent of all crackhouse denizens were female. It was maddening to see how many young mothers abandoned their children in pursuit of another hit. Often these women were forced to give sexual favors to support their dependencies.

During the eight years of Reagan's presidency, the ripple effect of crack flowed through all the social service agencies of our country— welfare, child care, medicare, you name the area of concern and crack's impact could be felt in it. At Family Court on any given day you'd see grandmothers struggling to hold families together by taking custody of their neglected or abandoned grandchildren. It was a tragedy that robbed grandparents of their rightful rest, strained their meager financial resources, and shortened their lives. In this multigenerational chaos few could raise their head above water or plan intelligently for the future.

For those who felt the fallout from crack's addictive power—the children of crackheads, their immediate families, friends, and neighbors— hope became a very hollow word. The world became defined by the 'hood, the block, or the corner where the search for drugs or their addicted loved one went on every day. As the '80s rolled on, the physical and moral decay begun by heroin was accelerated by angel dust and then the McDonaldization of crack.

As a consequence for many, materialism replaced spirituality as the definer of life's worth. An appreciation for life's intangible pleasures, like child rearing and romantic love, took a beating in places where children became disposable and sex was commodified. The go-go capitalism of Reagan's America (and its corporate greed) flowed down to the streets stripped of its jingoistic patriotism and fake piety. The unfettered free market of crack generated millions and stoked a voracious appetite for "goods," not good.

CRACK UP

IN MY NEIGHBORHOOD YOU WERE EITHER IN A GANG OR A GROUP—MOST WERE IN BOTH.

—SMOKEY ROBINSON, 1997

Gangsta rap (or reality rap or whatever descriptive phrase you like) is a direct by-product of the crack explosion. Unless you grasp that connection nothing else that happened in hip hop's journey to national scapegoat will make sense. This is not a chicken or the egg riddle—first came crack rocks, then gangsta rap.

Because the intense high of crack fades quickly, crack turned ordinary drug dealers into kingpins. After shooting up or snorting heroin, an addict resides in dream land for hours; a crack addict experiences a brief, incredible rush, then five minutes later desires another rock. Crack created a fast-food economy of quick product turnover. Because it was so addictive and profitable, competition within impromptu urban enterprise zones (i.e., urban street corners) grew fierce. With the money crack generated from its increasingly ghostly clientele, bigger and more lethal guns filled our cities. Entering the '80s, the Saturday Night Special, a .45 caliber automatic, had long been America's death inducer of choice; by the end of the decade a medley of higher caliber weapons (the Israeli Uzi and Desert Eagle, the German Glock, even the good old American Mossburg 12-gauge shotgun) pushed murder totals in Washington, D.C.; Los Angeles; Detroit; Gary, Indiana; and scores of other cities to record levels.

As dealers used these guns indiscriminately, residents in the drug-ravaged communities armed themselves as well, seeking protection from dealers and crackheads, and the climate of immorality they represented. Police impotence in cleaning neighborhoods of drug trafficking and our government's failure in drug interdiction (or complicity in the trade) produced cynicism and alienation in this nation that made Nancy Reagan's "Just Say No" campaign a joke and left her husband's "Morning in America" rife with gunsmoke from the night before.

Gangsta rap first appeared in the mid-'80s. It exploded at the end of that decade and has leveled off—just like crack use—in the '90s. The majority of this subgenre's sales are made in the suburbs. A lot of this has to do with the rebel credentials of hard rappers with teenage kids (which I'll explore in more detail later) and with the true nature of the contemporary teenage suburban experience.

Suburban kids—no longer just stereotypically white, but black, Asian, and Hispanic—have, since the '60s, always known a lot more about drugs than civic leaders have ever acknowledged. (Although there aren't as many drive-bys in suburban counties, they do indeed happen. Drug dealers don't necessarily all congregate on green lawns, but they have never met a mall they didn't love.) The dirty little secret of mainstream America is that kids of every age, particularly in high school and junior high, have access to a medley of controlled substances. The romance of the outlaw mystique of drugs and dealing is not foreign to young people—another reason why gangsta records, supposedly so distant to the white teen experience, is in fact quite familiar. Even the urban context of the records is not as mysterious or exotic, as commentators assert, since many suburban dealers and addicts use urban 'hoods as drive-through windows.

Another consequence of the crack plague was an evil increase in the numbers of incarcerated black males. In February 1990 a Washington, D.C.–based nonprofit organization, the Sentencing Project, issued a frightening report titled *Young Black Men and the Criminal Justice System: A Growing National Problem*. The report stated that one in four African-American males between twenty and twenty-nine—610,000 men in total—were either behind bars or on probation. In comparison, only 436,000 were enrolled in higher education.

The reasons for this number were legion—the crack trade, the aggressive sentencing of low-level drug offenses such as possession, the eroded economic base of urban America, a profound sense of hopelessness, ineffective school systems. The social repercussions, however, were sometimes less obvious. With so many young men in jail or monitored by law enforcement, most African-Americans had someone in their family or a friend involved with the justice system, both as perpetrator and victim. It is not surprising then that narratives dealing with crimes and its consequences—from the reality TV show *Cops* to urban movies like *Boyz N the Hood* and *Juice*, and, of course, hip hop records that talk of jail culture—have a special appeal.

More profoundly, the mentality of black culture was deeply affected.

The kind of dispassionate view of violence and overall social alienation that incarceration fosters was spread by prisoners and infected the rest of the community. Jail became not a cruel punishment but a rite of passage for many that helped define one's entry into manhood. And what being a man meant could be perversely shaped by imprisonment. For many young men their sex and romantic dealings were forever altered by the sexual activity that goes on behind bars.

While homosexuality is widely condemned in the black community, the committing of homosexual acts behind bars is rarely commented on. Because they often occur through rape or psychological coercion they are not viewed as acts of sexual orientation but manifestations of control and domination, both reflections consistent with a "gangsta mental" or gangster mentality. If sex is taken, from this viewpoint, it is not an act of love but power. Whatever the justification, it suggests that there's a homoerotic quality to this culture's intense male bonding. As an example of how values shaped by prison influence behavior outside it, sex be- comes about power, not affection. You bond with other men, not simply out of shared interest and friendship, but as protector and to gain preda- tor power. For some men, in and out of jail since adolescence, jail begins to supercede the presence of all other environments.

Suspicion of women, loyalty to the crew, adoption of a stone face in confronting the world, hatred of authority—all major themes of gangsta rap—owe their presence in lyrics and impact on audiences to the large number of African-American men incarcerated in the '90s.

CRIMINAL MINDED

Whenever people rail about the evils of gangsta rap, my mind floats back to a particular record and an interview that never happened.

In 1985, New York's KISS-FM had a Friday night rap show. I'd either write with it on in the background or lie in bed listening. However, every week there was one record that stubbornly refused to be background mu- sic. Whenever the station played Schoolly D's "PSK—What Does It Mean?" the mood of my night changed. A first-person narrative about being a vicious stick-up kid and a member of PSK (Parkside Killers) in Philadelphia, it wasn't just Schoolly D's words that got me. His cold-blooded delivery and the bracing, taunting track always chilled me. The intensity of my reaction to "PSK" has been matched by only two other listening experiences: hearing Robert Johnson's devilish Delta blues for the first time and experiencing Tricky's dense premillennium dread at a New York concert in 1997.

Though as an artist Schoolly D is not on the same level as the legendary Johnson or the innovative trip-hop pioneer Tricky, the Philly homeboy channeled something tortured and warped when he laid down "PSK." When I hear people talk of being repulsed by gangsta rap's cartoony brutality I understand it by invoking the unease "PSK" induced in me. Back in that more innocent age, Schoolly D's nonjudgmental attitude toward violence (as opposed to the cautionary tone of "The Message") was unusual and even shocking.

My second early gangsta memory involves my sole encounter with Boogie Down Production's cofounder Scott LaRock (Scott Sterling). It was backstage at Madison Square Garden during a huge, arena-sized rap show. The flavors of mid-'80s black pop culture were in effect: the teen star of America's then number-one sitcom, *The Cosby Show*'s Malcolm-Jamal Warner, sat in the wings watching L.L. Cool J rock the crowd; Mike Tyson, the then heavyweight champ from my native Brownsville and unrepentant bully, hit a girl with a forearm as he passed her and chuckled.

A moment later I was introduced to LaRock, who had just emerged as one of the hottest producer-entrepreneurs in hip hop. As part of Boogie Down Productions, LaRock had helped mastermind the brilliant *Criminal Minded*. Fronted by the brutal rhymes and oddly whimsical vocals of ex-homeless teen KRS-One (Chris Parker), this was the first album-length exploration of the crack-fueled criminality of Reagan's America.

Criminal Minded had been released in 1987 on the black-owned, Bronx-based B-Boy Records, which KRS-One took every opportunity they had in the press to trash. B-Boy controlled Boogie Down Productions for only one album. As a result, everybody in the business was after BDP, but Jive's Barry Weiss and Ann Carli closed the deal. I told LaRock I wanted an interview for *Billboard*. He took my notepad and wrote down his name and number. I said I'd call next week. That weekend on August 26, 1987, LaRock was murdered in the kind of gun-related stupidity we now take for granted.

Before he began his hip hop career, LaRock had earned his keep as a counselor at homeless shelters, which is how he'd hooked up with Parker. One of the young men in the BDP collective was D-Nice (Derrick Jones), a shy, attractive, and gifted fifteen-year-old DJ being mentored by Parker and LaRock. D-Nice's boyish good looks had attracted the unwanted attention of a drug dealer's girlfriend in the Bronx and her unamused boyfriend threatened Derrick with harm. On the Saturday afternoon after the Garden concert, LaRock, D-Nice, and a couple of BDP members drove to the dealer's 'hood hoping to squash the beef. Apparently the dealer or some of his associates knew BDP were coming. Aware of *Criminal Minded*'s violent content, perhaps they anticipated trouble, but LaRock was actually seeking a sit down. As the Jeep containing BDP members arrived on the dealer's street, a shot rang out and the bullet that entered the vehicle struck Scott LaRock dead. As with so much urban violence, no one was ever indicted for the murder.

The question of whether BDP's rep played any part in this preemptive strike will likely never be known, but whenever someone equates rap and gangsterism LaRock's death comes back to me. Looking back at his shooting, it seems a harbinger of a future where reality and rhyme often would tragically intersect. LaRock was not a violent man. He, in fact, spent much of his life trying to mediate conflicts in shelters where hopelessness ruled. The day he died he was on a peace mission for a friend. Yet with *Criminal Minded*, LaRock, as a musician and entertainer, had already tapped into the furiously self-destructive materialism of his age.

It is the irony of LaRock's life and death that make me question simplistic explanations of gangsta rap. Not all rappers who write violent lyrics have lived the words. Most exercise the same artistic license to write violent tales as do the makers of Hollywood flicks. A few of those who do write violent lyrics have lived the tales or have friends who have. Within any collection of rap songs—either by those making it up or those who have lived it—a wide range of narrative strategies are employed. Many violent rhymes are just cartoons, with images as grounded in reality as the Road Runner. The outrageous words of Eazy-E and Kool G Rap fit this category. Some are cautionary tales that relate the dangers inherent to street life—Melle Mel and Duke Bootee's words in the "The Message" is the prototype. Some are first-person narratives told with an objective, almost cinematic eye, by masters of the style Ice Cube and KRS-One. Some end with the narrator in bold, bloody triumph, techniques both Scarface and Ice-T employ well. A bold few end with the narrator dead and work as stories told from the grave, an approach both Tupac Shakur and the Notorious B.I.G. favored in sadly prophetic recordings.

Some violent rhymes are poetically rendered and novelistically well observed, as in the more nuanced work of Chuck D, Rakim, and Nas. Too Short and Luther Campbell can, in contrast, be as crude as the bathroom humor of Jim Carrey's *Dumb & Dumber*. Some are morally complicated by the narrator's possible insanity, which is a specialty of Houston's Scarface. Some are so empty and rote that only the most reactionary listeners would think they could incite anything beyond contempt. My point is that most MCs who've been categorized as gangsta rappers are judged thoughtlessly without any understanding of the genuine stylistic differences between them.

Besides, what's gangsta rap anyway? Listen to any of N.W.A's albums, as well as Eazy-E's solo efforts, Dr. Dre's *The Chronic* and Snoop Doggy Dogg's *Doggystyle*. In their celebration of gatts, hoes, gleeful nihilism, and crack as the center of their economic universe, these albums darkly display everything people fear about gangsta rap. But outside of this collection of records—most of them with brilliantly modulated vocals supervised by Dr. Dre—I'd be hard-pressed to agree to label any other major rap star a gangsta rapper. For example, the work of Ice Cube (except for his insipid West Coast Connection project) and Scarface are way too diverse and eclectic to fit a simplistic mass media stereotype.

The martyrs of '90s hip hop—Tupac Shakur and the Notorious B.I.G. (Christopher Wallace)—were quickly tagged gangsta rappers *after* their demise, though crack and crime were not their only topics. A lot of drivel has been written about these two dead young black men. Heroes for a generation. Victims of their violent recordings. Martyrs. Villains. Whatever. For a moment let's just discuss them as artists. If, over twenty years after it evolved out of the Bronx, hip hop is an artform, then these men built profoundly on that foundation. Far from being simple oppositional figures in an East Coast–West Coast soap opera, Pac and Biggie complemented each other, though outwardly they seem mismatched.

Biggie was round and spoke in a thoughtful Brooklyn-meets-the-Caribbean drawl he derived from his articulate mother, a Jamaican-born schoolteacher. Tupac was taut and spoke with an activist's urgency and an actor's sense of drama, a by-product of his mother's militant background and his theatrical training in high school. Biggie covered himself in layers of expensive clothing and the regal air that led him to be dubbed the "King of New York" after the '90s gangsta film. Tupac always seemed to have his shirt off, better to expose his six-pack abdominals, wiry body, and the words "Thug 4 Life" tattooed across his belly.

But inside, both young men possessed lyrical dexterity, a writer's strong point of view, and a bitter, street-hardened sense of irony. Ultimately, Tupac and Biggie, like most of the controversial and best rappers who came after Public Enemy's political spiels, were both poets of negation, a stance that always upsets official cultural gatekeepers and God-fearing folks within black America. African-Americans have always been conflicted by art that explores the psychologically complex, even evil aspects of their existence, feeling it plays into the agenda of white oppression. On a very direct, obvious level they have a point. Black people saying bad things about themselves can serve to reinforce racist attitudes among non-blacks.

Yet, without a doubt, political and social conditions must not, cannot, and will not circumscribe the vision of true artists. Tupac and Biggie were artists who looked at the worst things in their world and reveled in describing their meanest dreams and grossest nightmares. They embraced the evil of crack America and articulated it with style—but highlighting is not the same as celebrating. The celebrated work of director Martin Scorsese parallels this artistic impulse. His violent masterworks—*Mean Streets*, *Raging Bull*, and *GoodFellas*—are undeniably artful yet morally twisted and deeply troubling in what they depict about the Italian-American soul in particular and the human capacity for violence in general—yet no one accuses him of being a self-glorifing predator.

Scorsese is considered, perhaps, the greatest living American film-maker; Tupac and Biggie were labeled gangsta rappers in their obituaries. Yet the homicidal characters depicted by Joe Pesci and Robert DeNiro in *GoodFellas* could walk into any of Tupac or the Notorious B.I.G.'s records and feel right at home. Tupac and the Notorious B.I.G. didn't make records for the NAACP; they made harsh, contemplative, graphic, deliberately violent American pulp art.

Tupac's hip hop Jimmy Cagney and the Notorious B.I.G.'s Edward G. Robinson didn't die for their sins or the ones they rhymed about; they died for their lives—the lives they chose and the lives that chose them. Rap lyrics that describe violence are a natural consequence of a world where a sixteen-year-old is shot at close range over his jacket by class-mates, where a fifteen-year-old boy is fatally stabbed by another teen over his glasses, where a seventeen-year-old is stabbed to death after hitting another teen with an errant basketball pass. In a world where crack-empowered gangs run on a philosophy of old-fashioned, excessive, insa-tiable, and unending revenge—one that is supported by the plots of American classics from *The Searchers* to *Star Wars*—gangsta rap is just fur-ther exploration of this theme.

There is an elemental nihilism in the most controversial crack-era hip hop that wasn't concocted by the rappers but reflects the mentality and fears of young Americans of every color and class living an exhausting, edgy existence, in and out of big cities. Like crack dealing, it may die down, but the social conditions that inspired the trafficking and the un-derlying artistic impulse that ignited nihilistic rap have not disappeared and will not because, deep in the American soul, it speaks to us and we like the sound of its voice.

the "i" of me

WE CAN GO RHYME FOR RHYME
WORD FOR WORD, VERSE TO VERSE

    —BIG DADDY KANE,
      "RAW"

FOR CERTAIN AFRICAN-AMERICAN MEN, PRIDE AND ARROGANCE ARE bound together like electrical wiring. Twisted tight and full of energy these two qualities often become one supercharged current that burns away humility. In general this is perceived as a bad thing. Yet for generations of disenfranchised men this has been an invigorating source of self-empowerment.

In the venerable tradition of European literature there are many texts by dead white men (see Dante and Milton) that depict pride as one of the seven deadly sins. According to Dante's *Inferno*, pride is what got Lucifer cast out of heaven and led that fallen angel to create hell. Maybe for dead white men pride is a bad thing. However, for a living, breathing black man, arrogant pride can be essential. On a planet where to demonize, demoralize, disdain, and dis black people is a long-standing preoccupation, this kind of extravagant pride is often a system of survival.

For African-American males, this pride can be an aggressive manifestation of identity. It is the way Reggie Jackson stood at home plate and gazed satisfied at his home runs. It is the way grim-faced Nation of Islam members stand erect in suits, white shirts, ties, and shades as they survey the world. It is Michael Jordan hitting that last-second shot one more time. It is Jesse Jackson running for president twice and twice scaring the hell out of the Democratic Party. It is Henry Louis Gates, Jr., building a black academic empire at Harvard. It is Sammy Davis, Jr., writing an autobiography titled *Yes, I Can* despite working in an America that often says, "No, nigga, you can't." It is the wit of Ralph Ellison to name a book *Invisible Man*, knowing full well a black man never goes unnoticed. And it is the essential swagger that underpins hip hop. Black male pride is a weapon and an attitude. It is an attack on the negative and it is a way to spin the negative on its head.

"I" is a powerful word in the vocabulary of the African-American male. In telling his-story brothers are extremely subjective, and we revel in the chance to make others see things our way. The first word in Ellison's *Invisible Man* is "I." In some of the most important African-American male narratives of this dying century—Richard Wright's *Black Boy*, Claude Brown's *Manchild in the Promised Land*, James Baldwin's *The Fire Next Time*, Nathan McCall's *Makes Me Wanna Holler*, and the entire canon of rap—a powerful autobiographical impulse demands the exploration of the "I" of me.

Of course, among brothers "I" is not enough. The view must be expressed with style. Jesse Jackson once observed that some African-American leaders are tree shakers (like himself) and some are jelly makers who work more quietly (like Colin Powell). Most of our most celebrated leaders have been smooth-talking tree shakers. Dr. King. Malcolm X. Adam Clayton Powell, Jr. Plodding, bureaucratic, detail-oriented men have an equally crucial place in our community—without them it is all sound with no follow-through—but traditionally it takes flavor to rock a crowd, and we gravitate to men who provide that flavor.

Black male pride is profoundly manifested in the renaming of oneself. No matter how much we love our parents, African-American males throughout the twentieth century have been notably uncomfortable with the Christian-based names they were given. In the last twenty years or so, this has become less of a problem as this generation's black parents have opted for phonetic spellings that create new names. Juwan, Anfernee, and Antawn are just a few of the scores of new names that African-American families have added to the English language and, in the process, personalized the naming process, leaving behind John, Paul, Joseph, etc.

This renaming trend is an extension of a long process by which African-Americans have created new "I"s that speak to how they see themselves or wish to be seen. The blues, the root of most American music and the essential idiomatic African-American expression, is studded with new "I"s. Muddy Waters (once McKinley Morganfield), Bo Diddley (once Eugene McDaniels), Howlin' Wolf (once Chester Burnett)—all created gutsy new identities that spoke to a grand sense of self. In that same spirit of renewal through naming, Cassius Clay became the Nation of Islam's Muhammad Ali. So Joseph Saddler, inspired by kung fu flicks, became Grandmaster Flash. During the jazz era, African-American culture was rife with Counts and Dukes, names of regal grandeur. In the current age of lowered expectations and harsh sensibilities we have names like Public Enemy and even Ol' Dirty Bastard. Whether anointing oneself royalty or basking in words originally designed to demean, African-American males are restless in the desire for self-definition.

For all his individuality, the black man craves a context for that style, one that often comes as part of a male-dominated collective. It may be at a barbershop, a political campaign, in church, or a hip hop crew. Sometimes they are simply his boys from the 'hood. Sometimes these boys from the 'hood are labeled a gang. Sometimes they really are a gang. But whether the collective is his homies, a gang, a team, a crew, or a posse, it is important to move in unison. Using his "I" to strengthen a collective "we" is crucial to his nature.

The underlying desire to personalize each action can make others envy or hate us. That impulse informs our walk—the hipster's cool bop, the crisp stride of the corporate boy, the back-bending b-boy stance. In basketball, for example, how you score can be as important as scoring itself. The no-look pass, the behind-the-back pass, the crossover ankle-snapping dribble, and the 360-degree-hang-time-tongue-out space jam only result in two points, but what a pretty two points they are.

We love to take things that were once out of reach—the saxophone, the sampler, the pager—and reinvent the technology in our own image. The sax was invented by Adolphe Sax in the mid-nineteenth century, yet it didn't become a valued instrument until brothers got their hands on it in the '30s. The sampler was invented by sound scientists in the '70s but it was via the ears of hip hop producers that this technology found its deepest use. The pager, long a tool of doctors on call, became a staple of

American culture because of the curiosity and vision of black young people. It started as a tool for drug dealers, spread to the rest of the community, and, ultimately, has entered the everyday life of the nation.

HEROES AND ANTIHEROES

If you'd asked me in the late '80s what figure most embodied hip hop, I wouldn't have named a musician at all. My choice would have been Mike Tyson. Like all the iconic black fighters, Tyson was a bare-chested, powerful projection of the dreams of dominance that lay thwarted in so many hearts. Jack Johnson, Joe Louis, "Sugar" Ray Robinson, Muhammad Ali, and so many others, no matter their considerable differences in style and personality, could awaken a pride, an almost animalistic intensity, in black viewers that only a man besting another with his fists can create.

Despite living in an overwhelmingly white country, our heroes tend to be brown (though we gave Bruce Lee much love). We want them to rock the boulevard and penetrate the boardroom. They must have style, either in voice or gesture. They must get the girl and they must be cool in so doing. They must be fearless but not foolish. If they talk the talk they must walk the walk, or they are suckers and will get dissed. Our vision of heroism is not for the timid, the insecure, or the introverted. We like them bold, we like them to embody our blasculinity, and, be they revolutionaries or rap stars, we like to know they are ready to die—even though we truly don't want them to. Often our heroes are not heroes but antiheroes, at least anti in the view of others. They can be Robert Johnson selling his soul to the devil at midnight in Mississippi. They can be Superfly in his big-brimmed hat and Cadillac. They can be Mike Tyson in his fierce, reckless fury. Or, at least, as he used to be.

Tyson had moved from street fighting and gang banging to a more refined kind of violence. And the Malcolm X–like, true-life myth of his rapid rise from thug to champion was quite compelling for his peers, women and men who saw the gap between rich and poor widening and feared being left behind. Mike was one of them and vowed allegiance to their hunger in his actions and his words.

There was no artifice in vintage '80s Tyson, none of the cunning that

Robinson and Ali brought to the ring. Instead, Tyson guaranteed a brutal attack in black shorts that "punked" a string of opponents before the
first blow was landed, which somehow resonated outside the ring in the
'80s, a time of governmental and social insensitivity. Who had time for
the sweet science of boxing when a Tyson match promised instant grati-
fication and ritual emasculation, all within round one?

There was a part of America, white and black, that was never happy
about Tyson's rise. He was just too close for comfort to the national
nightmare of Bigger Thomas, as conceived by Richard Wright, and
Willie Horton, an ex-con made famous by that skilled authority on black
pathology, the late GOP operative Lee Atwater. Tyson lacked the pretty-
boy charisma of Ray Leonard and the humble, God-fearing peity of
Evander Holyfield, two types that so many Americans could digest easily.
(Holyfield, once managed by MC Hammer and praised in rhyme by
Snoop Doggy Dogg, had many non–East Coast rap supporters.) Tyson
was never at ease with our country's social niceties. His boredom with
traditional decorum has always emanated from behind the shades he
wore to innumerable pre-fight press conferences.

That same energy, the one unleashed in the ring and in his voracious
nightclub crawling, made Tyson a hero in places where hip hop ruled. As
a consequence he was mentioned in scores of rap records because his
force and irreverence earned the rappers' respect. When Will Smith was
still the Fresh Prince he made a song about him called "I Think I Can
Beat Mike Tyson" and, to show his gratitude, Tyson bruised the MC's
arms with punches during the shooting of the video.

In the '80s Tyson made the hip hop nation proud, but in the '90s
Tyson fell victim to its weaknesses. The permanent business of boxing
took control of his career and his money. Lack of discipline led him to
defeat at the hands of Buster Douglas, a lesser fighter, in Japan. Objecti-
fying women led him into a horrible mismatch of a marriage with an actress he saw on TV, and his sense of entitlement sent him to jail for rape
in Indiana.

Like so many of his generation Tyson rejected Christianity for Islam
while imprisoned, though he seems hard-pressed to maintain its aus-
terity once released. And then, in perhaps the most bizarre heavyweight
fight of all time, he bit off a piece of the ear of his great antagonist

Holyfield, a testament to the impatience and unfocused rage that often mars contemporary black youth culture.

For a true warrior, a loss of face, a public humiliation within the confines of the battle is the deepest blow. In some cultures such a fall from grace calls for a suicide by private ritual. In America, however, Tyson, still a young man, will fight again. But more important, both for him as a symbol and as a man, is how Tyson handles the years when publicly sanctioned brawls are over and he is confronted with the rest of his life.

The challenge Tyson, and his generation's particular brand of pride, faces is whether he has the staying power to thrive in a highly uncertain future. Muhammad Ali, silenced for years yet eloquent in his gestures, remains a vital force decades removed from his greatest triumphs. Tyson must somehow find his own version of that grace or all his once furious victories will have no resonance. They will just exist as a few notes in the melody of his failures.

chapter 5
black owned?

A TIME OF TENSION, RACIALLY FENCED IN
I CAME OFF (AND ALL THE BROTHERS BLESSED HIM)

    —3RD BASS,
        "PRODUCT OF THE ENVIRONMENT"

SOMETIME IN THE MID-'80S CHARLES STETTLER, THEN MANAGER OF the Fat Boys, charged me with racism. "You don't like me," he scolded, "Because I'm a white and I manage a black group." Stettler was the balding, glib European who'd skillfully masterminded the marketing of three overweight Brooklyn boys into rap stars. Under his guidance Prince Markie Dee (Mark Morales), Kool Rock-Ski (Damon Wimbley), and the Human Beat Box (Darren "Buffy" Robinson) amassed significant hits ("In Jail," "All You Can Eat," "Can You Feel It") and won major commercial endorsements.

Stettler convinced the Swiss makers of Swatch watches, then struggling to penetrate the American youth market with their colorful timepieces, to underwrite a national hip hop tour for the Fat Boys in a national television spot, a historic breakthrough in terms of corporate support and national exposure for hip hop. After the Fat Boys costarred with Run-D.M.C. in the 1985 feature *Krush Groove*, Stettler negotiated a deal for a starring vehicle called *Disorderlies*, perhaps the crummiest of many crummy rap flicks.

Stettler, who had renamed the trio the more comic Fat Boys after they'd won a New York talent show as the Disco 3, cannily exploited the boys' hefty waistlines to make them lovable clowns and not what they were—health-endangered kids from East New York in Brooklyn, one of the city's toughest 'hoods. He was the ringmaster orchestrating a lucrative merchandising and media circus based primarily on the group's weight, particularly the unhealthy looking Buffy, and that same teenager's gift for creating polyrhythms with his mouth.

If I had any real beef with Stettler it was because of his style, not his skin color. I have no inherent dislike of hustlers. It goes with the business—my good friend Russell Simmons is hardly shy about hyping his clients. Stettler and I just didn't vibe. Mind you, our bad chemistry didn't hurt his career any—over a decade later, Stettler's still in the game, as the manager of the nationally syndicated hip hop radio jocks Dr. Dre and Ed Lover—but our interactions are still chilly.

Yet Stettler's charge of antiwhite racism has lingered with me. Not because I felt he was justified, but because it dramatized for me how much antiwhite feeling Stettler must have encountered in his moves through the black music world. Antiwhite rhetoric flows through hip hop, and he had no reason to think I felt any different.

One of the prevailing assumptions around hip hop is that it was, at some early moment, solely African-American created, owned, controlled, and consumed. It's an appealing origin myth—but the evidence just isn't there to support it. Start with who "invented" hip hop: In its days as an evolving street culture, Latino dancers and tastemakers—later internationally know as breakers—were integral to its evolution, because of the synergy between what the mobile DJs played and what excited the breakers. Also, Caribbean culture clearly informed hip hop's Holy Trinity—Afrika Bambaataa, Grandmaster Flash, and Kool Herc. Two of them, Flash and Herc, were either born in the Carribean or had close relatives from there. In Bam's case, non-American black music had been essential to his aesthetic.

More heretically, on the owner front, I'd argue that without white entrepreneurial involvement hip hop culture wouldn't have survived its first half decade on vinyl. It is indisputable that black-owned independents like Sugar Hill, Enjoy, and Winley cultivated and supported hip hop from 1979 to 1981. But it was white small-businesspeople who nurtured it next. Scores of white stepmothers and fathers adopted the baby as their own and many have shown more loyalty to the child than more celebrated black parental figures.

The list of these folks is long and includes Tommy Boy founder Tom Silverman and president Monica Lynch, the late manager-producer Dave (Funken) Klein, publicist Bill Adler, artist and A&R man Serch (Michael Berrin), record executive-producer Dante Ross, Jive's Barry Weiss and Ann Carli, Select's Fred Munao, Tuff City's Aaron Fuchs, Priority's Brian Turner (a tremendous champion of West Coast and non–New York rap) and of course the Fat Boys' Charles Stettler. Lyor Cohen, Russell Simmons's longtime partner, first in Rush Management and later at Def Jam, has long been a behind-the-scenes force. Def Jam itself was founded by the adventureous producer Rick Rubin. Booking agent Cara Lewis has been a longtime champion in the shark-infested waters of concert appearances.

Interestingly, the majority of these men and women were Jews who carried on a long tradition of black and white collaboration in grassroots music that stretches back, at least, to the '40s when Jewish record men like Leonard and Phil Chess in Chicago and Jerry Wexler in New York led the pioneers who put electrified blues and R&B on vinyl. All of these people poured a great deal of time and passion into hip hop and, of course, many were handsomely rewarded. And, I say, why not? They believed when so many others didn't.

In 1989 Public Enemy was widely accused of anti-Semitism because of public statements given by its Minister of Information Professor Griff (William Griffen). This flap, which generated plenty of hand-wringing and column inches in the music press, resulted in Griff's removal from the group. Later lyrics in one of the band's greatest records, "Welcome to the Terrordome" on the 1990 *Fear of a Black Planet*, were interpreted to be anti-Semitic—again generating much morning talk show fodder. The great irony of these two infamous is-Public-Enemy-anti-Semitic controversies was how many Jews were working for and with the band at the time. Public Enemy were signed to Def Jam by the Jewish Rick Rubin. Their tours were organized by the Jewish Lyor Cohen at Rush Management in conjunction with agent Cara Lewis. Much of their spin doctoring at the time was done by the Jewish Bill Adler at Rush Management. And Chuck D and Hank Schocklee were partners in Rhythm Method Productions with two Jews, Ed Chalpin and Ron Skuller. If P.E. hated Jews, then they must have been applying the gangster ethos: "Keep your friends close and your enemies closer."

The truth is, during 1981 to 1985, hip hop's developmental period, African-American executives at black music departments and at black urban radio were not supportive. The buppies of the business who peopled the black music departments of the early to mid '80s and programmed radio stations were still putting time into Michael Jackson clones or the latest act from Minneapolis with keyboards programmed like Prince. They didn't understand, respect, or support hip hop.

Kurtis Blow, signed to Mercury in 1979, was the only rap star with a major label deal at the time. His contract didn't come through the black department—he was signed by a white English A&R executive. There was a real class schism working against hip hop at the time. This dislike of the music was hardly limited to blacks in the business, but of course their lack of enthusiasm had real practical consequences. If you're looking for one of those crucial turning points where the adult black population began to profoundly disconnect from its kids, where the foundations of the intergenerational tension rampant in the '90s began, you can find it in the attitudes of black music industry figures of the early '80s toward hip hop.

During my tenure as black music editor at *Billboard*, I regularly interviewed the buppies, and psuedo-buppies, who populated the offices of CBS, Warner Bros., PolyGram, RCA, MCA, and the other corporate imprints. The closer they drew to the top the stronger their attitude of "How long will this last?" They saw rap records, at best, as a fad and, at worst, as a blotch on African-America. This profound mistake occurred because these executives, armed with expense accounts and suburban homes, had fallen out of touch with—or deliberately rejected—black urban youth culture and were skeptical of any talent not recommended by attorneys and managers they hobnobbed with at the Jack the Rapper and Black Radio Exclusive conventions.

The corporate record companies had been committed to producing black talent a little over a decade when hip hop on small labels began appearing regularly on the charts. Because it was perceived as juvenile, unmusical, and with a limited audience, it didn't fit the prevailing crossover orthodoxy then epitomized by Michael Jackson and Lionel Richie. The twist is that hip hop prospered without them—by figuring out a whole different way to attract white music fans.

WALK THIS WAY

It is a fallacy that there ever existed a time when hip hop buyers were exclusively black. The first rap hit, "Rapper's Delight," was voted single of the year by the National Association of Record Merchandisers, hardly a collective interested in celebrating singles sold just to black teenagers. "The Breaks" was only the second 12-inch single ever to sell 500,000 copies, a format originally designed for disco. You've got to be deluded to think that no whites purchased "The Breaks" in large numbers. The same can be said of Afrika Bambaataa & the Soul Sonic Force's "Looking for the Perfect Beat" and Grandmaster Flash & the Furious Five's "The Message." The numbers betray the myth. All these records were crucial building blocks for the music, artistic triumphs, and multicultural successes—just the crossover market the big labels lusted for.

In fact, a straight line can be drawn from "Rapper's Delight" to the hip hop present by looking at popular rap hits whose sales testify to the devotion of the white teen audience for nearly twenty years.

Sugar Hill Gang "Rapper's Delight" 1979
Stayed on the *Billboard* pop chart for 12 weeks, though it only reached #36. The charts at that time were heavily skewed by pop radio play, which the record didn't get a lot of. Still, its 12-week stay reflected the record's appeal. Because sales were balanced out by pop air play during this period, the position of rap singles on the chart weren't always true baromters of their crossover sales. In Canada and several foreign territories "Rapper's Delight" was a top 5 record.

Kurtis Blow "The Breaks (Part I)" 1980
Only the second 12-inch single to be certified gold. For perspective, it should be noted that the first was the Barbra Streisand–Donna Summer duet, "Enough Is Enough."

Grandmaster Flash & the Furious Five (featuring Duke Bootee) "The Message" 1982
Social commentary that first made rock critics respect rap lyrics and inspired a generation of MCs. A gold single.

Herbie Hancock (with Grandmixer DST) "Rockit" 1983

Though it only reached #71 on the pop chart, it went gold in large part because the still-young MTV network adored its gimmicky video.

Chaka Khan (with Melle Mel) "I Feel for You" 1984

The first hugely commercial collaboration between a rapper and an established vocal star. It went to #3 on the pop chart, then went gold and pushed Khan's album, *I Feel for You*, to platinum. Adapted from a Prince song.

Run-D.M.C. "Rock Box" 1984

A hit MTV video helped propel this first rap-rock success. Helped make the trio's debut album, *Run-D.M.C.*, gold.

Run-D.M.C. (with Aerosmith) "Walk This Way" 1986

As culturally significant as "Rapper's Delight." Made Run and his crew superstars, revived the career of Aerosmith by remodeling one of their classics, and made the rock world pay attention to Rick Rubin's production skills. Run-D.M.C.'s *Raising Hell* sold three million copies.

Jazzy Jeff & the Fresh Prince "Parents Just Don't Understand" 1988

Everything that Will Smith (aka the Fresh Prince) has accomplished, from his television series to his movie stardom, flows out of this song and video.

Beastie Boys "Fight for Your Right to Party" 1986

This frat-party anthem led the landmark album *Licensed to Ill* to sales of four million plus, which at the time was the most albums sold by any rap act.

L.L. Cool J "I Need Love" 1987

L.L. created the rap ballad and rode it to #1 on the black singles chart, one million sales, and a two-million-selling album, *Bigger and Deffer*.

Salt-N-Pepa "Push It" 1987

This single sold one million copies and the accompanying album, *Hot, Cool & Vicious*, went platinum, both firsts for female rappers.

Rob Base & DJ E-Z Rock "It Takes Two" 1988

A genius, left-field dance hit with great sampled hooks and a quick-silver rhyme from Rob Base that sold one million copies.

Tone Lōc "Wild Thing" 1989

Another great dance single. Reached #2 on the pop chart and stayed on 25 weeks. The album *Lōc-ed After Dark* went #1 on the pop chart and contained another huge single, "Funky Cold Medina," that hit the #3 spot.

Digital Underground "Humpty Dance" 1989

If you wanna be nostalgic for when hip hop was fun, this record makes your case. Fun, funny, and sure to rock any house party. One million satisfied customers purchased it.

Young MC "Bust a Move" 1989

Went to #7 on the pop charts behind a brash, lively video by Tamra Davis (who'd already done Tone Lōc's two hits).

MC Hammer "U Can't Touch This" and "Pray" 1990

By sampling Rick James and Prince, and making kinetic dance-driven videos, Hammer created a formula that's worked in hip hop ever since—familiar samples and movement-driven visuals. As a result *Please Hammer Don't Hurt 'Em* sold 10 million copies, more than twice what the Beasties did just a few years before.

Vanilla Ice "Ice Ice Baby" 1990

The Osmond Brothers to Hammer's Jackson Five, Vanilla Ice enjoyed a #1 single and a seven-times platinum album, made a movie, was threatened by Suge Knight, and dated Madonna. It was his fifteen minutes, and they were action packed. Now stands as the universal symbol of hip hop wackness.

Naughty By Nature "OPP" 1991

Lead rapper Treach had a hard delivery over pop melodies, an infectious blend that led this clever record to #6 on the pop chart and two million sales.

L.L. Cool J "Around the Way Girl" 1990

No rapper has loved women more than L.L., and this celebration of urban womanhood went gold and set up L.L.'s best album, *Mama Said Knock You Out*.

Salt-N-Pepa "Let's Talk About Sex" 1991

Playful, cute, and yet frank. A gold girl-group record for the '90s.

Arrested Development "Tennessee" 1992

A true one-album phenomenon that led the group to the 1992 Grammy for best new artist. The *3 Years, 5 Months & 2 Days in the Life Of . . .* sold two million copies.

House of Pain "Jump Around" 1992

Another white rap one-hit wonder, but a damn good one.

Sir Mix-A-Lot "Baby Got Back" 1992

A #1 pop single that rapped the praises of the African-American backside. Who says hip hip isn't a force for good?

Kriss Kross "Jump" 1992

Teen appeal duo with backward gear, an undeniable pop hook, and shrewd production by young Jermaine Dupri. Atlanta's emergence into the hip hop game.

Naughty By Nature "Hip Hop Hooray" 1993

A hip hop anthem for the time capsule with an irritatingly memorable chorus and a simple, arm-waving dance move that replaced the wave at sports arenas nationwide. Spike Lee's biggest video.

Tag Team "Whoomp! (There It Is)" 1993

Inspired by the activities at an Atlanta strip club, it went on to be one of the biggest-selling singles of all time at four million sold. It is one of the records that people will forever identify with the '90s.

Dr. Dre "Nuthin' But a 'G' Thang" 1993/Snoop Doggy Dogg "Gin & Juice" 1994

The power of street knowledge manifested. Two massive hits that illustrate the intense, spacious, funk-based production of Dre and the singing, sinister, melodic voice of Snoop. Dre's *The Chronic* sold three million and Snoop's *Doggystyle* eventually sold four.

Coolio "Gangsta's Paradise" 1995

Employing the Hammer formula and an unusual hairstyle, this ex–gang banger found a new career as a pop star with a bite of Stevie Wonder's "Pastime Paradise" from the *Dangerous Minds* soundtrack.

Salt-N-Pepa "Shoop" 1995

Not a great hip hop group, but a fantastic pop singles act, the Queens from Queens rule again.

Puff Daddy (featuring Mase) "Can't Nobody Hold Me Down" 1997

In the wake of the Notorious B.I.G.'s murder and at the height of Puff's synchronicity with the age, this three million seller became the "Ain't No Stoppin' Us Now" of the '90s.

These records share plenty of similarities. They are overwhelmingly dance-oriented with up-beat lyrics and catchy, simple choruses that appealed to teenage girls and kids (the notable exceptions are the down tempo L.L. Cool J's "I Need Love" and Coolio's "Gangsta's Paradise"). Most sample a musical or vocal hook from a well-known R&B or pop song of the '70s or '80s. "Rapper's Delight" is one of the few that actually had musicians re-create the musical source—in this case Chic's "Good Times"—by employing a band. Quite a few in the '80s used rock guitar riffs in their hooks, a trend that has become as played out as laceless sneakers.

From "Rockit" on, the records were aided by vivid, fun videos that gave the performers larger-than-life personas and featured great dancing or some combination of both. The public's embrace of the kinetic, dance-oriented videos for innocuous records like "Ice Ice Baby" or "Bust a Move" was crucial in driving them to million-selling status. Listening to Young MC and Vanilla Ice's records without recalling the videos is like imagining hip hop DJing without the mixer.

To hard-core purists almost all the records on my list are crossover crap and not "true hip hop," a stance that, like a great many purist positions in all art, is short-sighted and ahistorical. Throughout the last twenty years these hits kept the general population excited or at least aware of the music and, within the industry, constantly proved nonbelievers wrong.

Bubblegum rap records, often made by one- (or perhaps two-) hit wonders, just one angle of intersection between hip hop and white buyers. The reception given "The Message" by rock media (*Rolling Stone* gave the song a five-star review) foreshadowed a long-standing kinship between the teenage male rock audience and hip hop. Perhaps the chief exploiter of this relationship has been Def Jam Records head Russell Simmons. Starting with "Rock Box," produced by Simmons with Larry Smith, Run-D.M.C. was promoted as a rock band. There was a rebellious, nonconformist attitude in rap that Russell saw as analogous to the rock attitude he experienced hanging out at punk clubs like the Mudd Club, Hurrah's, and the Peppermint Lounge in Manhattan.

The white hipsters who had been intrigued by hip hop in its graffiti and break dancing forms also became fans of the music, influencing the coverage of early rap records in periodicals like the *Village Voice, SoHo Weekly News*, and other Lower Manhattan journals. Early national television exposure on ABC's *20/20* was also catalyzed by this community. However, Russell, who left Queens to become a habitué of this downtown world, was after bigger game. He wanted mall America to become hip hop America, and in Rick Rubin—NYU student, long-haired guitarist, hardcore rap aficionado, and product of Long Island—Russell found a partner who shared his vision of rap as rock.

Rubin "reduced" rap tracks, moving the music away from the R&B that supported Kurtis Blow and the Furious Five to a hard, stark aural assault with antecedents in AC/DC's "Back in Black" and Billy Squier's

"The Big Beat"—the last of which had been an old-school break beat in the Bronx. The Rubin-reduced sonic masterpieces created with Run-D.M.C. (*Raising Hell*) and on several Def Jam acts (L.L. Cool J's *Radio*, the Beastie Boys' *Licensed to Ill*) added heavy metal timbres to the beat emphasis of old-school DJs, creating a new way of hearing hip hop. Moreover, encouraged by Russell and Rubin, their artists proved that hip hop albums could be more than a collection of singles and filler, they could be complete artistic statements in a way rock fans understood.

One of the peculiar things about African-American culture is that white interest in black art is what sometimes incites proprietory interest in that art within our community. Prime example: the emergence of the Beastie Boys. The rapid rise of this Manhattan-based trio of white MCs, whose debut, *Licensed to Ill*, sold four million copies, generated a racial chauvinism among black folks, making the Beasties the first whites (but hardly the last) to be accused of treading on 100 percent black turf.

The irony is that these young men were managed and zealously promoted by Russell Simmons. It was one of the rare moments in pop history that a successful white group practiced a black music style with a black person so intimately involved in guiding their careers. (The next most prominent example is Boston-based producer-writer Maurice Starr's grooming of teen idols New Kids on the Block and their subsequent management by Dick Scott, another black man.) While Rubin provided the production punch, Russell gleefully encouraged the various little acts of adolescent outrage that the band perpetrated to promote *Licensed to Ill*, for which the trio became justly notorious and now, happily, have matured out of.

Public Enemy, signed by Rubin and hyped by Russell, found its own unique balance of rap danceablity and rock aggression. Black people used to wonder how a problack nationalist group like P.E. garnered a large, loyal, white fan base. It was simple: Public Enemy rocked and rebelled, literally, against the status quo. There is an endearing part of the white American mind that as teenagers (and less often as adults) detests the outward manifestations of this nation's mainstream culture. To be sure, this youthful rebellion is often superficial, not politically astute, and can be highly hypocritical—but it sells a lot of records.

This limited rebellion led white teenagers to pump *It Takes a Nation of Millions to Hold Us Back* in 1988, Ice Cube's *AmeriKKKa's Most Wanted* in

sample this

MASE GOT THE LADIES, PUFF DRIVES MERCEDEZ
TAKE HITS FROM THE '80s, DON'T IT SOUND SO CRAZY

—MASE,
"BAD BOY," 1997

ON A SUNDAY MORNING IN 1988 I WAS A GUEST, ALONG WITH PRODUCER-songwriter Mtume and a couple of other music industry types, on Bob Slade's *Week in Review,* a radio show on New York's KISS-FM. We were kicking it about African-American culture and Mtume was wailing hip hop upside its head. The man who wrote '80s standards like Roberta Flack's "The Closer I Get to You" and Stephanie Mills's "I Never Knew Love Like This Before," Mtume is one of the most articulate, thoughtful musicians I've ever encountered. He was a political activist with Ron Karenga's nationalist U.S. organization in the '60s (with whom he sur-vived a shoot-out with the Panthers). He played with Miles Davis during his controversial funk period and went on to write and produce for Flack, Mills, Levert, and Phyllis Hyman as well as with his own band. Mtume's wide musical experience, balanced by his grounding in street politics, has given him a provocative perspective on the evolution of black culture and music.

Mtume spent much of this particular Sunday morning blasting hip hop record production for its slavish reliance on record sampling. He charged that "this is the first generation of African-Americans not to be extending the range of the music" and that the resulting recordings "were nothing but Memorex music." To further illustrate his creative disdain,

Mtume made a bold analogy: sampling James Brown's drum beats in a hip hop album was like me sticking chapters from James Baldwin in my books and claiming the words as mine.

Now let me be clear here. Mtume wasn't totally against sampling as a musical tool. What he was objecting to was the use of sampling as a substitute for musical composition. It upset him that so many hip hop producers had no understanding of theory, could play no instruments, and viewed a large record collection as the only essential tool of record making. He charged that this made for lazy musicians and listeners. If obscenity is what the general public chiefly criticizes in hip hop as a social statement, the musically astute have long expressed contempt for its rampant sampling.

Listening to KISS-FM that morning was Daddy-O (Glenn Bolton) of Brooklyn's Stetsasonic, a six-member crew composed of rappers, a DJ, and a live drummer, who boldly proclaimed themselves a hip hop band. Just as Mtume's cold-blooded critique of sampling reflected the widespread disdain of soul-generation musicians for the use of sampling (especially when done without crediting the source recordings), Stetsasonic's response to his comments spoke to hip hop's warrior aesthetic: when challenged, dis back.

Stetsasonic's answer was "Talkin' All That Jazz," a most articulate defense of sampling that became the band's signature hit. Released in 1988, "Jazz," which itself was based on a loop made from sampling '70s keyboardist Lonnie Liston Smith's instrumental "Expansions," argued: "Tell the truth, James Brown was old / 'Til Eric and Rak came out with 'I Got Soul' / Rap brings back old R&B and if we would not / People could have forgot." This was a reference to Eric B. & Rakim's use of several James Brown samples and singer Bobby Byrd's vocal in "You Know You Got Soul." Mtume didn't appreciate the line "You said it wasn't art / So now we're gonna rip you apart," and he certainly wasn't impressed with Stetsasonic's reply.

Sampling represents the kind of generational schism that tore through the rock world when folk purists chastised Bob Dylan for plugging in electric instruments in 1965 and jazz purists attacked Miles Davis for rejecting acoustic instruments in the early '70s. (Coincidentally, Mtume was Miles's percussionist for much of that period.) What continues to be debated is whether sampling is a tragic break with African-America's creative musical traditions or a radical, even transcendental, continuation of them.

NEW TOYS

Since the end of World War II, technology has been a driving force in moving black music ahead—it has given musicians tools and opened possibilities their old instruments never suggested. While Charlie Christian, an extraordinary jazz musician, was the first to explore the possibilities of the electric guitar, it was country boys from the South and Midwest, men like Muddy Waters and Chuck Berry, who electrified the blues, giving rural music a hard, loud, citified sheen that set the stage for rock 'n' roll. Monk Montgomery, a bass player in Lionel Hampton's dance-crazy postwar big band, was the first to tour with the Fender bass guitar, an instrument that, along with the electric guitar and larger trap drum kits, recalibrated the sound of American dance music.

Quincy Jones once told me that the bass guitar's sound was "so imposing in comparison to the upright bass . . . it couldn't have the same function. You couldn't have it playing 4/4 lines because it had too much personality. Before the electric bass and the electric guitar, the rhythm section was the support section, backing up the horns and piano. But when they were introduced everything upstairs had to take a backseat. . . . The old style didn't work anymore and it created a new language."

Similarly, Stevie Wonder's embrace of the Moog synthesizer in the '70s again revamped pop. As Wonder announced with *Music of My Mind* and then elaborated on in a series of masterpieces (*Innervisions, Fulfillingness' First Finale, Songs in the Key of Life*), sounds filtered through then-novel computer technology could give an adventurous composer access to traditional sounds (strings, horns) and a wide range of new sonic textures. Just as the big bands were overwhelmed by enhanced rhythm sections of the '50s, Wonder's synthesizer-driven albums had a ripple effect throughout popular music. One by-product of the synthesizer's versatility was that it eventually drove most of the great African-American bands of the '70s to either shrink or disband in its wake.

At the tail end of the '70s the Fairlight Computer Musical Instrument appeared out of Australia. Sampling was not the main feature of this machine, though many musicians utilized it for that. With a Fairlight you could digitize a real sound, manipulate its pitch or tone, and then replay it. English artists such as the estimable Peter Gabriel and lesser acts like Heaven 17 and the Human League utilized the Fairlight in the early '80s. So did R&B producer Kashif and Earth, Wind & Fire, on its abysmal *Powerlight* album.

Around 1981 the E-mu Emulator, the first pure sampler, was developed and put on the market in the United States. This digital device, and the many others that followed, possessed the ability to store, manipulate, and play back any sound that had been stored in it. No musical expertise was needed to use it, though there is an inherent musicality required to understand how elements from various recordings can be arranged to create something new. But to make it work, you just had to know how to push the buttons.

Legend has it that the Emulator was first used in hip hop to capture the drum sound from an old record, which became the centerpiece of rap record production, by accident. Marley Marl was doing a remix in either 1981 or 1982 and was trying to sample using his Emulator when "accidently a snare went through," as he told Harry Allen. He loved the sound of this old snare on his remix and realized "I could take any drum sound from any old record, put it in here and get that old drummer sound on some shit."

Kurtis Blow claimed that in 1983 he used a Fairlight to snatch the "one, two" countdown from "A.J. Scratch," making the first sample loop, using go-go band Trouble Funk's "Pump It Up," on his hip hop standard "If I Ruled the World."

Before hip hop, producers would use sampling to disguise the absence of a live instrument. If a horn was needed or a particular keyboard line was missing, a pop producer might sample it from another record, trying to camouflage its artificiality in the process. However, a hip hop producer, whose sonic aesthetic was molded by the use of break beats from old records pulled from dirty crates, wasn't embarrassed to be using somebody else's sounds. Recontextualizing someone else's sounds was, after all, how hip hop started. For example, producer Marley Marl became known for the "dusty" quality of his productions. In his records for

Big Daddy Kane, Biz Markie, and L.L. Cool J, you could damn near hear the pops, scratches, and ambient noise of old vinyl.

To the post-soul generation that makes and consumes rap—people who grew up using remote controls, microwaves, and video games—employing an E-mu SP-1200 (favored by Public Enemy's producers) or an Akai MPC-60 (utilized by Teddy Riley) to sample, then loop and surround with other percussive elements is making music and no amount of bitching can change that.

SAMPLE THAT

In 1979, the Sugar Hill house band replayed Chic's "Good Times" to provide musical backing for "Rapper's Delight." Eighteen years later, Sean "Puff Daddy" Combs sampled Diana Ross's "I'm Coming Out" to provide musical backing for the Notorious B.I.G.'s "Mo Money Mo Problems"—both sampled songs were written by the team of the late Bernard Edwards and Nile Rodgers. The Sugar Hill Gang, and many of the early studio band–generated rap records, used live musicians to replicate the feel of a DJ spinning. They may have been trying to create a sound that black radio DJs felt more comfortable airing, but it had nothing to do with the way authentic rap was made or sounded. Rather, this strategy reflected the sensibility of the soul-era producers who controlled the recording process at Sugar Hill, Enjoy, and elsewhere.

Sampling's flexibility gave hip hop–bred music makers the tools to create tracks that not only were in the hip hop tradition but allowed them to extend that tradition. For them the depth and complexity of sounds achievable on a creatively sampled record has made live instrumentation seem, at best, an adjunct to record making. Records were no longer recording of instruments being played—they had become a collection of previously performed and found sounds.

Hip hop's sampling landmarks were both recorded in the late '80s by two acts from Long Island. The power of the first, Public Enemy's *It Takes a Nation of Millions to Hold Us Back* from 1988, is not simply its evocation of the Black Panthers, the Nation of Islam, and fearless brothers confronting anti-Nigga Machines. All that rhetoric is intensified with heavy-metal vigor by a tapestry of samples that set standards few have come close to since.

Greg Tate described it as "a songcraft from chipped flecks of near forgotten soul gold. On *Nation* a guitar vamp from Funkadelic, a moan from Sly, a growl abducted from Bobby Byrd aren't rhythmically spliced in but melodically sequenced into colorful narratives. Think of Romare Bearden." The revered African-American painter used color, texture, and collage (photos, ads, fabric) in a visual approach that is comparable in many ways to what the Bomb Squad production team achieved with *Nation*. Pulling from the Nation of Islam's Sister Ava Muhammad, a John Coltrane solo, an Anthrax rock riff, and scores of other sound sources, *Nation* fulfilled the visionary promise of sampling as an agitprop tool.

Equally visionary was De La Soul's whimsical debut, *3 Feet High and Rising*, a 24-track collection of raps, songs, puns, skits, and amused good feeling that was released a year after *Nation*. While P.E. looked for sounds that articulated anger and contempt, De La Soul sought bemused, off-handed noises and deceptively childlike melodies: De La Soul's "Eye Know" features Steely Dan's "Peg" rubbing up against Otis Redding's "Dock of the Bay," and on "Say No Go" Sly Stone fragments meet the Hall and Oates hook from "I Can't Go for That." Over these crafty Prince Paul–produced tracks, rappers Trugoy and Posdnuos intone their lyrics with a witty, conversational ease.

It Takes a Nation and *3 Feet High and Rising* were both products of a more carefree environment regarding sampling. Producers in the '80s tended to make liberal use of musical samples and were not as concerned about copyright issues. That philosophy has been replaced by greater sophistication on the part of everyone involved—the record labels, the producers, and especially those with catalogs that have been heavily sampled, who are now eternally vigilant. After "Rapper's Delight" hit the charts in 1979, Edwards and Rodgers eventually sued and got full songwriting credit (and royalties) on the Sugar Hill Gang hit. The case was widely covered, but sampling still went on for years before attorneys really caught on to how lucrative sampling could be for the original sound creators.

There is an evident racial aspect to this wake up-call. It was only when progressive groups such as P.E. and De La Soul began expanding beyond black music for samples that the form truly attracted negative attention.

When rock or pop musicians found that—horror of horrors!— a rap group was using their music, they tended to go after the offense with an outrage that spoke to their contempt for the form. Old R&B performers on the whole were not aggressive enough, or maybe they were just more used to being ripped off. Prince Paul, a member of Stetsasonic when they made "Talkin' All That Jazz," was, along with De La Soul's other members, sued for using a bit of a song by the '60s band the Turtles on De La Soul's "Transmitting Live from Mars," resulting in a costly out-of-court settlement.

The most damaging example of anti–hip hop vindictiveness in a sample case came from a most unlikely source. In 1992, the gentle-voiced '70s balladeer Gilbert O'Sullivan sued Cold Chillin'–Warner Bros. signee Biz Markie for unauthorized use of his 1972 hit "Alone Again (Naturally)." But instead of sticking up Biz and his record companies for a substantial royalty on all records sold—which he was certainly entitled to—O'Sullivan successfully forced Warner Bros. to recall all pressings and stop selling the album until the song was removed. The resulting loss of visibility severely damaged Biz Markie's career as a rapper and sent a chill through the industry that is still felt.

Obviously, sampling hasn't disappeared from hip hop, but the level of ambition in using these samples has fallen. The high-intensity sound tapestries of P.E. have given way to often simpleminded loops of beats and vocal hooks from familiar songs—a formula that has grossed Hammer, Coolio, and Puff Daddy millions in sales and made old R&B song catalogs potential gold mines.

The most audacious uses of sampling in the '90s has not come from hip hop proper but from acts directly influenced by hip hop aesthetics (the Beastie Boys, Beck, Tricky, Forest for the Trees) and from those for whom hip hop is but one key point of reference (Prodigy, the Chemical Brothers). The gulf between instruments and sampling, bridged by hip hop, is now a given in progressive dance music around the world. Hip hop moved sampling technology to a central place in record making, the same way R&B did the electric guitar and bass in the '50s and Stevie Wonder did the synthesizer in the '70s.

That undisputable fact doesn't always cheer me. Sometimes when I hear a record I grew up with—say, Diana Ross's Bernard Edwards and Nile Rodgers produced "I'm Coming Out"—reused in a contemporary record, I get pissed. I rail against the lack of creativity in the hip hop generation. I long for old familiar sounds to remain in their original context and for younger musicians, with new approaches, to dominate the musical mainstream.

But those are the cries of an old-school purist and this decade's culture has little use for such arguments. My answer to the question—is or isn't sampling an extension of African-American tradition?—is a straightforward no *and* yes. If creating new notes, new chords, and harmonies is what the African-American musical tradition is about, then sampling is not doing that. However, if that tradition means embracing new sounds, bending found technology to a creator's will in search of new forms of rhythm made to inspire and please listeners, well then sampling is as black as the blues. Sampling has changed the way a generation hears, and hip hop was central to that change. To quote Run-D.M.C., "It's like that and that's the way it is!"

A side note: Up to this day Mtume, who spent much of the '90s creating the hip hop–flavored score for Fox's *New York Undercover*, continues to be a vocal critic of rap's overuse of sampling, doing it now from his regular spot giving commentary Sunday mornings on WRKS in New York. Even the fact that "Juicy Fruit," the biggest hit his band enjoyed, has become an extremely popular sample—used quite prominently (and one imagines lucratively) in the Notorious B.I.G.'s "Juicy"—hasn't softened his opinion, though he no longer calls it "Memorex music." No, on that he's moved on. These days he calls it "artistic necrophilia" and has a good laugh.

chapter 8

where my eyes can see

IT IS SAID THAT THE CAMERA CANNOT LIE, BUT RARELY DO WE ALLOW IT TO DO ANY-
THING ELSE, SINCE THE CAMERA SEES WHAT YOU POINT IT AT: THE CAMERA SEES WHAT
YOU WANT IT TO SEE.

> —JAMES BALDWIN,
> *THE DEVIL FINDS WORK*

OF EVERYTHING THAT HAS AFFECTED THE EVOLUTION OF HIP HOP—
cash, corporations, crack, sampling, crime, violence—none is more
important than music video. Through its images, the attitude and obses-
sions of urban America have been broadcast around the world, igniting
fascination and fear, indignation and imitation, in the minds of youths
on the other side of the globe (or continent) from America's urban
streets. More than the millions Hollywood has spent on hip hop flicks
and promoters have poured into concert tours, it has been the video that
made the culture mythic.

Beginning in the '60s, videos featuring black music, as well as most
white acts, were shot for use in Europe as image-building tools. MTV,
which initially programmed clips made in Europe, had a hands-off attitude toward all forms of black music in its early years. Black music wasn't
"rock 'n' roll" and MTV defined itself as a televised rock radio station,
though that didn't stop them from playing videos by white performers
who played R&B or reggae.

In the United States, Black Entertainment Television's inauguration
in 1981 was a boon to R&B, but it would be years before the network's
conservative management embraced hip hop. So while mainstream black

music from the Solar stable of stars (the Whispers, Shalamar, Midnight Starr) found immediate play on BET, from 1981 to 1988 videos for hip hop MCs were more likely be seen in London than the Bronx.

For example, the video for "Rapper's Delight" was recorded during a Sugar Hill Gang club performance in the U.K. and wasn't seen widely here even after the record's success in the United States. Again, Whodini's 1982 video for "Magic's Wand," shot around Times Square and in the lobby of MTV's future home, 1515 Broadway, was shown primarily in the U.K. to exploit the group's connection to the then hot producer Thomas Dolby.

In the mid-'80s I regularly watched *Video Music Box*, a pioneering hip hop video show broadcast on New York City–owned WNYE, channel 31 on UHF. Predating *Yo, MTV Raps!* by several years, *Video Music Box* came on in the afternoons after school and on Saturdays, and it was the only place you were guaranteed to see rap's videos. Hosted by Ralph McDaniels and Lionel "the Vid Kid" Martin (later to become one of hip hop's top directors), it was then the cutting edge of rap television broadcasting. For years, NBC ran *Friday Night Videos*, a show with rotating celebrity hosts, as well as veteran radio DJ Frankie Crocker, that slipped selected hip hop hits in the mix.

Budgets for R&B videos in the '80s were small, on the high end running $40,000 to $50,000, while rock bands were regularly cracking the $100,000 barrier. At this time rap videos were being shot for as little as $10,000 and sometimes less. In an attempt to expand his career, neophyte auteur Spike Lee shot a spec video of Grandmaster Melle Mel's "White Lines" in 1983, before making *She's Gotta Have It*. The ultra-low-budget video, featuring Lawrence Fishburne, was officially turned down by producer Sylvia Robinson, though a bootleg of the piece sometimes showed up on local video shows.

The few videos that did exist for black acts of any genre were primitive. They were often shot on videotape, not film, in nightclubs, on city streets, or in front of blue-screened backgrounds with cheesy scenery. Conceptual videos were rare, elaborate locations rarer, and real impact on sales minimal owing to the lack of domestic airplay.

Interestingly, even the early video output of Prince, easily the single most innovative black pop musician of the '80s, suffered from low-rent production. His early domestic videos were performance clips ("Little

Red Corvette," "1999") shot on his concert stage. The master shot was a wide look at the stage area with variety provided by close-up inserts of Prince seducing the camera and his band writhing on beat. In essence, these were more mini–concert films (like his later extravaganza *Sign O' the Times*) than creative videos. Prince didn't make his first real creative music video until 1984's "When Doves Cry" when, shooting on film, the images proved almost as provocative as the song itself.

The world of music video was, of course, changed forever by Michael Jackson's 1983 breakthrough *Thriller* videos—"Billie Jean," "Beat It," and "Thriller." Not only did he extend the conceptual reach and upgrade filmmaking style and budgets for acts of all colors, he specifically opened the doors for the era's other crossover stars—Whitney Houston, Prince, and Lionel Richie—at MTV. But, for hip hop, Run-D.M.C. played the pioneering role in video. Just as "Beat It" employed rock guitar to make Jackson more palatable to MTV programmers, the use of rock motifs made Run-D.M.C. MTV friendly. Over the course of three albums Profile released one guitar-driven single a piece—"Rock Box" in 1984, "King of Rock" in 1985, "Walk This Way" in 1986—each selling more copies and winning more MTV exposure than the last.

While the kings from Queens made breakthrough rap videos, perhaps the most important personality in hip hop video's development was that quint-essential hipster, Fab Five Freddie Braithwaite. As I noted earlier, Fab helped move graffiti writing from subway walls to art galleries. Through graffiti, Freddie became a bridge between the uptown urban artists and the lower Manhattan scene then enthralled with the punk–New Wave aesthetic. (That's why Freddie received such a lovely shout out in Blondie's 1981 hip hop celebration, "Rapture," bopping so prominently in the video's background.) However, Fab's work to promote graffiti would prove to be only one phase of his involvement with hip hop's visual components.

In 1983, Freddie not only acted in Charlie Ahearn's hip hop feature *Wild Style*, he recruited talent and worked as a creative collaborator on a project that captured the experimental flavor of New York hip hop before its discovery by the mainstream. Parlaying his role as uptown-downtown cultural gatekeeper, the sartorially aware Freddie (the man is never without his ubiquitous eyewear, usually shades, and a hat or cap) moved smoothly between b-boys, bohemians, and businesspeople.

That crosscultural heat is a key reason why Ann Carli, Jive's vice president of artist development, suggested Freddie try directing a rap music video. His first effort was historic: the powerful black-and-white video for "My Philosophy," the first single off Boogie Down Productions *By All Means Necessary*. Rife with images of posse solidarity, the band's 'hood (Bronx, South and otherwise), the legacy of violence (the late Scott LaRock's son), and black heroes (Malcolm X, Bob Marley), the "My Philosophy" video was a landmark in its use of band-identified geography, Afrocentric icons, and tribal imagery—established motifs that appear in videos to this day. Freddie quickly became the rap video director du jour, able to fuse his own bohemian tendencies with the persona of various artists.

As rap videos emerged as a viable business, two rival black-owned production companies grew to prominence in New York: Atlantis, operated by director Rolando Hutson and producer Pam Gibson, and Classic Concepts, with director Lionel Martin and producer Ralph McDaniels. Later in the '80s, Paris Barclay, Chuck Stone, and Millicent Shelton, while still working with relatively low budgets, would upgrade the visual ambition of rap video. In the '90s, the pop success of hip hop and R&B-flavored hip hop has finally resulted in budgets that rival, and now often surpass, those given to big rock bands or pop solo singers. Two young African-Americans, Hype Williams and Paul Hunter, have used the increased financial resources given to black videos to create the glossiest, most technically sophisticated, and fun videos around.

Not surprisingly, it was black labels, such as Def Jam, Cold Chillin', and Uptown, that were key supporters of Classic and Atlantis. Filmmakers Reggie and Warrington Hudlin, later to make *House Party I* and *Boomerang*, got their young careers off the ground with two early videos for Uptown. And it is Puff Daddy's Bad Boy, that has given free reign to Hype and Hunter.

Soon white directors and production companies began aggressively pursuing these gigs. The reason? The increasing exposure the music was receiving—exposure Freddie was crucial in providing. Because of his visibility and hip persona, Freddie was a natural choice to host MTV's first foray into rap. *Yo, MTV Raps!* debuted on a Saturday in September 1988, immediately racking up the highest ratings of any show in the young network's history. In February 1989, the high ratings led MTV to

air a daily version hosted by Dr. Dre, Ed Lover, and T-Money. Both
Freddie's Saturday version and the daily show of *Yo* were produced by
Ted Demme, nephew of famed director Jonathan. Demme would use the
show as a springboard—later directing the Lover and Dre vehicle, *Who's
the Man?*, and then moving on to mainstream comedies like *The Ref.*

Yo, MTV Raps! didn't just pull in viewers—it sent seismic waves through
the whole music industry. By giving hip hop music, dances, and gear a
regularly scheduled national platform, the broadcast was integral in in-
culcating hip hop's distinctly urban culture into the rest of the country.
Within the record industry, *Yo's* popularity on MTV, which in the
United States reached the largest record-buying audience in the world,
encouraged the making of more hip hop videos and, as a by-product, the
on-fly documenting of hip hop style.

An exciting interplay—a kind of videographic loop—developed between the consumers and performers. Performers would latch on to a
new clothing style in the street. That style would be showcased in a video
and the audience would then be turned onto the style, be it Run's hat or
Snoop Doggy Dogg's braids. Within a few weeks, an outfit worn in
Queens or Compton would suddenly become a national and sometimes
international trend. Or the dialogue would go the other way. If unlaced
Adidas was the new national trend, acts would quickly try to catch
up and affirm the trend by wearing unlaced Adidas in their video. This
cultural cross talk meant that while an artist featured on *Yo* usually
sold more records, he or she could really blow up with a distinctive, exciting look.

Yo's visibility spawned grassroots rap video shows, most of which were
found on local cable and or public access. Often broadcasting from local
nightspots or concerts, this rap video underground became part of the
fabric of the culture, shining a spotlight on local artists and scenes and
airing raw videos that MTV wouldn't. *Yo's* ratings forced the conservative
programmers at Black Entertainment Television to finally introduce its
own version, *Rap City*, a full year after MTV. Slowly BET allowed rap to
seep into its regular programming mix.

The Box, a Miami-based network that broadcasted a call-in music
video request line on cable systems across America, was the ultimate expression of the hip hop interactivity. It began on a UHF station in Miami in December 1985 with locals being able to call in and order videos

from a list that ran across the screen. By 1992, The Box was available in thirty-six states with one-hundred sixty affiliates on UHF and cable. The booty videos of Miami's own Luther Campbell (such as "Doo Doo Brown") became staples of The Box and exposed viewers to records that no local radio station was playing. To aid in exposing certain videos, promotion people would hire kids to call constantly to request videos.

The Box suffered a major blow in 1995 when New York's Time-Warner, which controlled cable in the city, replaced The Box with the History Channel, bowing to corporate pressure to lessen Time-Warner's involvement with hip hop. This was one negative victory that C. Dolores Tucker, William Bennett, and their ilk could claim. Despite the setback, The Box is still broadcasted around the nation and continues to play a significant role in helping edgy acts find an audience outside MTV and BET.

In the mid-'80s, traditionalists fought kicking and screaming to keep rap out of the mainstream, but it was too late. Rap proved to have two elements that could not be denied—style and star power. As an expression of urban dress in the '80s, hip hop knew no peers. Before the mass marketing of designer labels targeted this audience in the '90s, style was more a projection of function and taste. From the time of the Sugar Hill Gang's sideburns and vests in 1979 to the Cameo cuts and four-finger rings of Big Daddy Kane in 1989, hip hop style moved with a relentless rapidity.

Videos projected images of these ever-changing styles and the artists who wore them across the globe, as no other African-American music style had been before. In the '60s, the Temptations or James Brown could play *The Ed Sullivan Show*, other network variety shows, *American Bandstand*, local *American Bandstand* knockoffs, and the odd Motown-produced TV special. In the '70s, black popular music was showcased on *Soul Train*, *Midnight Special*, *In Concert*, *The Mike Douglas Show*, and a trickle of network specials hosted by African-Americans (Bill Cosby, Diana Ross, the Jackson Five, etc.).

However, compared to the exposure white entertainers like Glen Campbell, Sonny and Cher, or Tony Orlando could achieve, black music was shown only briefly and often in a very culturally hostile environment. Videos, in contrast, are repeated endlessly and usually presented by hosts who feel kinship to the culture. The images, just like the music, have a just-off-the-street immediacy that excites kids in Iowa and Tokyo just as much as those in South Central Los Angeles. Hip hop's larger-than-life personas certainly lend themselves to the visual. Stars of the '80s like Luther Vandross, Freddie Jackson, and Whitney Houston wore the glitzy garments of Hollywood aristocracy, while rappers were the kids on the corner, no matter how extreme their mode.

Big Daddy Kane with his Grace Jones-meets-Carl Lewis hair, Biz Markie with his humorously grotesque dances, and Roxanne Shanté's take-no-shit homegirl (perhaps an unconscious blueprint for Queen Latifah's career) are just three examples from the Cold Chillin' "Juice Crew" of mid-'80s stars who managed to be regular and yet project a star-bright persona. On camera, rap stars popped like champagne corks, creating personality cults that energized record sales and caught Hollywood's eyes.

PRIVATE DICKS AND MENACING HOODS

There are two kinds of hip hop movies. Those that helped create the culture and those that reflect the culture spawned by the first. The first set embraces the genres of blaxploitation, kung fu, and action films of various descriptions. The second set are music- and dance-driven vehicles, ghetto coming-of-age stories, and the odd gem that captures the truth of contemporary African-American life without hokey plotting.

In the '70s, leading civil rights organizations like CORE and the NAACP railed against the film genre known as "blaxploitation," feeling these movies would have long-term negative effects on black youth. Having been one of those youths, I must admit the effects have lingered, both on me and our culture. My wardrobe is still filled with turtlenecks and leather jackets because of how cool Richard Roundtree looked throughout *Shaft*. In a larger sense, blaxploitation, and the urban entertainment culture such films were part of, still resonate in America at the turn of the century.

Samples of dialogue from the movies have popped up on hip hop records for years (a sound bite from *The Mack* intros "Rat-Tat-Tat-Tat" on Dr. Dre's *The Chronic*). Beyond sampling, phrases from the films are often paraphrased and their imagery is regurgitated. The Players Ball scene in *The Mack*, in which the story's pimp protagonist is crowned

"Mack of the Year," has shown up in several videos. The female rapper Foxy Brown owes her handle to a Pam Grier vehicle, while Jim Brown, Fred Williamson, and black cult comedian Rudy Ray Moore (the star and writer of the raucous Dolemite series of comedies) make frequent music video cameos. Antonio Fargas, a ubiquitous presence in blaxploitation as loudmouthed comic relief (*Shaft, Across 100th Street*) before getting a regular check as Huggy Bear in *Starsky and Hutch* on TV, hovers over many videos; his preening vanity and over-the-top delivery have been referenced in hip hop by Eazy-E and Public Enemy's Flavor Flav (Rico Drayton).

Video store geek turned gritty auteur Quentin Tarantino injects blaxploitation's potboiler storylines and "nigga"-driven language into his movies. Ving Rhames's gangster Marcelius and Samuel L. Jackson's Jhericurled hit man in *Pulp Fiction* are bloody cousins of the uptown kingpins who strode the blaxploitation landscape. And, of course, there would have been no *Jackie Brown* without the busty, bullet-blasting canon of Ms. Grier's films.

The question is not whether blaxploitation, and its exploitation contemporary, the kung fu movie, still impacts us—a resounding yes—the real trick is to figure out *why*. Looking back to my childhood, I'd argue that the answer is aggressive black heroism. Shaft, Hammer, Trouble Man, and Slaughter were tough, no-nonsense, and as cool as the other side of a pillow. Even the antisocial coke dealer Priest in *Superfly* and the pimp Goldie in *The Mack* filled their films with a sly cinematic presence that only church ladies and NAACP spokespeople could resist.

Unlike the relatively passive Sidney Poitier, who marched through the '60s in a white shirt, tie, and dark suit as the embodiment of noble striving, the blaxpoitation guys and gals were funky as multicolored bell-bottoms and two-toned platform shoes. In keeping with the candy-colored aesthetic of the period, these movies dressed their stars in state-of-the-art threads that allowed them to live as large and insolently as we all dreamed we could.

Never in the history of American cinema had there been so many aggressive, I-don't-give-a-damn black folks on screen. That is so crucial. Blaxploitation movies reserved little space for the singing of Negro spirituals, turning the other cheek, or chaste kisses. In fact, characters who possessed these qualities were often the brunt of much-appreciated derision. In blaxploitation black people shoot back with big guns, strut to bold jams, and have sweaty, bed-rocking sex. Whatever story the often loopy plots tell, they are usually secondary to full-bodied action.

This is why, two generations removed from their double-feature glory, blaxploitation videotapes fill the collections of teenagers and the genre is evident in the iconography of hip hop and R&B. Where my generation was the first to experience the heady exhilaration of commercially available black aggression, the hip hop generation has embraced in-your-face as a guiding principle. For contemporary consumers, blaxploitation movies often seem crudely made and haphazardly conceived. Yet the brashness of the characterizations doesn't look back on a past filled with public humiliation; they clearly look to a present where the value of cocky attitudes, sullen faces, and gaudy materialism are celebrated.

The youth culture of aggression that hip hop has codified (and commodified) also has roots in kung fu flicks. Parallel to blaxploitation coming out of Hollywood was an influx of films from Hong Kong and Asia that, for a time, replaced Westerns as the grassroots morality plays of the age. Based on rigid formulas similar to films like *Shane* as well as Asian folktales, these kung fu flicks tend to center on a virtuous yet humble martial arts initiate called upon to seek revenge against some evil clan that has caused injury to his family, teacher, school, or village. The hero's initial reluctance to fight is balanced by his balletic vigor once engaged in battle. In countless films, revenge is finally exacted and scores of eager teens memorized the leg whips, chops, and badly dubbed dialogue.

While blaxploitation's appeal is naked black aggression, kung fu provides a nonwhite, non-Western template for fighting superiority. The flying, leaping, spinning angels and devils of what *Variety* labeled "chop socky" movies are yellow men who awed us with their ability. And there was no one more awesome than Bruce Lee, the diminutive giant of the genre. He first came to pop culture prominence as Kato, the driver-sidekick of TV's live-action comic strip hero the Green Hornet. After his idea for a weekly kung fu series was in fact made, though he was replaced at the last minute by a white actor, Lee went over to Asia where he found fame in a series of kung fu kickfests. His masterpiece is *Enter the Dragon*, in which his skills and charisma transcend and elevate the genre in a way analogous to what Bob Marley was doing in reggae at the same time. In black homes in the '70s it was typical to find a Martin Luther

King portrait in the living room while in the basement, next to the component set and the velvet black light Kama Sutra horoscope, hung a poster of Lee, a truly worthy nonwhite icon.

Though kung fu movies were passe by the time of "Rapper's Delight" in 1979, their role in hip hop culture still looms large. For example, it is doubtful whether Joseph Saddler would have renamed himself Grandmaster without hearing that title of respect in countless chop socky flicks. Likewise, the "furious" title of his five rapping cohorts adopted to describe their antic delivery harked back to the titles of kung fu movies.

In the '90s, the vogue for contemporary Hong Kong action movies that blend '70s martial arts with more elaborate special effects (as in the popular Chinese Ghost Story series) inform the rhymes, names, and cosmology of the Wu-Tang Clan. Though they in fact come from Staten Island, its nine members claim to belong to an ancient and secret sect searching for the thirty-sixth chamber of martial arts knowledge. While theirs is far from a coherent vision, the Wu-Tang have used their interest in Asian action movies to inject a sense of the mystical into hip hop.

The final and, perhaps, most crucial link between '70s pulp movies and late '90s youth culture are blaxploitation soundtracks. No one can dispute the enduring quality of Isaac Hayes's *Shaft* and Curtis Mayfield's *Superfly*. Both soundtracks, the products of '60s soul producer-writers using movie scoring to expand the sonic scope of their work, are jammed with wahwah guitars, sensuous Latin percussion, blaring horns, supple flutes, and vocal choruses that still inspire current music makers.

Dr. Dre, the dominant hip hop producer of the early '90s, made extensive use of freshly created flute, keyboard, and bass lines that added cinematic sweep to the tales of drive-bys and machismo that made him famous. As the definitive gangsta rap producer it is quite appropriate that Dre consistently pays homage to blaxploitation in his provocative immorality plays. D'Angelo, a son of soul with a hip hop pedigree, opens his live show with the "Theme from *Shaft*." The singer isn't in search of postmodern irony or nostalgia; the song is an affirmation of his own badness that his fans happily co-sign.

The best blaxploitation music—the themes from *Shaft* and *Superfly*, Marvin Gaye's "Trouble Man," Willie Hutch's "Brothers Gonna Work It Out" from *The Mack*, James Brown's "Down and Out in New York City"

from *Black Caesar*—have a theatricality and sense of place that no succeeding genre of African-American pop, including hip hop, have consistently matched. But hip hop has embraced the rhythmic underpinning of
the scores. Listen closely to the work of Premier, Marley Marl, and other
veteran producers and you'll get an inkling of how early hip hop DJs utilized beats and bits of rhythm from these records.

I remember, in the late '70s, that the soundtrack from *Shaft in Africa*
was prized by party givers. The album's hit was the Four Tops's "Are You
Man Enough," but the object of passion was a percussion break on an
obscure instrumental. The three pioneering DJs of hip hop—Flash,
Afrika Bambaataa, Kool Herc—were relentless record excavators who
would comb the aisles of Downstairs Records, a cluttered shop on
Forty-third Street in the heart of Times Square, for the unknown, awful,
and ignored. Hawaiian guitars, drum fills, and the galloping rhythms of
chase-scene instrumentals often ended up in their mixes, linking B-movie
music to the groove obsessiveness that would mature into a culture.

Other movies have played a role in hip hop's naming rituals, and other
exploitation genres—the spaghetti Western, the white urban detective
movies starring Eastwood and Bronson—have also contributed styles,
scenes, and phrases to hip hop. The titles of two '80s sci-fi action films,
RoboCop and *Terminator*, became popular street names, not always used
with endearment. While Public Enemy's Terminator X was definitely an
affectionate shout out to James Cameron's lethal killer, brutal or racist
policemen were often dubbed Terminators or RoboCops to describe
their abusive law enforcing. The low-budget, slightly existential gangster
film *King of New York* gave hip hop a title that the Notorious B.I.G. would
claim as his own.

However, no '80s film had a bigger ripple effect on hip hop than Brian
De Palma's 1983 *Scarface*. Savaged by critics at the time of its release, the
film has had a life of its own; its Cuban coke-dealing protagonist Tony
Montana became the patron saint of drug traffickers. As written by a
young, wired Oliver Stone and played with over-the-top vigor by Al Pa-
cino, Montana gloried in his outsider status, big guns, and mountains of
cocaine.

The phrase "the world is mine," which came from the original '30s
Paul Muni version of *Scarface* and used again by De Palma, became a
catchphrase that has shown up in all manner of hip hop artifact—

videos, album titles, and songs. New York's Nas used it on his critically acclaimed first album. So did the Houston MC who was so moved by the flick that he labeled himself Scarface and then used its violent imagery to shape his recording persona. The raw, aggressive, unbridled energy in De Palma's film—'80s avarice personified—make it an essential hip hop text.

NEW JACK CINEMA

In contrast, the most consistently disappointing cultural offshoots of hip hop have been the movies made expressly about it. Feature films or documentaries, by and large, have been either technically crude, clueless about the culture, juvenile, or unfocused missed opportunities. In 1993, I cowrote and produced a comedy about hip hop and its effects, *CB4*, so I can testify firsthand to the difficulty of locking it down on film. Because film lacks the immediacy of music videos, any film on the subject is, on some level, dated by the time of its release. Because hip hop moves so rapidly, any aspect of the culture—the clothes, the slang, the dances, the music—can make a film seem a bit behind the times. Even if the movie is released only six months after it is shot, in hip hop that can be an eternity. The dictates of plot or, perhaps more accurately, the formulas of Hollywood storytelling have rarely enhanced viewer understanding of any subculture, much less one with this many layers.

I would argue that the only movie to truly capture the hip hop experience in the '90s was not *Boyz N the Hood*, *Menace II Society*, or the concert film *The Show*. Though all three exhibit moments of clarity about hip hop, only one feature that I've seen expresses the true fabric of daily life that created and sustains hip hop. Ironically, the film's actual subject is another urban obsession—basketball.

The crew that made the epic documentary *Hoop Dreams* spent four years following two Chicago schoolboy basketball players and their families. Director Steve James and his dedicated filmmaking team revealed the fantasy life, rationalizations, sociology, and tragedy that shape the mentality of working-class black America. *Hoop Dreams* documented the artistic impulses and mercenary business practices that both elevate (a few) and destroy (many) gifted young black athletes. Because of its nuance, humanity, and refusal to perpetuate stereotypes, *Hoop Dreams* captures the landscape that most hip hop films distort.

Because *Hoop Dreams* was a super-low-budget project, it has the substance but not the flash of hip hop culture. Feature films should have an advantage over a *Hoop Dreams*, since their mission is to choreograph arresting montages of music, sound, and image. Yet, save a moment here and there, few features have found a visual language for hip hop as bracing as the music. The scene of Omar Epps stalking Tupac Shakur at a Harlem house party as Cypress Hill's "I Could Just Kill a Man" plays on the soundtrack at the conclusion of *Juice* is for me a thrilling hip hop moment. And there's that vivid sequence near the end of *Do the Right Thing*, when the stuttering prophet Smiley walks into Sal's burning pizza shop to place a photo of Malcolm X greeting Dr. King on the wall of heroes. With "Fight the Power" pounding in the background, it is a complicated, strong moment.

But just as sampling changed the nature of hip hop record production, videos have made it tough for movies to keep up when it comes to nailing hip hop's imagery. Scott Calvert's "Parents Just Don't Understand" for Jazzy Jeff & the Fresh Prince, Lionel Martin's "Night of the Living Baseheads" for Public Enemy, Dr. Dre's "Let Me Ride" for himself, or Hype Williams's "Flava in Your Ear" remix for Craig Mack are just a few that come to mind that contain more intense, joyous, challenging, fun moments of hip hop pleasure in their five minutes than any single rap-influenced film (except perhaps *Wild Style*) has mustered.

RAPTORS

While big-screen narratives have largely failed the culture, the raptor (i.e., rap-actor) has consistently added guts, fun, and credibility to motion pictures. Rapping is an extrovert's art in which projecting a self-created identity is essential. This is why, to the chagrin of many established black actors, rappers have been able to walk off video sets and into movies with surprising ease. There is no question that even in their most ridiculous roles Ice Cube, Ice-T, and the late Tupac Shakur brought a street-hardened verisimiltude to the screen. The iconic weight of Cube in *Boyz N the Hood* and Ice-T in *New Jack City* grounded both films. While the two

Ices flaunt credible tough-guy personas, Shakur displayed true leading-man charisma. Not only could he flash DeNiroesque viciousness (*Juice*) but he had a vulnerability (*Poetic Justice, Grid Locke'd*) that showed how much of his inner life was concealed by his outlaw pose.

Like ex–football players during the exploitative '70s, hard-boiled rappers personify black hypermasculinity. The surprising part is how many have ended up succeeding as comic actors. While P.E.'s Flavor Flav, a natural screen presence, never got his shot at comedy, a number of MCs have adapted their ability to deliver a rhyme to comic timing. Kid 'N Play (Christopher Reid and Chris Martin), an amiable, dance-oriented New York rap duo, used *House Party I*'s unexpected success and quality (care of filmmakers Reggie and Warrington Hudlin) as a platform for four other movies, a sitcom pilot, a short-lived variety show, and celebrity status larger than their rhyme skills. Another beneficiary of the raptor trend has been Tone Lōc (Anthony Smith), whose gravelly voice and sleepy eyes make him a captivating caricature on record and in videos. Since 1991 he has worked steadily on film and TV, appearing in *Poetic Justice, Posse*, and the massive hit *Ace Ventura: Pet Detective*, in which he held a conversation with Jim Carrey's articulate asshole.

One of the biggest surprises of the raptor epoch is not that some have become sitcom stars, but which ones. Queen Latifah, who debuted in Afrocentric garb and was one of the first really tough female MCs, and L.L. Cool J, who started as a shouting, bellicose maker of agitated b-boy anthems, did not seem like future situation comedy stars. Yet, as Khadijah, publisher of a black magazine, Latifah anchored Fox's *Living Single* for four years, while L.L.'s mugging approach and aptitude for physical humor got *In the House* picked up by UPN in 1997 after NBC let it go after one season. That these once stern-faced hip hop heroes are so comfortable in the seemingly restricting half-hour format speaks to their innate sense of showmanship.

In her film roles, Latifah has been much more fortunate than L.L. *The Hard Way* (which opened fitfully against *New Jack City*), *Toys*, and the limited release *Out of Sync* did little to enhance L.L.'s big-screen profile. Latifah's picks (bits parts in *Juice* and *Jungle Fever*) and a powerful featured role as a butch bank robber in *Set It Off* have all showcased her well. On any decent album the rapper-narrator takes on any number of guises—wiseman, fool, hero, victim, criminal, social commentator. To date, Latifah has skillfully managed to embody that kind of versatility as an actress.

The biggest raptor ever is, not coincidentally, one of the least street-oriented MCs. Will Smith, once the Fresh Prince, who now earns more than $10 million for movie roles (due to the $100 million grosses of *Independence Day* and *Men in Black*) never lied about who he was. Unlike other pop rappers such as Hammer and Vanilla Ice, who aspired to a veneer of toughness even as they recorded scores for teeny bopper dances, Philadelphia-born Smith was always a middle-class kid. Even before the 1988 "Parents Just Don't Understand" made Smith a mall favorite and attracted the eye of L.A. deal makers, he was viewed by many hard-core aficionados with suspicion.

His partner, Jazzy Jeff, one of the first great scratching DJs from outside New York, achieved street credibility with 1987's "The Magnificent Jazzy Jeff," but Smith's clean-cut looks and unabrasive voice was viewed as an annoyance by some of the same folks who made Chuck D their personal guru. Now after six years of network TV, an Eddie Murphyesque buddy movie (*Bad Boys* with Martin Lawrence) and two sci-fi extravaganzas, Will Smith is either Denzel Washington in training or Tom Hanks with a tan. Smith has won by applying that essential hip hop rule—keeping it real. His version of real just has more to do with the mall than the 'hood.

Hip hop has long been chastised for projecting a harsh urban reality (and pathology) to the world. Yet its star multimedia graduate is one of its most thematically benign students. This illustrates two related points: The pull of the American mainstream is unyielding and seductive, and it always seems to reward or promote the most unabrasive element of any subculture, no matter how rebellious it might have started. While Smith may have been too soft for the hard core when his career was centered around records, his hip hop past gives him just enough edge to titillate the world.

VIDEO KILLED THE HOUSE-ROCKING MC

The saddest consequence of hip hop video is that its prominence has removed live performance from the center of its aesthetic. The process began as early as 1983 with the growing sophistication of rap recordings, shifting DJs from the center of the culture as they were replaced first by MCs and, finally, producers. On stage, the change was manifested by the popularity of DAT tapes, whose superior quality made live DJs superfluous, because the tracks came across clean with no chance of the inadvertent record scratches or turntable shaking that hampered live shows. Unfortunately, lost in the translation was the interplay between a live DJ—such as Flash or Run-D.M.C's Jam Master Jay—the MCs, and the audience. DATs turned rap performances into virtual lip-sync extravaganzas sadly reminiscent of the bad television variety shows.

This mechanized quality, which put the rhythms in lock step and had MCs rhyming over their recordings, was bad enough. Additionally, however, what videos have done is force young performers, a great many with little or no on-stage experience prior to recording, to compete with videos packed with frantic edits, dynamic lighting, and dramatic camera angles. On occasion, a stage show (Public Enemy circa *Fear of a Black Planet*, N.W.A circa *Straight Outta Compton*) packs enough visual and musical variety to fill a stage for an hour or so, but most rap attractions, lacking the intensity of a Chuck D or Ice Cube, the textured beats of a Bomb Squad or Dr. Dre, or the comic relief of a Flavor Flav or Eazy-E, look smaller than life on stage. Their concert appearances are simply not as compelling as their videos.

Another factor contributing to the decline in hip hop showmanship is the posse culture glorified by videos themselves. The "all-for-one, one-for-all" ethos espoused by rappers (such as Snoop Doggy Dogg's "It Ain't No Fun If My Homiez Can't Have None") runs contrary to a smooth stage show. In concert terms that means the MC and his DJ (whether using a DAT or not) are never alone. The stage is shared by the MC's homeboys, with often as many as twenty or more piling on stage during a gig.

What can look empowering, a sign of unity in a well-designed video, looks cluttered and disorganized in a club or arena. The mass of sullen bodies—either standing still, drinking 40s, or, even worse, grabbing the mike from the star—distracts eyes from the person the audience has paid to see, while ruining the impact of lighting, staging, or any of the production values that separate a concert from a park freestyle. The logical conclusion of posse performance has been reached by the Wu-Tang

Clan, whose posse, instead of hangers-on, is packed with skilled rhyme animals who stalk the stage ready to "catch wreck" at a moment's notice. While in most cases the posse is somebody's cousin and the kid from down the block, Wu's killer B's attack is the example that proves the rule because with them the *posse* is the star.

At the same time that video had devalued live performance in hip hop, it has helped turn its audience from tastemakers into product consumers. From its in-the-park roots right up to the late '80s, MCs were anointed by the group of dedicated buyers, white and black, who constituted hip hop 's core consumers. It was through underground 12-inches, embraced by active buyers, that Run-D.M.C., Public Enemy, Ice-T, N.W.A, Too Short, and most other rap notables emerged. Now, however, video has made it possible for Hammer, Vanilla Ice, Arrested Development, and others whose appeal had little to do with real rhyme skills, to become national stars without having built a loyal grassroots following. Suddenly hip hop stars are created before they have true fans—a concept typical of pop music for decades but not introduced to hip hop culture until videos. On the basis of only one great or good video, one could blow up quickly, such as what happened to Kriss Kross in 1992 with "Jump" and Onyx in 1995 with "Slam."

This is not to say that underground regional acts no longer happen. As Master P's growth from local favorite in New Orleans in 1995 to having the number-one album on *Billboard*'s album chart in 1997 attests, the traditional pattern can still work. Video just changed the hip hop environment enough so that more sucker MCs have hits, taking up space from worthier artists. Some view this aspect of music video much more positively than I do, feeling it enables an act to rise quickly, which is certainly true. Video *has* made rap more democratic—but is democracy good for art?

Hip hop was, at one point, a true meritocracy. You battled in the park. You rocked the house on stage. You made 12-inches that created your audience. You toured and built a rep. If you survived all these stages, you became a rap star with some level of fame. In the '90s, you combine the right sample with the right video and you could blow up. That's the reality. It may be good for record sales and good for black video-production companies, but it is *bad* for the culture when a video editor with a sense of rhythm can be as important as a MC with a killer rhyme flow.

chapter 9

new jack swing to ghetto glamour

MUSIC PLAYS A MONSTER JAM
FEELS ALL RIGHT, JUST GOT PAID

—JOHNNY KEMP
"JUST GOT PAID"

BACK IN 1987 ANDRE HARRELL, FORMER MEMBER OF THE RAP DUO
Dr. Jeckyll & Mr. Hyde, ex–vice president of Rush Management and ad
salesman at WINS news radio, had finally moved in from the fringes. No
longer a MC with a gimmick (he and partner Alonzo Brown had performed in suits), a junior member of Russell Simmons's growing empire,
or the token black employee at a white business, Andre was a beneficiary
of the major label's sudden realization that hip hop was here to stay.

Jheryl Busby, MCA's head of black music and then the most powerful African-American executive in the industry, decided to finance the
California-based corporation's first rap label. Busby was the first prominent establishment black record man to get aggressively involved with hip
hop, a historic and long overdue event. The buppies and b-boys were finally, and quite lucratively, coming together.

Uptown was the highly symbolic name Andre chose. It wasn't simply
that he was from uptown—he was a native of the Boogie Down Bronx—
but the name represented a spirit and style the label was to stand for. But
what would the sound of Uptown be? I recall a conversation during the
early months of Uptown where Andre pulled my coat.

We were talking about records and I mentioned how dope I thought
"Rap's New Generation" by the Classical Two was. Anchored by a James

Brown sample and a funky looping keyboard bass line, the track had immediacy and was fresh in the hip hop sense of the word. "You think that's dope, huh?" Andre said with a grin. "Teddy Riley made that." Then he told me that the complex, dramatic drums and keyboards that energized Doug E. Fresh's instant classic, "The Show," were played by that same Riley, a teenage prodigy from Harlem.

The reason all this pleased the new label owner was that Andre was already deeply involved with Riley, who was producing the debut of MC Heavy D. & the Boyz and was negotiating to sign with Uptown as an artist. To his lasting credit, Andre knew that investing in Riley was good business. What no one could have known was that this kid would reconnect hip hop with R&B.

In the *Village Voice* Barry Michael Cooper labeled Riley's approach "New Jack Swing," and the tag stuck. "There is no space to breathe in Riley's music," Cooper wrote in 1987. "The orchestration slams you, the drums tear out your heart. Riley's music is Robo Cop funk in full effect; go-go music gunned down by rap and electronics, then rebuilt with more vicious beats and an incharge, large attitude."

"New Jack" was late '80s slang for the extra-fly class of gold nameplate, high-top, fade-wearing urbanities. "Swing" came from the button on the Linn drum machine that created the swing beat Riley often used as the basis for his intense syncopation. Combined, Cooper's phrase spoke to the fresh twist Riley brought to the music as he was able to bridge the gap between what, in the late '80s, were warring aesthetics.

Riley's musical gifts had been evident since childhood. At five he could play gospel piano and by twelve he'd mastered drums, trumpet, and saxophone. In the mid-'80s Riley's uncle Willie purchased Harlem's Rooftop roller rink–disco, a nightspot that became a popular hangout for Teddy and other would-be stars, including ex–Treacherous Three member Kool Moe Dee.

During his formative years, a burly, brusque, stylishly bald man named Gene Griffin emerged as a father figure to Riley. Griffin owned an indie label, Sound of New York, that enjoyed success with the mid-'80s club anthem "Last Night a DJ Saved My Life" by In Deep. However, there was another side to Griffin's business interest—he was convicted on a drug possession charge just as Riley's career was taking off. As a result, Griffin would serve two years of a six-to-ten-year sentence. Instead of separating the two, Griffin's incarceration only solidified Riley's commitment to his mentor. When Griffin was in prison, Riley signed a lucrative song publishing deal with Zomba Music, Jive Records' sister company, who rightly believed his catalog would one day be worth millions.

So while Andre was out touting Riley, the young phenom was already in business with two other influential entities. The bad news for Andre was that he would never have the total control of Riley's services he would have preferred. The good news for Riley was that his three alliances—with Uptown, with Griffin who after his release became Riley's manager and production partner, and with Zomba—all steered projects his way. In the late '80s Riley's sound was so ubiquitous he seemed more a one-man movement than a producer with a distinctive style.

Riley was the first producer-writer to glide easily from MCs (Heavy D., Kool Moe Dee) to vocalists (Keith Sweat, Johnny Kemp, Bobby Brown) eliminating the barriers between hip hop beat production and R&B song composition. This allowed him to influence all the reigning forces in black pop—Jimmy "Jam" Harris, Terry Lewis, Kenny "Babyface" Edmonds, Antonio "L.A." Reid, Dallas Austin, Jermaine DuPri, Prince, and even Michael Jackson, for whom he'd replace Quincy Jones as chief producing partner. Bell Biv DeVoe's remarkable 1990 single "Do Me!"—with its motto "Hip hop smoothed out on the R&B tip with a pop feel appeal to it"—would have been impossible without the musical opening Riley had created. Moreover, hip hop producers responded to Riley's use of funk keyboards, drum programming, and dynamic understanding of groove. Dr. Dre, for example, one of the truly great hip hop producers, was clearly inspired by Riley; it is evident when you listen to his work on *The Chronic* and beyond.

Because he understood gospel, the synthesizer riffs of P-Funk's Bernie Worrell, rap cadences and sampling, Riley brought a truly post-soul sensibility to bear on the culture. Unlike, for example, the excellent Sugar Hill house band, who came out of R&B, or Rick Rubin, whose sonic sensibility came from hard rock, Riley was a musician raised on hip hop, a distinction crucial to all his work. On an early hit like Kool Moe Dee's breakthrough "How Ya Like Me Now" Riley sampled James Brown's "Night Train," had a keyboard echo the "Salt Peanuts" refrain from the

Dizzy Gillespie jazz classic, and concocted a dense rhythm track filled with thick layers of synthesized percussion.

As new jack swing exploded from 1987 to 1989 Riley seemed to be involved in every important nonrap project of the period: He produced and wrote Johnny Kemp's anthemic single "Just Got Paid"; produced and cowrote much of Keith Sweat's album *Make It Last Forever*; arranged on Al B. Sure!'s debut album, *In Effect Mode*; produced and cowrote Bobby Brown's hit single "My Prerogative," and debuted his own band on Uptown, Guy.

It is unfortunate that Guy, which represented the most undiluted example of new jack swing and featured ex–gospel singer Aaron Hall, the best vocalist Riley worked with, didn't achieve the same commercial success of Sure!, Sweat, or Brown. While *Guy*, the band's self-titled first album, did go platinum it never spawned a massive pop single or enjoyed the wider recognition it deserved. Still that first album, as well as much of the follow up, *The Future*, are Riley's truest masterpieces. Aside from his trademark feel for rhythm, the richness of Riley's keyboards, and his sensitivity in producing vocals—his own limited chops as well as Hall's melismatic runs—are landmarks.

Though musically his work with Guy is Riley's most important early achievement, Bobby Brown's 1988 "My Prerogative" is more culturally significant. Unlike Hall, Sweat, and other new jack swingers, Brown's public image was always very closely associated with rap. When he starred in New Edition, the kiddie vocal quintet from Boston that mixed R&B vocals and rap, Brown had been the angry, rebellious one. Even within New Edition's tightly choreographed stage show Brown was always a little rawer, more overtly sexual than the other four members. Eventually that buck-wild attitude spilled over into Brown's dealings with his group mates, leading to disputes with three of New Edition's other members and his departure. Amid rumors of drug abuse, management chaos, and a 1986 lackluster solo debut album, *King of Stage*, many predicted Brown would disappear back into the Boston housing projects that spawned New Edition.

Louis Silas, a smart MCA A&R executive who worked under Busby, hooked Brown up with the top young producers of the day—L.A., Babyface, and Teddy Riley. While L.A. and Babyface handled most of 1988's

Don't Be Cruel, Riley's relentless "My Prerogative" was its first single and centerpiece. Built around a testosterone-powered bass line, "My Prerogative" had a stomping macho feel accentuated by Brown's lyrics. "Everybody's talking all that stuff about me / why don't they just let me be." The autobiographical song depicts the singer as a man hounded by enemies and yet defiant in his contempt, a display of aggressive paranoia that was becoming a staple of urban culture.

Moreover, Brown's raspy shout, far removed from the velvet tones of older R&B divas Luther Vandross and Freddie Jackson, harked back to the days of soul men like Wilson Pickett, yet also had an intensity that matched L.L. Cool J. Brown would sell four million copies of *Don't Be Cruel,* more than any single new jack act. On tour in 1987, opening for New Edition and Al B. Sure!, Brown confirmed his star status by both blowing the other two acts off the stage most nights and getting arrested in a couple of cities for humping female audience members after inviting them on stage.

Riley's impact on the careers of the acts he produced was so powerful that most (Kool Moe Dee, Al B. Sure!, Bobby Brown, Wreckx-n-Effect, James Ingram, Today, Redhead Kingpin) couldn't sustain their popularity when he moved on. The only exceptions have been Heavy D. and Keith Sweat, who from their first recordings projected strong personalities.

Even Riley himself, despite creating some fine work with Michael Jackson ("Jam," "Remember the Time"), lost focus for a while in the early '90s. Arguments with Aaron Hall led to the dissolution of Guy. His business and personal relationships with Griffin soured, but not before his mentor got cowriting and producing credit on a score of Riley hits. In 1990, Riley relocated from New York to Virginia Beach where he went through several managers and a couple of record deals.

UPTOWN! UPTOWN!

Yet if Riley's entanglements and overwork slowed him for a time, the influence of new jack swing continued to grow. Andre Harrell used Riley's musical aesthetic to guide the development of Uptown, not simply as a record label but as a lifestyle leader. When, in 1992, Andre landed a multimedia deal with Universal/MCA valued at $50 million (which would lead to the creation of the hip hop cop show *New York Undercover*), it was because Andre had been so skillful at creating a mystique around his operation. All the original Uptown signees, Heavy D., Guy, Al B. Sure!, and later Mary J. Blige, Jodeci, and Soul for Real, from Andre's perspective, represented in dress, videos, and public appearances an urban look that wasn't raw like Def Jam or too smoothed out like adult black pop. Years later, the tag "ghetto fabulous" or, depending on the speaker, "ghetto glamour" was used to characterize this look.

Andre had some very strong opinions about the black audience, about who was and was not supposed to be attracted to Uptown's music. For *Vanity Fair*, Andre broke it down into four types:

The first are ghetto niggers, who come from poverty-stricken environments and have the minimum society has to offer. Ghetto niggers have a natural sense of edge. Then there are lower-middle-class black people, who conform to what they think white people like in order to get ahead. You call these people colored folks. Then you have people who are the upper echelons of the black community. They are second generation, educated, suburban, upper-middle-class, probably elitist intellectual Negroes. And then the best of all these situations, from ghetto to colored to elitist intellectuals, is to be black. When you be who you truly are in any situation and feel good about yourself. If you don't feel like you have to conform in your dress or your attitudes, you become a black person. You cross all boundaries. And that is the idea behind Uptown. It's a lifestyle.

The Uptown acts, as well as non-Uptown signee singer Keith Sweat (who Andre once called "the perfect Uptown artist" because of his musical and sartorial style), didn't reflect the hard-core reality of urban youth but their Moet-sipping, Rolex-wearing aspirations. Uptown was as materialistic as most hip hop expressions, but it wasn't nihilistic or genocidal. Still, there was an edge to Uptown recordings. Uptown staff producer Eddie F's work on Heavy D. records, because they were informed by Riley's work, made the Overweight Lover's dance-oriented tracks tougher and cooler than anything from his lighthearted hip hop peers the Fresh Prince, Hammer, or Young MC.

At no time during Uptown's ten-year reign did it release any act that would upset C. Dolores Tucker. The closest it came was near the end, with a Queens rap quartet, the Lost Boyz, who had a veneer of hardness but a soft core more in common with Heavy D. than Ice-T. Testimony to Uptown's success (and the popularity of the softer touch) is that from 1986 to 1995 Uptown enjoyed platinum and multi-platinum albums by six different acts.

PUFFING UP

About midway through Uptown's run, Andre took on a young intern he'd met at a Washington, D.C., party. Sean Combs was a wanna-be record man attending Howard University, making more of a rep as a party giver and dancer than as a student.

He began work at Uptown traveling by Amtrack from D.C. to New York to work the phones, listen to unsolicited demos, and do gofer work. By then Uptown was operating out of MCA's Manhattan offices and so, in deference to this more professional atmosphere, the future fashion leader wore white shirts, suits, and ties his first weeks on the gig.

Combs's more colorful side quickly emerged. He dropped out of Howard but, instead of going back to his native Mount Vernon, he moved into Andre's spacious New Jersey home, which was already the site of raucous parties—parties that got even bigger when Combs injected his new jack energy into the mix.

The relationship between Andre and Sean Combs was classic student and teacher, though the exchange went both ways. Andre, then in his late twenties, was a natural observer and theoretician. He prided himself on interpreting the urban market, spotting talent, and making records to fit a niche. Just as he had with Teddy Riley, early on Andre saw something special in Combs's eye for fashion, willingness to take risks, and ear for music. To the consternation of some of Uptown's older heads, Combs, a college dropout, began influencing Andre's decisions. Riley was the first major producer to have been raised on rap; Combs would be the first significant hip hop–reared record executive to move so rapidly from consumer to power broker.

During his early days at Uptown, Combs—who took on various monikers, including Puff, Puffy, Puff Daddy, and PD—befriended Jessica Rosenblum, a bright, worldly, young Jewish woman with a passion for black music and party giving. In tandem with Rosenblum, Combs began promoting parties under the banner "Daddy's House." These parties gave Combs his first taste of public acclaim. Hanging at his events became obligatory for record industry types, rappers, gangsters, and fly girls. The ghetto glamour that Uptown projected on record could be found in the flesh at Daddy's House. Between his Uptown gig and his parties, Combs seemed on his way to a great career when tragedy stuck in December 1991.

Combs, Rosenblum, and Heavy D. promoted a huge party at the City College campus gym in Harlem, the same campus where Russell Simmons met Kurtis Blow, the same gym where I experienced my first transcendent hip hop moment and my first rap riot. The centerpiece of the day was supposed to be a celebrity basketball game. Instead there was a stampede at the door of the overcrowded gym. People tripped on the steeply inclined entry steps and fell atop each other. Some attendees were stomped. Other had bones broken. Nine people died and scores of others were seriously injured.

The deaths and the resulting front-page headlines would have been enough to destroy most careers or at the least cast a big cloud over anyone's reputation. Andre, then on vacation in the Caribbean, flew back and hired the celebrity attorney Alan Dershowitz to represent Combs. A press conference was organized at which Combs's representatives shifted the blame onto City College's security force and school administration. They argued that the promoters should not have been held responsible for managing the crowd, that the school should have been more cooperative, and that the deaths were not their responsibility.

Public opinion shifted. The tragedy, while not forgotten, became viewed as a CCNY mishap, and the public burden was lifted from Combs, Heavy, and Rosenblum, all of whom have done well since then. Rosenblum's own company, Stress Management, has grown, looking after many New York–based producers and DJs. Combs hasn't just survived; he blossomed in the City College aftermath, displaying a resiliency that has proven to be his greatest strength, cementing his role as a major influence on hip hop culture.

A prime example of Combs's influence is his work with Jodeci. Al B. Sure! and producing partner Kyle West worked closely with the quartet from North Carolina during the recording of their Uptown debut, *Forever My Lady*—the band's most disciplined songwriting effort thus far—and Jodeci member DeVante Swing would later become a distinctive producer. Combs didn't play a central role in Jodeci's musical development. His primary contribution to Jodeci was to transform the look of these Southerners, using his instincts for ghetto glamour to turn them into the rebellious alternative to the clean-cut Boyz II Men. As the *Source* described it: "He [Combs] nationalized Jodeci's baggy pants look, the just-below-your-navel Calvin Klein look and the infamous 'Puffy' attitude—pouty faced brashness tempered with I-can-do-anything-matter-of-factness."

Combs's involvement with Mary J. Blige's career was much more intimate. Given total freedom to complete an album of hers that had long been in gestation, he used the opportunity to make it the definitive female new jack swing album or, as some joked, new jill swing. With *What's the 411?* Blige immediately became one of the most influential artists of the '90s by bringing the female vocalist back to the center of African-American youth culture.

Blige, unlike most R&B performers, doesn't sing with an overwhelming gospel inflection but with a dark, bluesy feel that gives her work a tart, world-weary quality that invokes the street, not the church. "She represents all the honeys in the urban communities of Detroit, Harlem, Chicago and Los Angeles that's growing up and going through regular everyday things that are a part of hip hop culture," Combs told the *Source's* Adario Strange. "We can make war with them or we can make babies. Mary J. Blige will sing, but if you try to play her, she'll smack the shit out of you."

On *411* Blige's attitude is supported by some of the best young post-Riley new jack swing producer-writers; including Kenny Greene, Jeff Sanders, and Clinton Wike of the underrated vocal trio Intro; Dave "Jam" Hall, who funneled Riley's lessons through his own beautifully structured work; and Combs, in tandem with his then close collaborator Chucky Thompson.

411 represents the first total manifestation of Combs's aesthetic. Where on Heavy D.'s *Blue Funk*, the Puff Daddy treatment was ill-suited for the buoyant rapper, there is an unsatisfied, worldly yearning in Blige's voice that fit Combs's ear and eye for fashion perfectly (he was also very influential in styling her image and conceiving her videos). Blige's even darker, sample-dependent second album, *My Life*, produced primarily by Combs and Thompson, continues this tight collaboration. Though some of the vocal production is weak (Blige's singing on Rose Royce's "I'm Goin' Down") and the melodies self-consciously unoriginal (many combined R&B classics with new words), *My Life* proves that the first album was no fluke.

BAD BOYS

One of the keys to Uptown's success was an expensive system of quality control. During the height of its prominence Uptown released only about three albums a year—records didn't hit the market until Andre and his young staff thought they were dope. That meant a lot of tracks were rejected. That meant a lot of studio time was wasted. That meant albums regularly went over budget. Combine that picky production philosophy with Combs's youth and accompanying poor paperwork, and soon Uptown's economic picture was more or less out of control. MCA auditors were often on Uptown's ass about invoices and unused studio time. On at least one occasion a top MCA financial officer flew to New York to interrogate the staff about Uptown's unorthodox procedures.

These financial conflicts came at the same time Andre was pressing MCA for more control of the marketing and promoting campaigns and money used on Uptown's records. Uptown had been funded during a period when its parent company, MCA, was having a tremendous run of hits with urban music (the Jets, Jody Watley, New Edition, Ready for the World, Pebbles), a success masterminded by Jheryl Busby. When Busby left to become chairman and part owner of Motown in 1988, Andre's chief advocate at MCA's West Coast headquarters was gone. MCA felt Uptown should spend less money to generate its hits; Andre argued Uptown should be expanded and given greater autonomy to maximize the label's crossover sales. Beneath the public image of success at Uptown, Andre was waging an underground battle with his corporate partner.

This pressure on Andre spilled over into his relationship with Combs. "Uptown was growing and getting bigger," Combs told *Rolling Stone*, "and Andre was having to deal with corporate concerns. I couldn't understand that from the creative side, so I started getting on his nerves and bugging out and being real rebellious. It became a situation where it was two kings in one castle, and it was his castle, so I found myself in the moat." One afternoon in 1994 things came to a head and Andre fired Combs. Neither man has ever given specifics on the cause of the blowup and, on a personal level, they have remained close enough for Andre to be named godfather to Combs's son, Justin.

With Combs suddenly on the market, offers came in from all the major distributors. Enter Clive Davis. Since founding Arista in the mid-'70s, Davis had built the most successful adult contemporary label of the era with mellow music flowing from Barry Manilow, Air Supply, Ray Parker, Jr., Dionne Warwick, Aretha Franklin, and Whitney Houston. Davis specialized in selling midtempo love songs and big, booming ballads. People often forget that in the '60s, while running what was then CBS Records, Davis had been the architect of that corporation's move into rock, signing Sly & the Family Stone, Santana, Janis Joplin, Chicago, and others. And it was under Davis that CBS made one of the groundbreaking deals in black music history—agreeing in 1970 to finance and distribute Gamble and Huffs' Philadelphia International. This deal established the tradition of alliances between black-run boutique labels and major distributors, as opposed to the Motown model of independent distribution. By the mid-'70s most successful black pop music was released through such deals.

In the '90s, with the rise of R&B-flavored hip hop, Davis was back on familiar turf. Within a two-year period he made deals with Babyface and L.A. to create LaFace, with young producer Dallas Austin for Rowdy, and, finally, with Combs to form Bad Boy. By placing his bets on the right horses Davis remade Arista's image from the home of Whitney's power ballads to a place that black music's leading creators called home.

The story of Bad Boy has been, well, notorious due to the brief, tragic life of its signature act, the late Christopher Wallace (aka Biggie Smallz aka the Notorious B.I.G.). His still-unsolved shooting in Los Angeles in the spring of 1997 will be remembered (rightly or wrongly) as the last tragic gasp of the infamous East Coast/West Coast conflict. I'll discuss that later. The point to focus on here is that Biggie's spectacular career was just a part of Combs's amazing accomplishments in his label's first years.

Never in the history of postwar black pop has a single man done so much so well. He produces, he writes, he raps, and he runs a label. Others have done all this but never as successfully. In 1997, as an artist Combs had two successive number-one singles, "I'll Be Missing You" with Faith Evans and "Mo Money Mo Problems" with Notorious B.I.G. and Mase, a feat only the Beatles, Elvis Presley, and Boyz II Men have accomplished.

Combine that with "Can't Nobody Hold Me Down" by himself and Mase, and the Notorious B.I.G.'s "Hypnotize," and Combs's Bad Boy became the first label since Motown's glory days to have four number-one singles in the same year. Since Bad Boy's inception, every album produced by Combs on the label has been certified at least gold and usually platinum. His *Puff Daddy & the Family* album sold four million copies in 1997.

No one—not Berry Gordy, Kenny Gamble, Russell Simmons, or Quincy Jones—has simultaneously been as successful an entrepreneur, producer, and artist. During a memorable week in July 1997, Combs had the number-one record in the country ("I'll Be Missing You"), appeared on the cover of *Rolling Stone*, and released a solo album, *No Way Out*, that debuted at number one, selling 561,000 units, the second biggest debut week of the decade.

One of the most distinctive qualities of the post-soul era is the restless versatility of its most prominent figures. Spike Lee doesn't just make movies—he writes books, he owns an advertising agency, he acts (okay, it's barely acting). Shaquille O'Neal doesn't just play basketball—he raps, he runs a record company, he acts (okay, it's not really acting). There are many cases of this multimedia mania, where one refined skill is a platform for other (albeit mediocre) efforts. Sean "Puffy" Combs is the most extreme example of this impulse and, to date, the most successful. Despite an air of tragedy that lingers around him from City College to B.I.G., he is a born-and-bred hip hop success story.

THE EMPIRE STRIKES BACK

While Combs has moved from tragedy to triumph with dizzying speed, Uptown, the label that gave new jack swing its first home, ceased operation in 1997. The funny thing was that Uptown wasn't like Philly

International or Dick Griffey's once-successful Solar label, great black-run labels that slowly lost their musical urgency. In 1996, Uptown's last active year as a label, it released Jodeci's multiplatinum *The Concert, the Afterparty, the Hotel* and was breaking two new acts, the vocal quartet Soul for Real and the rap group the Lost Boyz.

So what happened? In 1995, the long simmering conflict between Andre and MCA reached a point of no return. With his contract up for renewal and Andre still pushing for greater control, MCA exercised its buy-out clause and took the label from him. And, in a very effective form of character assassination, MCA implied to the press that Andre might have misappropriated funds.

Just as Combs's exit from Uptown had been a hot topic in industry circles, where Andre would land after departing from Uptown filled industry gossip columns in the summer of 1995. Tainted or not, it didn't stop Andre from landing the most prestigious position in black music—the presidency of Motown Records.

In 1988, Motown had been purchased by a consortium that included Boston Ventures, an investment baking operation, and MCA Records. It was this deal that lured Jheryl Busby from MCA to Motown. Busby did what he could to update the roster and make the historic company a giant again. Under his leadership Motown moved from MCA to PolyGram, who bought a controlling share in the '90s. Busby's Motown developed Boyz II Men, a vocal quartet from Philadelphia signed by New Edition member Michael Bivens, into the biggest record sellers in the label's storied history. The quartet's first two albums sold a combined twenty-one million copies worldwide. This was the very good news.

The extremely bad news was that nothing else Busby marketed seemed to work. From Stevie Wonder to Johnny Gill to Another Bad Creation (ABC), Motown acts had singles that worked and sold some albums, but they were all dwarfed by Boyz II Men, which, in the eyes of Busby's detractors, seemed a fluke, not a sign of his smarts. Motown never got a serious foothold in hip hop, which is a key reason Andre was recruited to run Motown.

If Andre had just moved over to Motown quietly, which apparently is what PolyGram wanted, his tenure would have started fine. Instead Andre took over Berry Gordy's company in the loudest way imaginable. He ran an ad campaign all around the country—in subways, on billboards, in the industry trades—that pictured him in a leather chair, back to the camera, holding a cigar in his right hand. The caption read "It's On!" Andre intended the snipes to put Motown back on the youth culture map. It didn't work out quite that way.

Executives at PolyGram, including its chairman Alan Levy, were pissed. People around the business were either offended or amused by it. And many consumers, not tuned into industry politics, just wondered, "Who the hell is that?" The snipes, plus a mountain of press including the cover of *New York* magazine, made Andre a target. Whatever pressure he'd felt at Uptown was magnified one hundred degrees running America's best-known black business.

In August 1997, less than two years into his tenure, Andre, yet to match his initial hype with hits, was forced to resign. The transition had been difficult for him and the ex-Uptown staffers who had joined him at Motown. There was the difference in corporate culture between the newcomers and the Motown holdovers. There was the difference between running a boutique operation and the full-size operation that was Motown—PolyGram executives criticized him for spending exavagantly and overpaying employees. Finally, there was the psychological pain, perhaps not fully acknowledged, of losing your baby. Andre jumped from one highly pressurized situation right into another and, along the way, turned the pressure valve up to ten. He left Motown without a Boyz II Men or even a minor success like ABC to mark his tenure. Following his success at Uptown and his troubled tenure at Motown, Andre opened HE (Harrell Entertainment), where he will again test his theories and eye for talent.

While Andre was struggling to place his stamp on Motown, Teddy Riley, the new jack swing man himself, put his career back on track. After running through several managers, Riley seemed to settle himself around 1994, and this business stability eventually manifested itself in his music.

BLACKstreet, the band formed by Riley to replace Guy, at one point seemed to have as many different members as Menudo. (BLACKstreet's initial vocalist was an Aaron Hall clone.) They debuted on the soundtrack to *CB4*, a movie I produced, with the single "Baby Be Mine," which wasn't bad, but it was far from classic Riley. True to form, Riley quickly went in another direction. On the band's two albums *BLACKstreet* and *Another Level*, Riley has been both a leader and a follower. His up-tempo records, while rhythmically still intense, have a tendency to recycle melodies from '70s classics in an annoying, derivative way.

Yet when the older, wiser Riley is on his game, he's probably a better songwriter now than in his new jack glory. "Joy" and "Before I Let You Go" from the first BLACKstreet album and "Don't Leave Me Girl" from the second reflect a musical maturity and production acumen few other hip hop–generation musicians display. He's even attempted to coin a phrase, "heavy R&B," to characterize his recent work. While the 1997 smash single "No Diggity" swaggered with familiar new jack swing cockiness, Riley's music has matured nicely. Unlike so many pioneers who create a style and are then made obsolete by their imitators, over ten years later Riley remains a force and is gifted enough to remain a major player well into the twenty-first century.

national music

WE USED TO BE DOWN WITH Y'ALL NIGGAS
ALL Y'ALL HAD FOR THE WEST COAST WAS CRITICIZM

      —ICE CUBE WITH THE WEST SIDE CONNECTION,
      "ALL THE CRITICS IN NEW YORK"

IN 1989, ICE CUBE, FLUSH FROM HIS SUCCESS WITH COMPTON'S N.W.A,
came to New York to work with the Bomb Squad, the production team
behind Public Enemy. The resulting album, *AmeriKKKa's Most Wanted*, was
a hip hop landmark that made it seem like the music, for once, had a
united front. Seven years later he released the acerbic anti–East Coast
diatribe, "All the Critics in New York," with the West Side Connection.
Read the words quoted above and feel Cube's hurt. Just below the surface
of his contempt, you can tell he wanted love from New York, which, for
whatever reason, he feels he didn't get.

Unlike many, I didn't see "All the Critics in New York" as the opening
salvo in a new bicoastal war, but rather as a manifestation of an ongoing
love-hate complex the Big Apple seems to foster in the rest of America,
especially the West Coast. Way before rap records and remixes, New
York engendered a hostility and fascination from other parts of the
country that can border on obsession. This melting pot teems with arrogance, creativity, and willful multiculturalism, and it has been upsetting
redneck congressmen, concerning clergy, and irritating conservatives at
least since Gershwin wrote "Rhapsody in Blue."

In hip hop terms, this insecurity flows from the irrefutable fact that
the music originated here, and New Yorkers, with that swagger the world

detests and envies, have never let anyone forget it. East Coast–West Coast defines the debate way too narrowly. It has always been the vast, less concentratedly urban body of the nation versus New York, an aesthetic battle of country funkified folks against the egotistical double standards of my hometown. Ice Cube wasn't just speaking for South Central; he was articulating a disdain-attraction for New York City that is larger than rap.

In African-American culture, this tension has been apparent throughout the twentieth century. Langston Hughes captured this country-city contrast in his Jesse B. Semple stories about a Southern man who moves to Harlem, bringing a naivete to his observations about the big city that was by turns wise and goofy. The Ad Libs's doo-wop chestnut from the '50s, "The Boy from New York City," personified the cool style that the Big Apple purportedly represented. More profound was New York's relationship to jazz and the blues. While the jazzman, urbane, sophisticated, and way too-hip-for-room is ingrained in the city's DNA, the blues has never been embraced here. The blues was simple, too rural in content, too raw in delivery, too damn country.

A similar duality was apparent in the '70s when New York was the epicenter of the disco world and black-owned WBLS, the number-one rated station in New York, supported Donna Summer, Chic, and the Bee Gees. Meanwhile large funk bands (the Bar-Kays, Maze featuring Frankie Beverly, Cameo, the Meters, Con Funk Shun) with a raw rootsy feel and a heartland following had a hard time getting heard in New York. P-Funk (Parliament-Funkadelic) and Bootsy Collins eventually got so big that New York radio couldn't deny them, but the mania in the Big Apple didn't match what you'd find for P-Funk in D.C., Detroit, or Los Angeles. New York just didn't embrace uncut funk the way much of the rest of the country did. Combine that with New York's overall feeling of superiority, and you have a mix of taste and attitude that affected rap music very early on.

In a hip hop context, the contempt of New Yorkers for non–New York rap began with the disdain in Manhattan for New Jersey's Sugar Hill Gang. Then the Bronx, represented by Boogie Down Productions, debated Queens's MC Shan about the birth of hip hop on "The Bridge" and "The Bridge Is Over." Then New York dissed Philly, then Philly and

New York ridiculed rap records from outside the Northeast. And the Northeast attitude, that everything made outside the eastern corridor was substandard, was accepted by the first generation of rap consumers.

The first non–New York MCs to find a national audience were from Philadelphia, where the violent Schoolly D, the mild-mannered Jazzy Jeff & the Fresh Prince, and the feisty Roxanne Shanté won fans outside the city limits. Acts out of the city of brotherly love were promoted by a couple of late-night radio broadcasts, particularly by Lady B—the Philly counterpart to New York's Mr. Magic—on WHAT.

The Fresh Fest tour of 1984 and the Run-D.M.C. headlining tours that followed pushed the music's borders farther west. These stadium-size gigs allowed performers to proselytize like hip hop evangelists. Kids in D.C. where go-go was the local music, in Oakland with its rich and varied culture, and Los Angeles where a mobile postdisco party scene was thriving all came to see the kings from Queens. Not only were they converted as listeners—many customers came away convinced they could perform too.

In 1988, I did a piece for the *Village Voice* titled "Nationwide: America Raps Back" that argued, "Rap's gone national and is in the process of going regional. That seems like a contradiction, but actually it's easily explained. Rap spread out from New York to attract a loyal national audience. Now America is rapping back." As evidence I cited several factors: the founding of Rap-A-Lot Records in Houston, who would bring us the Geto Boys, and Luke Skyywalker (soon to be Luke Records) in Miami, who would release the 2 Live Crew; the fact that in a number of markets (Dallas, Houston, Cleveland, Detroit, Philadelphia, Miami, Los Angeles) certain rap records would sell more there than in New York City, suggesting regional tastes were developing; and the local support systems for rap that were springing up across the country, from Houston's huge rap clubs, Rhinestone's and Spud's, to progressive programmers such as Lynn Tolliver in Cleveland who aggressively mixed rap with traditional R&B.

But the most important distinction I found was the ability (or inability) of local rappers to regionalize their work. Case in point: a compilation *Boston Goes Def* that contained fifteen cuts from that many different rappers. Yet in all those tracks I counted only two specific references to

Beantown, no stories specific to Boston, and production styles that echoed what you'd hear in New York. There was nothing special or unique about what was coming out of Boston.

Out in L.A., the best-known rapper was born in Newark, New Jersey. Ice-T (Tracy Morrow) is a rhyme visionary whose debut work fused the rhymes of old-school jail chants, the lyric flavor of con man–author Iceberg Slim, and his own flair for tales of L.A.'s dark side, both figurative and racial. His 1987 *Rhyme Pays* album on Sire sold about 300,000 units, a respectable number for a debut, but far from the platinum levels New Yorkers were already regularly posting. One reason I felt Ice-T hadn't tapped into what we now know is a vast audience for L.A. rap was that, at least on his first record, he was too New York identified. His close friend and original Zulu Nation member Afrika Islam supervised production and recorded *Rhyme Pays* in the Big Apple. So while Ice-T was touted as the first L.A. hip hop star with a major label release, his credentials were tainted. His work didn't provoke the anti–New York feeling that was just under the surface of the national hip hop audience.

Miami's 2 Live Crew's *2 Live "Is What We Are"* made history in 1988 by becoming the first non–New York rap act to sell over 500,000 copies of an album. It succeeded precisely because it didn't sound a damn thing like New York; it was, in fact, defiantly country. The observation I made about that record, and national rap in general, to end the *Village Voice* piece still holds up:

> To my ears it was crude on all levels; the raps were witless ("Throw the D"), the elocution sloppy, and the recording quality awful. Yet its fast tempos (surely influenced by Miami's enduring disco romance), in-yo-face word, and down home flavor made it, for a time last spring, the South's hottest rap record.... And, maybe, that's the point. The rap that'll flow from down South, the Midwest and the West Coast will not, and should not, feel beholden to what came before. Just as hip hop spit in the face of disco (and funk too), non–New York hip hop will have its own accent, it own version of b-boy wisdom, if its to mean anything.

WEST SIDE, WEST SIDE!

Though New York birthed hip hop, the culture definitely has some L.A. roots. In the late '60s an L.A. trio calling themselves the Watts Prophets (Otis O., Richard Dedeaux, and Dee Dee MacNeil) built a local following by creating poetic call-and-response chants. To some poetry aficionados, their hard-to-find 1971 album *Rappin' Black in a White World* is considered a classic on par with the recordings of their better known East Coast counterparts, the Last Poets and Gil Scott-Heron. The trio's only real mainstream exposure came performing a lover's rap on Quincy Jones's 1975 album *Mellow Madness*.

Breaking, though refined in New York, was deeply influenced by locking and popping, two dance styles out of Los Angeles that got national exposure on *Soul Train* in the '70s. Locking and popping were upright dances in which dancers used their arms, legs, and torsos in isolated, semirobotic moves requiring great body control. During the hip hop dance mania of the early '80s, both these L.A. styles were featured in low-budget films made in Cali. You'd see these dances often at the Radio, a club in downtown Los Angeles that became a West Coast version of the Roxy, where white hipsters and black b-boys mixed in the days before gangs got out of control. The music was provided by DJs from both coasts, such as New York's Afrika Islam and Grandmixer DST of "Rockit" fame and locals Evil E (later to be Ice-T's spinner) and Chris "the Glove" Taylor, who would cut a single for Motown.

More grassroots were the '80s jams organized by Uncle Jam's Army, a collective of DJs and promoters who gave events at venues as large as L.A.'s 16,000-seat Sports Arena. The music at all these parties, be they at Radio or Uncle Jam's events, were dominated by New York acts. Even local MCs who were showcased usually worked on top of East Coast instrumental tracks. The first real L.A. hip hop sound tended to be electropop influenced by Afrika Bambaataa's early hits. Many of Dr. Dre's (Andre Young) early productions with his first band, the World Class Wreckin' Cru, had a "Planet Rock" feel, such as "Surgery" on which he scratches over a hectic electropop bed. Even the style of clothing Dre, DJ Yella (Antoine Carraby), and his comrades in the crew sported could have been worn by Bam—lots of leather, maxi coats, facial makeup—though they also recalled West Coast bands like Earth, Wind

& Fire. (Later Eazy-E used pictures of Dre in his glitzy gear to ridicule his former friend during their notorious feud.)

L.A. actually had a significant advantage over the New York scene in the '80s. KDAY, an AM station looking to carve out an identity in the crowded radio market, adopted a hip hop format under program director Greg Mack. The best of New York ruled of course, but records from Miami, Philly, Seattle, Oakland, and, increasingly, the L.A. area itself made the playlist. Many of the city's club jocks did on-air mixing, including the duo of Dre and DJ Yella. Listening to the latest sounds from around the country affected Dre's production style, turning him from the electropop of the Wreckin' Cru (who enjoyed a national hit with "Turn Out the Lights" in 1984) toward a darker, more complex, funk-based approach.

At this point Dre and Yella began hanging out with a shrewd, diminutive sometime "dope man" called Eazy-E (Eric Wright) who had constructed a mini-studio in his mother's Compton garage and started Ruthless, his own label. Around the corner from Eazy-E's house was a kid with some rhyme skills whose older brother was tight with the wanna-be mogul. Eazy promised the kid, Lorenzo Patterson, whose rap name was MC Ren, a chance to record. Another teenager, known around the area for putting obscene lyrics to rap hits, had befriended Dre and, after a stint in a local group called CIA, began putting rhymes to Dre's beats. His real name was O'Shea Jackson; his rap name became Ice Cube. Along with this core group were several other regulars: the D.O.C. (Tracy Curry), a talented lyricist with a grainy baritone, rolled in from Texas; MC Train, Ren's DJ, who would clock dollars producing J. J. Fad's *Supersonic* and would later provide the scratches on Ice Cube's *Wicked*; Sir Jinx, who would later be Cube's DJ and production partner; and Arabian Prince, a rapper and producer who would eventually fall out with the crew and go on to do his own solo albums.

They all gravitated to Eazy's garage. He was a surprisingly charming man with a wry, though clearly warped sense of humor, and he was willing to invest his drug money in a new hustle. With an eye to the possible marketing of New York rap, Eazy imported a group from the Apple, HBO, planning to record them in Compton. New Yorkers balked at the West Coast–flavored tracks and rhymes, and reportedly it was Dre's idea that Eazy record himself instead.

So, quite appropriately, in 1988 the first single on Ruthless was "Boyz N the Hood" by Eazy-E, which was followed up by two other Cube-penned Eazy vehicles, "Dopeman" and "8 Ball." Some time in this year Eazy hooked up with Jerry Heller, an old-school record biz member of the "permanent business" who had been involved with some heavies in the '70s (Pink Floyd, Elton John, Journey), but he clearly wasn't doing that well if he was managing a L.A. rap group in 1988. Heller's luck was about to change.

THE BEATLES OF GANGSTERDOM

WHEN WE DID N.W.A . . . THE MAIN THING IT WAS: NEW YORK HAD ALL'A THE BOMB GROUPS. NEW YORK WAS ON THE MAP AND ALL WE WAS THINKING, MAN—I AIN'T GONNA LIE, NO MATTER WHAT NOBODY IN THE GROUP SAY—I THINK WE ALL WAS THINKING ABOUT MAKING A NAME FOR COMPTON AND L.A. . . . KRS-ONE HAD "SOUTH BRONX," P.E. WAS TALKIN' ABOUT LONG ISLAND, RUN-D.M.C. TALKIN' ABOUT QUEENS AND ICE-T WAS TALKING ABOUT L.A. WE WAS LIKE "DAMN! FUCK IT, WE COMIN' FROM COMPTON!"

—MC REN, IN THE *SOURCE,* 1994

Jorge Hinojosa, a talkative promoter who was Ice-T's first manager, excit-edly walked me through the offices of Sire Records in 1988. He had something for me to hear. I'd been interviewing Ice-T for a piece in *Billboard,* but Hinojosa was so ecstatic about this group I thought the record was by a new client. He put "Straight Outta Compton" on the turntable and played it real loud. I believe he spun it twice, the first so I could orient myself, the second so I could really listen.

But it would take me many more than two listens to truly understand N.W.A. First of all, I didn't think these fools could rap. Okay, maybe that kid Cube had a flow. Maybe Ren. But that kid with the high-pitched voice was the epitome of wack. No flow. No cadence. Just irritating. The track itself wasn't bad. Had some drama to it. It sounded like some watered-down Public Enemy. And, Jorge, just where the hell is *Compton?*

My old-school New York, P.E.-is-God ears couldn't really hear N.W.A yet. It was too obscene. Too radical. If that was Compton, then it was too Compton, wherever that was. But I'd soon learn, along with the rest of the country and the world, that these Jheri-curled suckers deserved respect. While Eazy's early singles were the opening salvos from the garage, "Straight Outta Compton" was the full-blown sound of revolution.

Stripped of East Coast's "positive" rhetoric, emboldened by Ice-T's foray's into gangster storytelling, and informed by the evil energy that crack had sent coarsing through black L.A., N.W.A would send New York rap into a spasm of denial that lasted half a decade. It is hard to re-member now, after years of condemnation, studio gangsterism, and plain old bad imitations, how damn fresh N.W.A sounded. It was tough. The rhymes were vivid—mostly composed by two of the best lyricists ever, Ice Cube and the D.O.C.—and Dre's mastery seemed to grow with every record.

The community of buyers around the country—multiracial audiences who went to the Run-D.M.C. extravaganzas, urban children for whom crack was increasing violence in the 'hood, suburban teens who saw rap as rebel music like rock—embraced this music. Its success would unlock the dark imaginations of young black artists, freeing them to use raw lan-guage to say things on vinyl no generation of African-Americans had felt comfortable expressing in public.

Between the debut of the album *Straight Outta Compton* in the fall of 1988 and the end of 1990 a slew of West Coast "reality" rappers sur-faced with major label deals (Above the Law, Boo Yaa Tribe, Too Short, Mob Style, Compton's Most Wanted, King Tee), while acts on indie la-bels throughout the Southwest and Midwest got meaner. Hostility toward New York built—as did hostility *from* New York—as these rap-pers found that New York acts, radio, and live audiences seemed con-temptuous of them.

The graphic illustration of New York's insecurity was Tim Dog's "Fuck Compton," released in 1991. Tim Dog, a member of the Bronx underground crew the Ultramagnetic MCs, thought he'd issued the ulti-mate dis record. Instead the rap revealed just how fearful, and jealous, so many in hip hop's home were of these interlopers.

N.W.A, along with Luther Campbell in Miami, the Geto Boys in Houston, and Too Short in Oakland, would reinvent the very definition of what a good rap record was. The judgments of New York's arbiters would no longer be absolute. The harsh, nasal intonation of the Big Ap-ple became just one of many accents flowing from the Jeeps and boom boxes of the nation. It was joined by the twangs of Texas and Louisiana by way of Long Beach singsong, the little heard syncopations of Cleveland and Seattle, and sounds from almost every major black population center talking about their cities, 'hoods, and streets. In the heyday of soul music, regional sounds and local acts had always enriched the music in an authentic way. Now rap was experiencing a similar side effect of its national growth.

Now DJ Quik, another Compton star, or Too Short, the Oakland sexologist, didn't need New York sales or tour dates to go platinum. At the same time, acts from the New York metro area hailed by locals as the music's saviors—the Poor Righteous Teachers, Brand Nubian—didn't travel well past the Mason-Dixon line. As a result, much of New York rap became insular and defensive. As Tommy Boy president Monica Lynch wondered in a 1991 opinion piece in the now defunct *Break Beat* magazine, "Has New York Fallen the Fuck Off . . . Or What?"

It wasn't simply that New York rap was suddenly wack. De La Soul and the other colorful b-boy bohemians of the Native Tongues collective (A Tribe Called Quest, the Jungle Brothers, Monie Love, Queen Latifah) brought a reflective, ghetto-meets-Greenwich-Village outlook to rap that, much as Tracy Chapman was doing in pop and Living Colour in rock, suggested the diversity of thought among college-aspiring black youth. There was an irreverence to De La Soul and jazzy cool to Tribe that was refreshing during the rise of gatt talk.

In 1989, N.W.A began to break up—Cube left that year, Dre jumped ship in 1992—and the embittered lyrics that represent the fallout between the members were sprinkled around numerous records. N.W.A disses Ice Cube on the *100 Miles and Runnin'* EP. Ice Cube strikes back with "No Vaseline" on *Death Certificate*. Eazy-E disses Dre in the title of his *It's On (Dr. Dre) 187 umKilla* album. Dre dissess Eazy throughout *The Chronic*. They were all installments in rap's most interesting ongoing soap opera.

Yet the real impact in rap music as a commercial force wasn't that one of the great groups had broken up. What really happened is that by dispersing its talent, N.W.A expanded its sphere of influence. N.W.A turned out to be the beginning, not the peak, of Compton's talent. From Ice Cube's 1990 masterpiece *AmeriKKKa's Most Wanted* to Dr. Dre's *The Aftermath* in 1996, the ex-members of N.W.A had a run of sales unprecedented in hip hop, which rivals that of any disbanded rock band. Dr. Dre sold three million copies of *The Chronic*. Eazy-E sold five million: *5150 Home 4 Tha Sick, Its On* (*Dr. Dre*) *187 umKilla*, and *Eazy-Duz-It*. Ice Cube sold six million copies: *AmeriKKKa's Most Wanted, Kill at Will, Death Certificate, The Predator, Bootlegs & B-Sides*, and *Lethal Injection*. Ren sold one million of his *Kizz My Black Azz*. If you factor in non-N.W.A members who were either affiliated with the group (the D.O.C.'s *No One Can Do It Better* in 1989 went gold) or were signed and/or guided by ex-members (Ice Cube's protégés Da Lench Mob went gold with *Guerillas in the Mist*; Dre's muse Snoop Doggy Dogg sold four million copies of *Doggystyle*; Eazy-E's discovery Bone, Thugs-n-Harmony sold three million copies of the Eazy-E executive produced *Creepin' on ah Come Up*), the impact of this collective multiplies. It is a staggering achievement, one that belies the turmoil that hovered over every one of these records.

While Teddy Riley created new jack swing, Dr. Dre ruled gangsta rap. Even on records he didn't produce, Dre's approach to sampling, use of funk grooves, and high-pitched keyboard backings informed most of West Coast hip hop. Though he has made some fine nongangsta recordings (Michel'le's soulful 1989 self-titled effort), Dre's signature works will remain N.W.A's *Straight Outta Compton*, his own *The Chronic*, and Snoop Doggy Dogg's *Doggystyle*. The last two recordings are sonic masterpieces that utilize crisp, cleanly engineered tracks, live bass and keyboard playing, musicians, and Dre's wonderful ear for arrangement to tell tales of African-American self-genocide.

The beauty of Dre's musicianship and the seductive ugliness that it supported is a true hip hop statement, full of genius, pain, and contradictory values. As a video director, Dre has shown himself to be equally shrewd. His videos submerge the violent lyrics under a veneer of bikini-clad cuties at parties, homies driving vintage Cadillacs, and a good-time vibe that has more to do with the Beach Boys' vision of California than the Crips. They were perfect for the blondes and frat boys who swayed to Dre's beats but didn't understand all the words.

Equally contradictory, and quite charismatic to boot, has been the peripatetic career of Ice Cube. He made his best album, *AmeriKKKa's Most Wanted*, in New York, then years later dissed New York in a rambling *Source* interview. He shaved off the Jheri-curls, co-signed the Nation of Islam ideology of self-help and self-respect, and made a bundle hustling

St. Ides malt liquor in the ghetto. He is a bankable Hollywood star who still craves hard-core credibility. Consistency is not Ice Cube's calling card.

Because of his keen analytical mind, a novelist's care for narrative, and a biting rhyme flow, Ice Cube is one of the most fascinating men to ever rock a mike. His creative gifts are varied and restless. He's a doer. He doesn't want to star in movies—he writes, produces, and directs. His scripts, of which 1995's *Friday* was the first to be produced, are funny in ways that don't sacrifice toughness and suggest the discipline he brings to all his endeavors. As a follow-up he directed the comedy *Players Club*, set in a strip club. As a musical talent scout he hasn't been as visionary as Dre or Eazy (though sponsoring female rapper Yo-Yo was cool), but by hiring the little known video director F. Gary Gray to direct *Friday*, Cube put a compelling young black director on the map.

Of N.W.A's big three, Eazy-E proved to be the truest to his particular game. Eazy boasted he got into hip hop to feed his ego, make money, and get women. And he did just that. Greed proved his downfall. If he hadn't alienated Ice Cube and Dr. Dre by taking manager-partner Jerry Heller's side against that of his homies, his organization, Ruthless, might still be rolling on. But then how much more vision was he supposed to have? Between Dre, Ice Cube, the D.O.C., Ren, and Bone, Thugs-n-Harmony, Eazy proved himself one of hip hop's great talent scouts. Perhaps, being a gangsta himself, he realized it was only a matter of time before he got jacked, so why share anything?

Eazy's empire was ended by an O.G. a bit realer than he was. According to legend (and lawsuits which died with Eazy-E) Marion "Suge" Knight, the force behind Death Row Records, and several men alledgedly threatened Eazy-E with baseball bats and made him an offer he couldn't refuse. When this meeting was over, Eazy had relinquished any claims to the contract of Dr. Dre. Even after that scary story surfaced it was always difficult to feel sorry for Eazy or Heller. After all, Eazy's label was called Ruthless and, on vinyl at least, Eazy had smoked enough brothers to make you think he could handle himself. In the end, a more ruthless man intimidated Eazy out of the key to his empire. Even after he died of AIDS on March 26, 1995, there wasn't the same outpouring of love for him that the later deaths of Tupac or Biggie would generate. For most, Eazy-E's life was a cautionary tale, not one of a martyr.

BOW DOWN

In 1992, Suge Knight and his attorney (and longtime drug dealer mouthpiece) David Kenner made a deal for Death Row Records with millionaire Ted Fields's Interscope Records that altered hip hop's landscape in a way analogous to the Def Jam–CBS union in 1986. The Def Jam deal had put an aggressive promoter (Russell Simmons) and a top producer (Rick Rubin) in business with a mighty conglomerate. Similarly, this Death Row–Interscope marriage put a tough guy promoter (Suge Knight) and a brilliant creator (Dr. Dre) in business with a well-financed enterprise. Together, Death Row and Interscope would take the nihilistic celebration of the L.A. gang mentality that Eazy-E and N.W.A popularized and make it pure pop.

Suge and Fields spent millions on big videos and elaborate promotional and marketing campaigns. It didn't matter whether Interscope was distributed by Time-Warner or, later, MCA-Universal, the strategy was the same—gang bang glory, charismatic stars, and an us-against-the-world bravado in keeping with hip hop's ethos. The difference was that where Eazy-E just kept the money and chuckled about it, Knight's hubris had him gloating about an empire built on head knocking.

One of the beauties of American capitalism is its short memory. A family can go from criminal activity to the White House in one generation (from bootlegger Joe Kennedy to President John Kennedy). Another is that by creating subdivisons and joint ventures a major corporation can often distance itself from the more disdainful activities of its subsidiaries—the kind of deniability president's so love. So it was that Interscope could allow Death Row to function without scrutiny—or at least they were able to deflect the most extreme criticism from themselves. Fields was a large Democratic contributor; at the same time, he helped to jump-start Death Row. Even as President Clinton attacked Sister Souljah for inciting racism in 1992, one of his big contributors was in business with a company whose principle products were considered to have a nefarious impact on young minds that dwarfed anything Souljah was up to.

EAST COAST–WEST COAST

With Death Row, Suge Knight, and Tupac Shakur in the West corner wearing red trunks and Bad Boy, Puffy Combs, and Notorious B.I.G. wearing Versace trunks in the East corner in a bout covered by the editors of *Vibe* and the *Source*, the great East-West hip hop battles of the mid-'90s ended as grotesquely as Holyfield-Tyson II. I guess the belt goes to Sean Combs, who has not only survived but prospered to an unbelievable degree, but it is a bloody prize indeed. It is clear now that the feud wasn't a feud at all, but a figment of the paranoid minds in the Death Row camp. Yet, for a time, it was as destructive to hip hop as crack was to the black community.

As intimately chronicled in the hip hop press and every newspaper in America, Tupac was shot on November 30, 1994, in the lobby of Times Square's Quad recording studio. This was the key event, or at least the most potent symbol, of the so-called war. Tupac was on trial for sexually assaulting a groupie the year before—one of the many felony charges he'd accumulated since emerging from Digital Underground in 1991 into solo stardom on Interscope Records. He was on his way to add vocals to a remix for Uptown act Little Shawn—a way to pick up a quick $7,000. Among those hanging out upstairs in Quad's three studios were Andre Harrell, the Notorious B.I.G., and Puffy Combs. Downstairs, by the building's elevators, two gunmen pumped five shots into Tupac and stole $40,000 in jewelry, apparently leaving him for dead.

But Tupac was very much alive. The next day he was wheeled into a Manhattan courtroom to hear himself pronounced guilty of sexual abuse and later be sentenced to 1½ to 4½ years. The combination of his conviction on what many saw as a dubious rape charge and his survival of the close-range shooting elevated Tupac from being merely charismatic to the role of icon.

Sometime between his sentencing and his imprisonment in upstate New York, Tupac got it in his head that Puffy, B.I.G., and others in New York's rap community (Harrell, Little Shawn, Little Caesar of Junior M.A.F.I.A.) had him set him up for the hit. These unfounded accusations could have remained simple tabloid fodder if Suge and David Kenner hadn't visited Tupac in jail, then put up a $1.4 million bond to secure his release, pending an appeal of his rape conviction. They then arranged

for Tupac to move from Interscope to Interscope's Suge-operated sub-
sidiary Death Row. Just as he did for Dr. Dre, Suge had come to Tupac's
rescue, earning his loyalty and portraying himself as the liberator of another wronged black star.

Like Clint Eastwood's Man with No Name, Suge depicted himself as
a vigilante who would subdue the bullies who threatened the town. The
problem, of course, is it is only after the initial threat is handled by the
vigilante that you find out what the Man with No Name really wants.
The combination of Tupac's thirst for (verbal) vengeance, Suge's bel-
ligerent mentoring, and their mutual overripe West Coast chauvinism
was quite potent.

Tupac was already a star prior to hooking up with Death Row—his
previous album, Me Against the World, had sold two million copies led by
the woman-friendly singles "Dear Mama" and "Keep Your Head Up."
The Death Row identification hardened his image and his lyrical outlook, making him seem less complex and more easily categorized as a
gangsta or, as he enjoyed being called, a thug. The resulting postjail release, hip hop's first double album, All Eyez on Me, sold four million copies.

Tupac became Death Row's chief mouthpiece, celebrating the label at
every opportunity, bad-mouthing Comb's Bad Boy label, and continuing
to live his life as inside one of the rhymes. "I have no mercy in war," he
declared in a Vibe interview published after his death. "I said in the beginning I was gonna take these niggas out the game, and sure enough I will.
Already people can't look at Biggie and not laugh. I took every piece of
his power. Anybody who tries to help them, I will destroy." Even as Dr.
Dre began to withdraw from Suge's inner circle (starting his own label,
Aftermath, also affiliated with Interscope) and Snoop Doggy Dogg focused on a trial for attempted murder (he was cleared by a jury of his
peers), Tupac publicly reveled in thug life.

Only after his fatal shooting on September 7, 1996, by an unknown
gunman in Las Vegas following a Mike Tyson fight and his death six days
later, did it come to light that Tupac had actually been working toward
exiting Death Row and starting his own label.

After Tupac's demise, the true darkness within Death Row came to
light: Drug dealer and sometime entertainment investor Michael Harris
(he'd financed Checkmates, a Broadway play that starred Denzel Washington) claimed he'd given Suge the seed money to start Death Row through

their mutual attorney David Kenner. Suge's parole was revoked for helping beat down a young black man in a Vegas hotel lobby just hours before
Tupac's death. Afeni Shakur, Tupac's mother, discovered that her son had
only a few hundred dollars in the bank at the time of his death. Later, after suing Death Row, Afeni won control of some one hundred fifty of
her son's unreleased tapes and began releasing them on her own Jive-
distributed label in 1997.

By the end of that year the lucrative, violent tale of L.A. rap that had
begun in Eazy-E's garage and then had shifted to Death Row (largely financed by Interscope) seemed to run out of steam. Gangsta lyrics, at
least the West Coast version, sounded exhausted (Snoop Doggy Dogg's
Tha Doggfather) and many of its key figures were dead, in jail, or in retreat.
Without Suge running it on a day-to-day basis, Death Row limped
along, no longer intimidating or omnipotent. Dr. Dre is certainly gifted
enough to revive the scene, though his public statements and his signing
of ex–En Vogue member Dawn Robinson suggest a new, more pop-
song-oriented direction for him.

The style that had begun with Ice-T, was popularized by N.W.A, and
skillfully packaged for mass consumption by Dr. Dre and Suge Knight is
over. It generated paranoid fear and sold millions of records, some
among the finest hip hop records ever made, and, even if inadvertantly,
played a role in creating the climate that resulted in the death of two im-
mensely gifted young men.

This music will serve as an essential part of the historical memory of
Southern California in the '80s and '90s. Just as the Beach Boys spoke for
an idealistic vision of the area in the '60s and the Eagles presented a
cynical, mellow view in the '70s, the recordings from the Compton/
Long Beach axis tell the story of the poverty, guns, and despair that
everyone noticed after the 1992 riots—riots that had been happening on
CDs all along.

chapter 11

the sound of philadelphia—dunking

ALL THE JEALOUS PUNKS CAN'T STOP THE DUNK
COMIN' FROM THE SCHOOL OF HARD KNOCKS

—CHUCK D OF PUBLIC ENEMY,
"DON'T BELIEVE THE HYPE"

MUSIC AND AFRICAN-AMERICAN ATHLETICS HAVE BEEN LINKED SINCE Louis Armstrong sponsored a baseball team, Armstrong's Secret Nine of New Orleans, in 1931. Stylish as always, he came to games dressed in a white hat, striped tie, a blazer, vest, white pin-striped pants, and two-toned shoes, with a bright diamond on his left ring finger. In those days, black baseball was the repository of black style, a place where the players displayed a daring game rife with base stealing (including home), pitchers sold wuf tickets to hitters, and the fans themselves came dressed as if it was Saturday night.

After the decline of the Negro Leagues, boxing took center stage in African-America's blend of sweat and style. Black folk "in the life" always came to fights in their finery, to celebrate Joe Louis and "Sugar" Ray Robinson just as we do now to see Mike Tyson and his contemporaries. That same class of high rollers have always been prime consumers of black entertainment throughout this century, be it at jazz gigs, soul shows, or rap concerts. At a New York Knicks game circa 1998 celebrity row will be occupied by model Tyra Banks, Spike Lee, and Puff Daddy, icons of black pop culture there to savor the intensity of NBA basketball. Though none come to NBA contests quite as well dressed as "Pops" Armstrong, the vibe remains the same.

It is no surprise, then, that musicians and athletes, linked in the public mind as white social symbols and black role models, have always felt a kinship. They share celebrity status across racial lines, competence in highly pleasurable and competitive activities, and make way more money than the average African-American. Back in New York in the early '60s, if you went into a restaurant on Harlem's 116th Street you might have run into Sam Cooke, Cassius Clay, and Malcolm X sharing a bean pie and talking religion, just as in the mid-'90s Mike Tyson, Tupac Shakur, and Reverend Jesse Jackson could be spotted talking about punching power in Vegas after a fight. The synergy of black celebrities is powerful—they are connected by the pressure of white scrutiny, black adoration, and dealing with sudden, bewildering sums of money.

The steamy poetry of the bandstand and dance floor has long found exquisite parallels in the intensity and fancy footwork of the African-American sportsman. That's a fact of cultural life that predates, and will likely outlast, hip hop. Yet there is a deep connection to be found in the evolution of two contemporary definers of black male genius, basketball and hip hop, in the last three decades.

My focus isn't Michael Jordan or Magic Johnson or other obvious suspects. Instead, consider how one franchise, chiefly through three dominating, innovative players, illustrates the interplay between the aesthetics of ball and music. The franchise under inspection: the Philadelphia 76ers.

STYLE WARS

In the early '70s, when hip hop's aural building blocks were being laid into place by funk bands, disco producers, and well-miked rock drummers, a battle was getting underway on the hardwood floors of professional basketball. In one corner was the National Basketball Association, a league born in 1947 in which the ancient verities of the game were celebrated—the pick and roll, the give and go, the brownish orange ball—and flamboyance was defined by Boston coach Red Auerbach's habit of lighting up a victory cigar after yet another Celtic triumph. The NBA played the establishment game down the line—with the exception of the odd renegade like Elgin Baylor, the first man in the league to walk on air, or Earl "the Pearl" Monroe, who dribbled and shot as if he'd tuned Thelonious Monk's piano.

In the other corner was the American Basketball Association, the wayward child of a few self-proclaimed millionaires and hustling liars who gave birth to the red, white, and blue ball, the three-point shot, and multimillion-dollar salaries for nineteen-year-olds. What will save these rogue souls on Judgment Day is that they gave free reign to big-Afroed, headband-, wristband-, and tube-sock-wearing brothers. Black street flair, long suppressed by the NBA (and in NCAA Divison I) was unleashed by the ABA and forever changed not just the look but the very nature of the sport.

Along with the leaping ability African-American men brought to the game came a desire not just to win the game but to do so with flair. To win efficiently was simply not enough fun, and ball without self-expression was not fun. A key reason basketball has become such a repository of black male style is that the game allows individual expression within a team concept. You can go one-on-one in basketball and still help contribute to the success of the team—as long as it is done within the structure. Like the multicolored outfits with the flaired pants and platform shoes ABA players wore off court, its stars refused to play a buttoned-down game. In from the basketball wilderness came Connie "the Hawk" Hawkins who held the ball like a grapefruit in his huge hands. Straight out of high school came the relentless Moses Malone, while Spencer Haywood took his multifaceted skills from college to millionaire status in a shocking deal that ultimately led to a Supreme Court case. The ABA was chockfull of such stories, each team and damn near each player an epic unto himself.

The ABA, because many of its games weren't broadcast or were poorly attended, exists in the '90s as a kind of fairy tale, where extravagant claims can be backed up only by the smiles of tall, graying men. But one legend cannot be disputed. Julius "Dr. J" Erving, he of the windblown Afro, flying goatee, and airborne game, was a man who brought streetball athleticism and creativity to the pros. To watch Dr. J in the ABA, as I did on several occasions as a child, was to see gravity defied with a funk backbeat. Though raised in the black middle-class community of Hempstead, Long Island, Erving earned his wings competing against street-hardened players in schoolyard battles at Harlem's Rucker Tournament.

Old-school New York ball fans will tell you Dr. J was far from the best player they saw as a teen, much as old-school rappers sometimes belittle the achievements of new-school hip hop stars. Still, it is hard to argue about the level of Erving's game once he matured.

A 1997 Converse commercial evoked the "Right On!" majesty of Erving's game with images of his aerodynamically impossible dunks, backed by Stevie Wonder's "Higher Ground." It is a soulful sixty-second glimpse of why Dr. J was a legend. It also salutes Erving's earlier, often overlooked impact on American sneaker culture. Erving's identification with Converse was so complete that the sneaker never recovered from his retirement. From the time of his retirement in the early '80s until now Converse has been virtually invisible on urban streets. Trying to revive a brand through a retired athlete is testimony to his greatness and Converse's sad place in the '90s cultural landscape.

By the time the leagues merged in the bicentennial year, Erving's Afro was smaller, the goatee was gone, and his swoops to the hole were done more selectively. Still, he was a skywalking genius and the Philly 76er team he had joined was no conservative, old-school outfit. The Philly squad, in fact, played as close to an ABA game as was then possible in the older NBA league. At center was Darryl Dawkins, nicknamed "Chocolate Thunder," a 6′ 11″ 260-pound man-child who'd entered the NBA at nineteen. In the process Dawkins had become known for shattering backboards (he did it twice), naming his dunks (Earthquake Shaker, Turbo Delight, Sexophonic, In Yo' Face Disgrace), and claiming birth on the planet Lovetron.

The 76ers had a streaky guard from my old neighborhood of Brownsville who began life as Lloyd Free, took a nickname ("All-World,"—'70s slang hyperbole for excellence), and finally had his name legally changed to World B. Free to celebrate his love for both mankind and off-balance twenty-five-foot jumpshots. George McGinnis, an Indian schoolboy legend, a star at Purdue, and one of the ABA's leading lights before bolting to Philly, was not overjoyed at playing second fiddle to Dr. J, so he pouted when he wasn't forcing one-handed, off-the-wrong-foot pop shots from the lane.

Even the 76ers white boys were, in hip hop parlance, ill. Doug Collins was a floor-running guard who loved to flip up underhanded scoop shots and fast break like a fool—even in the half-court offense. In Gene Shue, the man who had let Earl Monroe run wild with the Baltimore Bullets, the 76ers had a coach who encouraged freelancing, fast breaks, and a game of reckless abandon that suited Dr. J and his backboard-breaking, off-balance-shot-taking, high-flying cohorts.

The 76ers didn't win the title until 1983, but with Dr. J in the lineup they were always a leaping, dunking highlight film of a team. Over time, Erving was surrounded by players with sounder fundamentals (Moses Malone, Bobby Jones, Maurice Cheeks); pushed and pulled by them, he developed his nondunking skills so that by the end of his career he was a better all-around player than he'd ever been.

Dr. J appeared in Coke commercials (later getting a piece of a Philadelphia distributorship), become a major sex symbol, and moved Converse from the era of canvas to leather. He had evolved from ABA renegade to all-American role model, a switch that made it easy for him to move into network broadcasting. In the mid-'80s as Erving was smoothing out on the R&B tip, his mantle as Philly's charismatic airmaster was overtaken by an extraordinary physical specimen once labeled "the round mound of rebound."

Where Julius Erving was tall and elegant as a Mandinka warrior, Charles Barkley had an ass wide enough to box out elephants. Where Erving learned diplomacy, Barkley flaunted a thoughtless, off-the-top-of-his-head speaking style. Where Dr. J's game came out of the age of funk, Barkley reached his explosive prime just as hip hop matured as art. In 1987 when Chuck D bellowed "throw down like Barkley" on "Bring the Noise" it wasn't because the Leeds, Alabama, born player was a hip hop head. It was because, on and off the hardwood, Barkley moved with a bullheaded rage that seemed a physical manifestation of the Bomb Squad's hammering tracks. Because Barkley was relatively short for a power forward, at a reported 6' 6" (in truth he's closer to 6' 4"), and had a chunky fireplug frame, it was astounding to watch him outleap and muscle taller men with classic athletic bodies.

However, Barkley didn't just frustrate foes on the floor. He irritated opposing fans as well. In New York, Boston, and everywhere else the 76ers visited regularly, Barkley reveled in being the player they loved to hate. He was notorious for shouting at fans, giving hecklers the finger, and, in one case, spitting at a fan and accidentally hitting a little girl. On the first Dream Team in 1988 Barkley brought his unrefined attitude to the Olympics, elbowing his overmatched opponents and disrespecting any unfortunate foreigner assigned to guard him. "My dream," Barkley once told some openmouthed reporters, "is for a fan to come at me in an alley and grab me—and be pounded through the concrete." (He more or less got his chance when an obnoxious guy threw ice on him in Orlando in 1997. Barkley responded by throwing him through a plate-glass window.)

During his years in Philly, Barkley was equally disdainful of his team-mates, coaches, and the local media. Yes, the once proud franchise fell apart around him, but he had no problem calling other Sixers "wimps" and "complainers." "I wouldn't want to be a diplomat," he once said. "I wanna be Charles, I'm gonna be real. I'm what life's about. I don't play games or put up fronts. I don't tell people what they wanna hear. I tell them the truth." Sounds just like an excerpt from a *Source* magazine interview.

Well before Dennis Rodman—and at the same time as Madonna, Spike Lee, and Public Enemy—Barkley's contrary, bad-boy persona won him media attention, column inches, and a lot of cash. In his many na-tional commercials Barkley played on his roughneck image, whether he was playing polo while speaking the King's English or slam-dunking Godzilla. Like other '80s icons, and rap as a genre, Barkley commodified rebellion for the consumption of the masses.

THE ANSWER

In 1992, Barkley badgered the Sixers into trading him to Phoenix, a deal that sent the 76ers from respectable mediocrity to abject awfulness. With no Erving or Barkley, the franchise, for the first time in twenty years, lacked a dynamic, defining presence. Yet in failure there's opportunity. By becoming profoundly bad the 76ers put themselves in position to draft one of the many new jack underclassmen making cameo appearances in college ball.

In the early '90s, a new generation of sub-twenty-two-year-old players began to make a profound impact on the NBA, one that perhaps we'll see be as important as the entry of ABA stars in 1976. Teenagers only a cou-ple of years out of the schoolyard are now getting multimillion-dollar contracts and mammoth sneaker deals that rival Michael Jordan's Nike contract, often before they've played one NBA game. The once heart-stopping above-the-rim style introduced by Dr. J and standardized by Barkley's generation is now an expected skill. The combination of cash and skill affords them a level of celebrity it took Erving and Barkley years to attain. These teen jocks take for granted their extraordinary visibility, often equating it to the musical impact of the rap music they blast in the locker room.

Where Charles Barkley was a cool rap reference in the '80s, the players of the '90s invest in rap production companies and, on occasion, rap themselves. In 1995, three members of the Orlando Magic—Dennis Scott, Brian Shaw, and Shaquille O'Neal—had rap material in record stores. In fact, the 1994 version of the 76ers featured Dana Barrows, three-point specialist and one of the NBA's best MCs. However, the 76ers didn't truly enter the hip hop present until the 1995 draft when they made North Carolina's Jerry Stackhouse their number-one pick.

In college Stackhouse's flying dunks made him a veritable baby Jordan and, during his rookie season, he enjoyed all the perks—a signature sneaker deal and regular appearances on ESPN's Sportscenter for his highlight film jams—as well as the standard undressing Jordan reserved for hotshot rookies. The problem was that while Stackhouse had an on-court hip hop game, he did not have an equivalent off-court persona. In an age when antiheroism (or the illusion of being an antihero) excited hip hop fans, Stackhouse's calm, relatively bland demeanor made no impression on the culture.

Sixers management provided that flavor in a major midseason trade that brought the game's more notorious young stars to Philly. In basketball circles, Derrick "D.C." Coleman was as controversial as any gangsta rapper—prodigiously talented, cocky as hell, and famous for an attitude as nasty as his fadeaway. With the New Jersey Nets the Detroit homie had displayed a versatile, undisciplined game that eventually frustrated the team's management and landed him on a *Sports Illustrated* cover as the symbol of underachieving new jack stars. Upon arriving in Philly in 1995, D.C. announced he had a new attitude but, between lingering injuries and poor practice habits, little changed in his game except everyone's inflated expectations for it.

In 1996, with a new motorcycle-driving, young owner, Pat Croce, and a spanking-new arena, the Sixers entered a new era by drafting not just a fine player but the best available b-boy. Allen Iverson entered the league barely over twenty, yet he had been playing a man's game for years. In Virginia he led his high school to state championships both as football quarterback and basketball point guard. Bubbachuck, as he was known in his native Newport News, dominated athletes in his state though only six feet tall and weighing only one hundred sixty pounds. Despite his size and weight, he can soar like Erving and dunk with authority like Barkley, plus he is a better dribbler than either, perfecting the crossover dribble that defines hip hop b-ball.

Iverson's life also has resonance for young African-Americans because it was almost derailed by that familiar institution, the justice system. During a race riot at a Virginia bowling alley, Iverson was accused of attacking other teens with chairs. Convicted on charges of "maiming by mob" and sentenced to five years in prison, it looked like Iverson's sports career was over at seventeen. Fortunately for Iverson, Virginia's then Governor, Douglass Wilder, the only African-American governor of this century, granted the player conditional clemency. Wilder asserted that Iverson had been tried under an "antiquated law" that had "only been invoked one time in Virginia's history." Eventually a court cleared Iverson of all charges, but he was now tainted goods. His mother, Ann, a woman only fifteen years her son's senior, reached out to Georgetown coach John Thompson—a formidable presence in collegiate athletics, both for his former center's large body and his outspoken positions on NCAA rules affecting black students.

Since rising to prominence in the '80s Thompson had always taught a hard-nosed, defensive style well suited to NBA-bound big men, such as Patrick Ewing, Alonzo Mourning, Dikembe Mutombo, Othella Harrington. (On a side note: during the '80s—the school's title-contending years—the Hoyas' blue and silver jersey, adorned by a pit bull, was a staple of '80s hip hop style.) But Thompson was more than an aggressive coach. As a critic of how college basketball rules restricted the recruiting of black student-athletes, Thompson had been as resolute as his squad's playing.

For Iverson, Thompson did the unthinkable—he changed his coaching style. The Hoyas still excelled at hyperphysical "D" but now the center offense was turned on its head. As point guard, Iverson had control of the ball and during two spectacular campaigns at Georgetown he usually didn't release it until he'd shot. Even in college, Iverson didn't just play well—he dominated the tough Big East conference and established himself as one of the age's exceptional players.

In 1996, with Thompson's blessing, Iverson became the first Georgetown player to leave school early for the NBA. Drafted number one by Philly, Iverson scored a huge sneaker deal with Reebok (negotiated by Michael Jordan's manager David Falk) and came into the NBA a marked man. Despite many "player haters" Iverson immediately established himself as a presence, making guards wobble as he shook them with his crossover and challenging big men in the paint. Iverson has a combination of speed and power that is special. Moreover, he has a combative, hip hop–bred attitude toward the league's elders. When Iverson said he didn't respect anyone on the court after an encounter with the Bulls, many took it as a dis to Jordan, Rodman, Scottie Pippin, etc. It was one thing to call Rodman "a freak." That was, after all, understandable. But his perceived dis of Jordan made national headlines, though Iverson claimed he'd been quoted out of context.

What Iverson meant was that when he stepped on court, it didn't matter who the competition was—superstars or nobodies. Rookies just weren't supposed to talk this way. Iverson wasn't boasting; this was how a true hip hop head would view the world. Tradition, hierarchy, and institutions are all things ripe to be challenged. Those perceived as the best are not deferred to but must be confronted head-on. (It was funny, at least to me, to hear Barkley join the chorus who condemned Iverson. As a young Sixer, Barkley once called a team meeting without consulting team leader Erving—a terrible sign of disrespect in team sports.)

Despite, or partly because of, the mainstream media's often negative coverage of him, Iverson became the living embodiment of hip hop's boldness and taste for controlled rebellion. As a product of Newport News, a small city with a strong migratory connection with New York City (many families there have roots in the area, including mine), Iverson's personality has a definite Big Apple flavor that is reflected in his dress, even the cadence of his speech, and his behavior.

People were understandably upset when Iverson admitted to carrying a gun, though in truth many of his peers carry pieces as security against the car jackings and armed robberies wealthy black men are often subject to. When a posse of his boys and Stackhouse's friends got into a shuffle outside a Sixer practice Iverson defended them all, a sign of solidarity with his homies central to the culture. Not surprisingly, Stackhouse was traded to Detroit a year later, as his game was smothered by Iverson's dominance of the ball and of the public imagination. When viewed in a hip hop context, a lot of the controversies surrounding Iverson's rookie campaign are just part of the usual baggage of stardom.

True to hip hop form, Iverson has formed his own production company, Crew Thick; the first artists signed were two of Iverson's pals known as Madd Rugid. And, Iverson's appearance, with his hat to the back, on the cover of *Rap Pages*, a national hip hop mag, certified his place in the culture's constellation.

Iverson's longevity is, of course, yet to be determined, but he and Stephon Marbury, Kevin Garnett, Shareef Abdul-Rahim, Kobe Bryant, and others—players raised on rap's bravado—are now the game's immediate future. What is exciting about them is that despite the huge salaries, they have strong warrior vibes. This group may strike Julius Erving as unpolished and Barkley as disrespectful. But they are not arrogant, lazy fat cats. The desire for props, the undercurrent of all hip hop competition, burns bright in these brothers. Just as the naysayers ridiculed ABA flair, this generation will have to overcome a lot of negative speculation. And, as in much coverage of rap music, the more benign among them (Garnett, Abdul-Rahim) will be used to make the more bodacious brothers look bad. Just don't sleep on them. The truth is that Iverson and company, with the spirit of hip hop in their hearts, have the will and the growing skills to make twenty-first century ball even better than today's.

capitalist tool

MY ADIDAS STANDING ON 2-5 STREET
FUNKY FRESH AND, YES, COLD ON MY FEET

—RUN-D.M.C.,
"MY ADIDAS"

HIP HOP IS NOT A POLITICAL MOVEMENT IN THE USUAL SENSE. ITS advocates don't elect public officials. It doesn't present a systematic (or even original) critique of white world supremacy. Nor has it produced a manifesto for collective political agitation. It has generated no Malcolm X or Dr. King. It has spawned no grassroots activist organization in the order of the Southern Christian Leadership Conference, the Black Panther Party, NAACP, or even the Country Music Association.

Hip hop has actually had surprisingly little concrete long-term impact on African-American politics. It has made its mark by turning its listeners onto real political icons (Malcolm X), radical organizations of the past (the Black Panthers), and self-sufficient operations of the present (the Nation of Islam). It spread the word about the evils of apartheid. It articulated and predicted the explosive rage that rocked Los Angeles in 1992. It has given two generations of young people a way into the entertainment business and an uncensored vehicle for expression. Chuck D once said he hoped Public Enemy would spawn thousands of black leaders. To the degree that his band opened the eyes of its listeners to political thought, Chuck D and his crew have probably affected many more young people than that.

Hip hop's major problem as a political movement is that MCs are not social activists by training or inclination. They are entertainers whose visability and effectiveness as messengers are subject to the whims of the marketplace. For all Public Enemy's impact—and there were at least four years when the band embodied the best of this culture—its ultimate strength lay in making and selling records.

But this doesn't mean there has been no political impact from hip hop—far from it. From the Chuck D–designed b-boy in a gun sight logo to the Muhammad Ali–Drew "Bundini" Brown interplay of Chuck and Flavor Flav, from the Security of the First World's onstage brandishing of toy Uzis and militaristic garb to the Bomb Squad's bombastic aural attack, Public Enemy made politics seem cool. In the process they also made politics a commodity. To be sure, this was a marketing tool with a wider purpose but, in effect, it was no different than what L.L. Cool J did for romantic themes or N.W.A did for gangsterism. In the great pop culture wave constantly rippling across our shores, black nationalistic rap crested and, for the time being, has receded along with the career of P.E. and acolytes Paris, the X Clan, and others.

While hip hop's values are by and large fixed—its spirit of rebellion, identification with street culture, materialism, and aggression—it is also an incredibly flexible tool of communication, quite adaptable to any number of messages. That's one reason it has endured. That's why no one style has been essential for over three or four years at a time. That's why it has been so easy to turn every element of the culture associated with hip hop into a product, be it Tommy Hilfiger selling leisure wear, academics writing a thesis, breakfast-cereal makers hawking sugar-covered wheat, or presidential candidates seeking an issue.

Hip hop didn't became commodified in a simple, connect-the-dots manner. It morphed, like an alien in a sci-fi flick, to serve its different masters. Yet, unlike so many other underground cultural expressions, hip hop has managed to remain vital, abrasive, and edgy for two decades. The culture's connection to the African-American working and underclass, people usually without a media voice, enables it to communicate dreams and emotions that make outsiders uncomfortable. When even Sony Play-station features a gentle childlike rapper, it doesn't fatally undercut or mitigate the force of roughneck MCs like Mobb Deep or Wu-Tang. Somehow hip hop survives even the crassest commercialism or, at least, it has so far.

There are scores of stories that illustrate hip hop's essential mutability. They are literary, cinematic, fashionable, and political in ways that
have nothing do with black nationalism, for hip hop is the ultimate capi-
talist tool.

FASHION SHOWS

The June 1997 issue of the *Source* featured a foldout cover of the Wu-
Tang Clan logo, a striking montage of the group members' eyes and, on
the back side, a two-page spread of these Staten Island boys. It was an effective attempt to sell the magazine and promote the group's highly anticipated *Wu-Tang Forever*. It was the *Source* fulfilling its role as a celebrator
of hip hop culture.

While the inducement to purchase the June 1997 issue was an opportunity to gain insight into Wu-Tang, a look inside showed that the *Source*
sold much more than records. Of the magazine's sixty-seven full-page
ads, twenty-nine were from clothing companies. In the August edition of
Vibe, the ratio of clothing ads (twenty-six) to total full-page ads (ninety-
three) wasn't as large, but it was still hefty. And the ratio wasn't the only
difference. *Vibe*'s higher ad rate and more mainstream orientation meant
its advertisers were mostly larger national brands (Calvin Klein's CK
Jeans, Union Bay, Ralph Lauren's Polo). The *Source*'s clothing constituency included a few national names but was largely composed of
smaller boutique companies (555 Soul, Pure Playaz, PNB), many of
which were either partially or solely minority owned.

This dichotomy between *Vibe* and the *Source*, between larger white merchandisers and grassroots ethnic designers, speaks to the multiple approaches and overall evolution of what may be the most multilayered
(pun intended) aspect of hip hop—its style. Even more than dancing,
record production, and rhyming, hip hop fashion has mutated amazingly
over the last twenty plus years. A photo chronicle of hip hop fashion that
broke it down by era, region, designers, crews, and personal idiosyncrasy
would celebrate not just style but the very nature of how clothing reflects
the tempo of the times. For the purposes of this narrative I'll simplify a
tale that has as many tributaries as the Nile.

In a 1985 essay in the book *Fresh, Hip Hop Don't Stop*, journalist Sally Flinker opened a piece on urban fashion by stating, "A true hip hop spirit doesn't need—or want—a designer label on his jeans. His own name, or his tag, is the only commodity to promote, and it's borne proudly on the backs of denim jackets, huge nameplate necklaces, and belt buckles." Flinker argued that a "heightened sense of identity, of putting across one's personal image" was essential to this post-soul aesthetic. In hip hop's first phrase, Flinker was right. Gang mode—a dungaree jacket turned inside out with the name Savage Nomads or Jolly Stompers drawn on the back—was the original hip hop fashion. So were hooded jackets or sweatshirts, worn by graffiti writers to hide their identity and protect their heads from the wire fences at subway yards. Enough gold chains to finance a condo, often with the owner's adopted street tag on nameplates; baseball and painter's caps, worn sideways or painted; sweat suits, usually Adidas, and shell-toed sneakers either with fat laces or no laces—all of these were where hip hop fashion began. The brand name gear—be it Lee cords or Ban-Lon shirts or Tommy Boy Record's popular promotional ski caps—tended to be inexpensive, utilitarian, and low maintenance. Personalizing the gear—with stenciled-on names, use of clashing colors, or wearing clothes out of season—was essential. Dancing in a crowded club in a leather ski parka with fur trim came out of hip hop's early days and has not totally disappeared.

There was an improvisational quality to style in the old school, which I'd define from a fashion viewpoint as the late '70s up to about 1983. That was the moment when high fashion designers began taking these street styles, and the Day-Glo colors used to tag subway cars, quite seriously. First into the game was black designer Willi Smith who hired several graffiti artists (Dondi White, Futura 2000, Zephyr) to do a well-received, playful T-shirt line. In 1984, the then hot designer Stephen Sprouse integrated the Day-Glo colors and graffiti-styled prints into his work.

Still the fashion establishment wasn't yet buying it. When a L.A. video production company approached several designers about using breaking and rap as a backdrop for showcasing their lines, most rejected the idea. Only Norma Kamali gave it a try. In 1984, the resulting video, "Street Beat," showcased her clothes and the moves of the *Breakin'* stars Boogaloo

Shrimp and Shabbadoo. Later a reedited version, with new footage of Chaka Khan dropped in, became the video for Khan's single hit "I Feel for You."

FAT LACES

It was in 1985 that the athletic wear manufacturers began to see how the link between hip hop and their products could pay off big time—and, unsurprisingly, it was Russell Simmons who made the connection real.

Run-D.M.C.'s "My Adidas" was a tribute to the seminal hip hop athletic shoe at the height of its appeal. Russell Simmons and his Rush Management team were determined to turn that record's message into money. Athletes regularly scored endorsement deals from athletic wear companies and Michael Jordan was already on his way to revolutionizing the marketing of sports gear with his landmark Nike deal. Russell wanted a piece of the pie for Run-D.M.C.

Run-D.M.C.'s 1986 headlining appearance at Madison Square Garden provided the right venue for Russell to prove his point. With several Adidas executives from Germany standing in the wings, Run-D.M.C. was rocking 20,000 New York b-boys and girls at Madison Square Garden. Before performing "My Adidas," Run told the crowd to hold up their Adidas sneakers. A sea of three-stripped athletic sneakers emerged like white leather clouds over the heads of most of the fans. When Run walked offstage that night "the Adidas representatives told me that I would have my own line of Adidas clothing," he told the *Source* in 1993. "That was the most memorable event in my life" (at least until he became born again). Within a year, Adidas and Rush Management had negotiated a $1.5 million deal with the rappers to market Run-D.M.C. sneakers and various accessories, including a Run-D.M.C. jersey I still treasure.

With this deal a line had been crossed. Instead of just adapting existing styles and working with "found" materials, the hip hop community was now having things made expressly for them by major manufacturers. As a result, other deals were made. (Whodini made a small deal with Lacoste Sportif and L.L. Cool J a large one with Troop.) Happily, though, the creative energy was still soaring—evidenced when the next major trend emerged from the underground.

SUPERFLY

In 1990, I took a trip up to Harlem in search of the new fashion flavor. This is what I saw:

> Another Saturday night at Dapper Dan's. It's near midnight on 125th and the hip-hop boutique . . . is amped. Dap, a slim, serious man dressed in khaki shirt and pants and trademark red loafers, is showing off a table full of pants and pullover tops plastered with Bally logos. Three brothers in full gear—space boot sneakers, gold capped teeth, knuckle rings—fondle the merchandise. One pulls on a lime-green top. The other tries on Halloween orange shorts with Bally printed across the groin. Dap and two of his team of African seamsters watch. Finally Dap tells them, "Whatever you want can be hemmed in 30 minutes. Just tell me what you want." The brothers continue to survey the goods. Just-Ice, notorious rap gangster and otherwise sweet guy, cruises in from his show at the Apollo. He needs a new outfit for the midnight show, doesn't have time to run up to the Bronx, and wants to know can he put something on his bill.

Dapper Dan's shop was one of the sites where the relationship between mainstream fashion and hip hop was altered. It was on the street outside that shop that Mike Tyson, on his way in to pick up a custom-made "Don't Believe the Hype" leather jacket, punched out Mitch "Blood" Green in 1988. It was inside that shop that the faux Gucci outfits Eric B. & Rakim wore on the cover of *Follow the Leader*, were stitched. It was at Dan's shop, and in the others that followed his lead, that large swatches of material embossed with designer emblems (Gucci, Louis Vuitton, Fendi, MCM) were cut to fit hubcaps, Jeeps, and furniture, where elite Italian and French brand names were married to hip hop style.

The appropriation of high fashion items began in the late '70s with Cazals, a line of designer glasses frames that homeboys often wore without any glass as pure style. The Gucci and Fendi shift, in which ghetto designers used upscale logos mirroring the way rap producers sampled beats, took this game to another level. Once the taste for designer gear was whetted, Run-D.M.C.'s admonition "Don't want nobody's name on my behind" was history.

Old-school symbols of self-identification (nameplate belt buckles, stenciled T-shirts) gave way to the culture's total immersion, even obsession, with expensive status gear. Young urban adults and even teens became regular visitors to the Fifth Avenue stores of high-profile clothiers, occasionally intimidating customers and attracting the close attention of security guards. This shift, which would prove more enduring than hi-top fades, Lacoste Sportif sweat suits, and the Louis Vuitton logo on car seats, would be monitored by manufacturers large and small.

Homemade gang emblems drawn and spray-painted onto jackets and dungaree legs were part of the New York scene during the days Bambaataa, Herc, and Flash were spinning in Bronx parks. Over ten years later another gang-generated style would rise out of the West. When the Oakland Raiders moved to Los Angeles in the '80s, their logo—a scowling pirate backed by crossed swords and the word "Raider" above his head—was adopted by kids in both of the city's major gangs, the red-garbed Bloods and blue-wearing Crips, as well as teens caught in between. The team's silver and black projected strength without declaring which "set" you were down with. Then the city's hockey franchise, the Kings, a team never known for its toughness, shifted from the blue and gold it shared with the basketball Lakers to the Raider's silver and black. The Kings' revamped bold logo quickly became essential to the West Coast hip hop uniform, nicely complementing the boastful violence of the emerging gangsta style. In fact, N.W.A's original look—the Kings and Raiders paraphernalia, augmented by sunglasses called "Locs" and the stiff Dickies jeans and jackets—recast athletic wear in a new sinister light. In cities around the country gangs and drug operations gravitated to different sports merchandise. In New York, a Yankees blue cap with its white "NY" meant certain drugs were available. In Boston, one gang liked to wear the green and yellow parkas and caps of the Green Bay Packers.

Because gang members, particularly the more successful crack dealers, were so visible in the 'hood, the sellers of athletic apparel began courting them. When the new Air Jordans or the latest Chicago Bulls parkas were due in, retailers would get the word out to local dealers. These young dealers, many with romanticized views of themselves as outlaws not simple crooks, became tastemakers directing both their customers and neighbors toward new merchandise.

While the oversize parka and wool cap has been a hip hop cultural artifact for most of its history, the heavy winter boots as year-round attire flowed out of their use by crack dealers clocking on corners. In the tradition of appropriation that is integral to the scene, Timberland boots—high quality footwear worn by folks in New England and the Midwest for decades—suddenly became official urban style. Tims, as they were nicknamed, were for several years the Air Jordans of boots, they became equally ubiquitous in music videos, on stage, and in the streets.

While Tims-mania generated millions, its owners were clearly uncomfortable with the unexpected identification of its brand name with urban youth. When word of mouth of Timberland's lack of enthusiasm for the hip hop audience hit the streets (a message aided by Luggz and other competitors), Timberland disappeared from the culture as quickly as it had emerged as a staple. By 1996, the only ember left of the fire was that a top Virginia-based producer went by the tag Timbaland. Other than that, Timberland was as over in hip hop as the Sugar Hill Gang.

There are other stories of mainstream brand names rejecting an association with hip hop. In the early '90s, A Tribe Called Quest's Q-Tip had several requests for Polo street wear rejected by reps for the Ralph Lauren affiliated–company. The stated reason was that they were worried how it would affect the company's image. A few years later Lauren's operation had turned a new leaf, using the defiantly dark Caribbean-American visage of model Tyson Beckford to sell everything from shades to underwear. Part of Lauren's reevaluation was surely influenced by the astonishing marriage between hip hop and Tommy Hilfiger. The elfin-looking American designer, since his company's founding in 1985, had built a rep for making colorful, loose-fitting sportswear. Lacking the haughty veneer of Gucci or Chanel or the all-American aura of Ralph Lauren, Hilfiger's brand was accessible in a manner similar to the clothes early hip hoppers gravitated to.

Grand Puba, ex-member of Masters of Ceremony, sometime-member of Brand Nubian, and the possessor of an intriguing off-kilter flow, has always been a hipster favorite, largely because he has remained as much a cult figure as a record seller. The lifelong New York–area resident once told the *Source*, "If I only sold records in New York, you know, I felt content with that," which was sweet to the ears of East Coast true believers. So when Puba began mentioning Hilfiger's clothes in his work, including during a guest appearance on Mary. J. Blige's *What's the 411?*, it served as a seal of approval that led other rappers, industry figures, and active consumers to make Hilfiger part of their wardrobes.

Around 1992 Puba and his crew, freshly dipped in Hilfiger wear, encountered Tommy and his brother Andy just off a plane from Hong Kong at JFK airport. Tommy didn't really know who Puba was but Andy, a music fan, knew of the rapper's music and his affection for their product. As a result of that chance encounter, Puba and his crew were invited up to the show room and given free rein to take whatever they wished.

Over the next few years Puba's endorsement and Hilfiger's friendly response rippled through the culture. More MCs wore clothes from the designer's Tommy Jeans line, more MCs mentioned "Tommy Hill" in rhymes (Q-Tip, Raekwon), and more consumers, white and black, followed suit. Moreover, Hilfiger, at his brother Andy's encouragement, began adapting his clothes to the hip hop–driven youth market. Since brand identification was such a powerful attraction, Hilfiger found that kids wanted his logos larger, more plentiful, and more colorful. Hilfiger accommodated them and this evolving style became known in the fashion biz as "urban prep," a way of dressing that took prep-school clothes and stretched them to fit the loose, baggy feel of '90s teen garb. Many young black designers were hired on to implement this change. One of Quincy Jones's daughters, Kadada, a hip hop tastemaker who dated L.L. Cool J and later Tupac Shakur, became a free-floating asset for the Tommy line, dressing Michael Jackson in the gear for a *Vibe* cover, appearing in Tommy ads, and, for a time, formerly working for the designer.

A backlash against Hilfiger's sudden prominence resulted from a rumor that the designer dissed the black market on *The Oprah Winfrey Show*, a tale that took on the power of urban myth though no one could produce a tape on which he did so. The truth was (as is often the case) quite the opposite. Hilfiger, who initially knew little about hip hop, befriended Russell Simmons and Quincy Jones and became a strong supporter of *Vibe* through advertising and copromotions. In 1996, Hilfiger was the number-one apparel company traded on the New York Stock Exchange, due primarily to his embrace of hip hop and the large suburban audience excited by that urban prep look.

The amazing thing about the hip hop–driven growth of designers like Hilfiger and Lauren is that it did not drive smart African-American companies out of business. On the contrary, the entry of the bigger brands expanded the market and, in some ways, enhanced the position of the better designers. The larger brands not only made white kids more conscious of style, they made more adventurous dressers "keep it real" by seeking black designers. The Afrocentric impulse never totally died but, like everything else in this field, evolved into something else.

Instead of sporting Malcolm X T-shirts, many black and hip white consumers decided they wouldn't be caught dead wearing the fashion equivalent of a Hammer record. In an economic manifestation of cultural nationalism, these consumers now buy their fashion black. Moreover, they are often rewarded stylistically since the black-run apparel enterprises tend to be more progressive in their choices of fabric, logos, and colors.

The greatest hip hop African-American fashion success story belongs to Karl Kani (Carl Williams), a Brooklyn native based out of Los Angeles. Karl Kani Infinity had estimated sales $50 million in 1997, making the twenty-nine-year-old designer's operation the largest black-owned apparel firm in America. The road to this accomplishment wasn't smooth. When urban youth first adopted the jail style of baggy jeans damn near sliding off their butts, it was usually Kani's line that sagged around their ankles. Around 1991, he pioneered extra baggy pants and sweaters with his bold signature adorning each piece.

At that time, Kani's work was distributed in partnership with the Los Angeles–based Threads 4 Life–Cross Colours line, a brand known for baggy denim overalls highlighted by a garish red, yellow, and green logo. The teaming of black East and West Coast design aesthetics was unprecedented, as both managed to tap into urban taste and black pride. Ads for Cross Colours used to boast, "We want it understood that only Cross Colours is made by true brothers from the 'hood." As a division of Threads 4 Life, Kani's company generated $34 million in 1993. Later that year the bubble burst. Mismanagement and unpaid bills ground this combination to a halt and, to a great degree, opened the market for the Hilfigers of the world to move in. While the brothers who founded Cross Colours have yet to fully recover, Kani bounced back. After buying back his trademark name, Kani launched his new operation in November 1993 with $500,000 in the bank.

Kani's street rep was still strong. So was his design eye and his proven relationships with national retailers. Though no longer the newest, coolest line on the street, Kani managed to create an air of stability around him that, along with black businesspeople from the corporate mainstream, put him on the cover of *Fortune* magazine's August 1997 "New Black Power" issue. Since 1996, he has moved into couture, designing suits, slacks, and blazers. Around the country other innovative African-American apparel companies have followed Kani's lead, people like Maurice Malone, ex-Mecca designer Tony Shellman (whose Enyce was funded by the Italian Fila company the way PolyGram backs Def Jam), Sir Benni Miles who successfully launched a line of nylon skull caps, and Fubu, a New York–based concern whose work exploded in the streets in early 1998.

FASHION FORWARD

Coming out of the first two decades of hip hop, there are two conflicting trends in fashion that, not coincidentally, speak to battling aesthetics within the overall culture. On the one hand is a coterie of slick, dressed-to-impress types whose embrace of high fashion names recalls the deification of Gucci and the like. Their signatures are the glitzy taste of Puff Daddy's Bad Boy camp, the late Gianni Versace's gaudy gear, and Foxy Brown's celebration of Dolce & Gabbana. In the past, the high stylers— the Dapper Dans of the world—were making uptown appropriations of the originals that were gleefully illegal and subversive. Now it just comes off as "I'm paid" consumerism with no subtext.

More encouraging are the folks who are holding on to the do-it-yourself philosophy that created hip hop. Chuck D has had his own clothing line, Rapp, for years, while Naughty By Nature and Wu-Tang both have stores and 800 numbers to receive orders. Russell Simmons has been slowly growing his Phat Farm out of his original SoHo location and L.A.'s expensive Fred Siegel boutique. Throughout the industry, rap entrepreneurs and local designers have been hooking up in hopes of building not just a Def Jam but a Kani-style enterprise.

I have no clue where hip hop style will go next, but the curiosity and ambition that have altered urban dress these last twenty plus years is no where near abating. While dollars will continue to be siphoned off by open-minded mass marketeers, the volatile nature of the culture means there will always be room for African-American entrepreneurs to innovate and, hopefully, build enduring companies.

PULP FICTION

I first read Barry Michael Cooper in the pages of the now defunct weekly *SoHo Weekly News*. It was a review of Chic's *Risque* album, which was so smart and entertaining I wish I'd written it. Not long after that I met Barry at a listening party. He is a large, brown-skinned brother with a serious demeanor and a thoughtful, world-weary voice that belies his hearty laugh. Despite growing up in the heart of Harlem, Barry has an innocent, idealistic quality that is more apparent in his agile, buoyant prose than the topics he addresses.

It turned out that Barry had read and liked my *Amsterdam News* review of Paul Schrader's *American Gigolo*, a 1980 movie we both admired for its alienated central character, its depiction of a chic, amoral Los Angeles, and the sleek Armani suits sported by Richard Gere. We talked a great deal about Schrader's use of Smokey Robinson's "The Love I Saw in You Was Just a Mirage" over a sequence of Gere's gigolo lovingly fondling his shirts, a striking confluence of romanticism and materialism. We agreed the scene was a quiet harbinger of the hip hop era in that it suggested material love could satisfy deeper than physically for those with broken moral compasses.

From early on Barry has had aspirations to shape, not just chronicle, the age. He produced and played keyboards on a couple of indie 12-inches and is always particularly sensitive to the uses of computerized keyboards in his criticism. However, Barry truly made his mark as a reporter-forecaster of the emerging culture of drugs, guns, and sampled beats that exploded in tandem with crack. Whether it was a jailhouse interview with Larry Davis, (the legendary Bronx drug courier for corrupt cops), covering a Central Park rape case, or coining the phrase "new jack swing" to describe Teddy Riley's sound, Barry was always on the edge.

His signature piece of journalism was "Kids Killing Kids: New Jack City Eats Its Young," a *Village Voice* cover story on Detroit's brutal, sophisticated drug scene. Written in 1988, it showed that the Motor City's dealers and its youth culture were trailblazers in experiencing the possibilities and corruption that crack presented:

> The get over class in New Jack City understands that gangster style is both form and function. To have gangster style you have to get "getting paid"—making so much gusto (money) until its goofy. . . . Then you can have an acquired taste by means of extortion, the ability to buy panache and aristocracy. But that's what also unnerves me about the emigre of New Jack City; the way he flashes his green card. Whether it's the kid that goes to Gucci to spend $3,000 on a wardrobe displayed no further than the L.L. Cool J show, the crackhouse or the projects or the kid who comes home to a $200,000 cul de sac and a good night's sleep after killing a rival crackdealer and two of his crew, and all the while mom and dad are in the den doing taxes on the PC—it alarms me that the need to "show & prove" is that extreme.

Barry's reporting was so thorough that he was warned to stay out of Detroit by local gangsters and so vividly written that it attracted the attention of two aggressive black film producers, George Jackson and Doug McHenry. The pair had been developing a movie about Harlem's heroin kingpin Nicky Barnes for Warner Bros. The original story, written by Thomas Lee Wright, was set in the '70s. But Jackson and McHenry, who had produced *Krush Groove* and *Disorderlies*, were aware of how the rise of hip hop and crack had changed urban street life. So they recruited Barry to create a "new jack" Harlem drug dealer for the go-go '80s.

Black music critics writing for an alternative weekly don't often get recruited to write a Hollywood melodrama. Certainly it's a tribute to the immediacy and punch of Barry's work. It also speaks to the impact of post-soul culture that black producers at a major Hollywood studio making a black flick can hire a black writer with no screenwriting experience simply because of his street knowledge. In the blaxploitation era, none of the people in such a position were of color. Hip hop put a premium on authenticity and Barry benefitted from this changed climate.

Barry's journalism provided the iconic title—*New Jack City*—and he conceived a slew of memorable characters (Nino Brown, Gee Money, Pookie), cramming the rise of crack into a tight narrative that radiates with the ear for slang he'd brought to his nonfiction. Moreover, Barry was able to accomplish something rare for a screenwriter; he put a personal stamp on the material. *New Jack City* was not only set in Barry's 'hood, but it featured a conflict between two men, brothers in the drug game, who would clash fatally over the limits of loyalty. In *New Jack City* the relationship between Wesley Snipes's Nino Brown and Allen Payne's Gee Money is central to the plot, giving the fast-paced film part of its emotional kick.

Barry's two other produced screenplays, *Sugar Hill* and *Above the Rim*, both released in 1994, are Harlem crime dramas featuring brothers in conflict. Though other writers, along with directors and actors, had input into each script, all three of Barry's movies are obsessed with the beautiful grime and troubled families of uptown New York.

Pulp fiction (the real stuff, not the arty recycling written by Quentin Tarantino) is disdained by most "respectable" or at least educated folks. Among African-Americans, where chronicling criminal lifestyles is always a touchy issue, Barry's films have been derided as contemporary blaxploitation. In truth, Barry's three films, as well as his yet to be produced screenplays, are extensions of his journalism, just as Nick Pilegi's gangsta scripts (*GoodFellas, Casino*) flow out of his days covering the Mafia. Moreover, Barry's work, which has provided Snipes, Tupac Shakur, Chris Rock, Ice-T, and Michael Wright with memorable roles, is in the authentic pulp fiction tradition of Iceberg Slim and Donald Goines—as are the gangsta rhymes of rappers such as KRS-One and Ice Cube.

Crossover has engendered a kind of crossback phenomenon, too. Just as hip hop smoothed Barry Michael Cooper's entry into moviemaking, it also created a climate where obscure black pulp fiction could find a publisher. In 1996, W. W. Norton, a venerable mainstream publisher, began a line called Old School Books, the title obviously an homage to its use in hip hop circles. Under the guidance of pulp fiction fanatics Marc Gerald and Samuel Blumenfeld, the line has reprinted novels that speak to the dark side of the soul era. In a way analogous to rap—but far from as visible—the Old School Books authors, whose titles cover the period from 1958 to the mid-'70s, looked at American life with harsh, desparing eyes.

A couple of the Old School Books authors are famous, Chester Himes and John Williams, and the line has reprinted two of their obscure novels:—Williams's *The Angry Ones* and Himes's *The End of the Primitive*. However, the heart of the line is dedicated to rescuing lost writers like Clarence Cooper, Jr., (*The Scene, Black!*), Herbert Simmons (*Corner Boy*), and Charles Perry (*Portrait of a Young Man Drowning*). Not all the books are crime based—Williams's novel is about the frustrations of a wanna-be buppie in the still segregated '60s—but as the editors wrote in an introduction to one of the first volumes of Old School Books, "It is a world of the desperate and the deranged; the doomed and the damned; a world where the sun never shines."

In the same year, a U.K. counterpart appeared as an import in the States. Payback Press acquired the rights to Gil Scott-Heron's long-out-of-print novels, *The Vulture* and *The Nigger Factory*, Melvin Van Peebles's *Panther* (the basis for son Mario's movie), and Iceberg Slim's *The Long White Con*. With introductions penned by Ice-T to several titles, Payback Press, like Old School Books, links reality rap, whether you call it gangsta or not, to forgotten hard-boiled prose, making it clear that explorations of nihilistic racism and the most brutal nightmares of African-America are part of an occasionally disreputable legacy that should not be ignored. Luckily for the post-soul generation of black pulp storytellers, their connection to music frees the Ice Cubes and KRS-Ones of the world from the obscurity and frustration of their artistic ancestors.

BOTTLE BAGS AND SODA POP

As far back as I can remember, beverage companies have been hawking malt liquor in black neighborhoods. Colt 45 was the brew I saw consumed by parents playing spades at kitchen-table card games and by boys tossing cilo dice in schoolyards. It wasn't as disreputable as drinking cheap wine, as socially acceptable as Miller or Budweiser, or as upscale as cognac, but Colt 45 had its own cache. It was the alcohol of choice for herd-living, macho brothers who took a cocky pride in brandishing the tall white cans.

When I was a teen in the '70s, Olde English 800 was on the rise. Colt 45 was your uncle's buzz; Olde E was younger and dumber. Its tall gold-

and-brown cans promised a quick, intense high, which, if purchased right after school on Friday, would have you silly by sundown. But Saturday watch out. An Olde E hangover is brutal. If Colt 45 was a R&B brew, Olde E was old-school rap's favorite libation. It became as associated with Run-D.M.C. as black hats and Adidas sneakers. D.M.C. even penned a poem in praise of Olde E's charms: "Crack the quart, put it to your lip / You tilt it slightly and take a sip / Now by now you should know the deal / 'Cause that one sip you already feel."

Back in the '80s, malt liquor in store-promotional posters either featured some macho double entendre slogan or a thick, scantily clad sister posed near the logo. Malt liquor ads never had the upscale veneer of cognac. ("I assume you drink Martel?" was one memorable ad line.) Nor did they aspire to the drink-it-at-ball-games-and-picnics appeal of Budweiser. Malt liquor was for roughnecks way before MC Lyte popularized the phrase.

Malt liquor ads had long used symbols of black macho (Fred Williamson was a King Cobra spokesman) and music-driven spots on black radio. So it wasn't that surprising that a new brand seeking to woo the hip hop generation would employ MCs as spokespeople. What was remarkable was how shrewdly they hit their target. St. Ides ignored mainstream rap stars like L.L. or Heavy D. and went right for the hard core. The brew debuted out West with a radio spot featuring a chilly performance by King Tee, an Ice-T protégé who dragged a shotgun across the cover of his debut album. I thought his sixty-second St. Ides spot was actually better than his album. Certainly that spot received more exposure on black radio than anything the L.A. rapper would release on his own.

As the brew moved East so did its choice of rap spokeperson. A TV ad directed by *Video Music Box* host Ralph McDaniels featured members of the Wu-Tang Clan when the crew were still just underground heroes. Using King Tee and Wu-Tang sent a strong message to malt liquor's core consumers—St. Ides is for roughnecks like you.

Then St. Ides pushed the envelope. When they signed Ice Cube around 1991 to be the chief spokesman his street credibility was high, coming off his stellar performance in *Boyz N the Hood* and his *Kill at Will* EP. And for a time the St. Ides's crooked "I" logo and Cube were intertwined and inescapable in America's 'hoods. His trademark scowl hung in bodegas, grocery stores, and 7-Elevens, while his elaborate James

Bond–styled TV ads rivaled his videos. The St. Ides marketing acumen and Ice Cube's visibility made the connection between hip hop, black youth, and malt liquor so uncomfortably intimate that Chuck D, rap's sometime policeman, commented negatively on the phenomenon in "I Million Bottlebags": "They drink it thinkin' it good / but they don't sell it in the white neighborhood / How many times you see a black fight a black / After drinkin' a bottle / Or malt liquor six pack?"

Given how forcefully anti–malt liquor Chuck D was, it is strange that Cube appeared in a St. Ides radio spot that sampled the voice of Public Enemy's leader. Chuck D, rightfully pissed at this inappropriate appropriation of his work, sued St. Ides's distributor, the McKenzie River Corporation, for $5 million and made an out-of-court settlement that reputedly provided the down payment on an Atlanta home.

When Snoop Doggy Dogg ascended to the status of new hard-core hero, St. Ides replaced Cube with the Death Row star. For his campaign, the brewers had a doglike caricature drawn of the MC that was employed to help introduce Crooked, a fruity beverage aimed at expanding the brand's base. So closely associated did St. Ides and Snoop's identification become that the same artist who did Crooked ads drew the scatological artwork (images that C. Dolores Tucker would later attack before the Congress) for Snoop's *Doggystyle*.

While St. Ides displayed a keen eye for the right hard-core rapper to push their brew, the makers of the benign, nonalcoholic soda Sprite have been equally shrewd. Sprite, once a poor relation to 7-Up with an undefined audience, began specifically targeting the hip hop audience in the mid-'90s. Wisely, the brand showed no interest in the roughneck approach. Instead, Sprite has gone for a less confrontational, more conversational approach. Its first TV spots featured music and images of A Tribe Called Quest. The colorful spots had a bright color scheme and trendy visuals that seemed aimed at adolescents and young women. The tag line for these spots was "Obey Your Thirst." Sprite then went to a more nuanced set of black-and-white spots that featured ex–Brand Nubian Grand Puba and the ex–Main Source Large Professor freestyling in a recording studio control room. The spots had an understated, soft sell feel—more like a documentary than an ad—that was aimed at rap connoisseurs, the kind of aware fan who knew who these two underground New York MCs were and would have been suspicious of a hard sell.

It was hip hop snob appeal, a bit of target marketing that Sprite would refine with a 1997 campaign updated with images from Charlie Ahearn's 1983 cult film *Wild Style*. Sequences from the original hip hop movie were restaged using contemporary stars (Nas and A.Z. freestyling on a Brooklyn stoop). By employing images from a film that never got wide release and is even hard to find on videotape, Sprite refined its rap snob appeal and displayed a deep understanding of rap's old-school history and that history's meaning for an active, smart segment of its consumer base. They even added more hip hop–oriented lines of copy: "Sprite has many styles 'cause you're stayin' true to what you do." I'm not sure it made Sprite an essential part of hip hop parties but it gave the product a connection with very cool aspects of the culture that certainly repositioned the beverage. Who would have imagined I'd be spending this much space on Sprite ads in a hip hop book?

SOULJAH'S STORY

I often saw Lisa Williamson speak at seminars and rallies in the late '80s and was always impressed. It wasn't hard to imagine her as one of African-America's next great leaders. Her voice contains a warming fire of love for her people and her mind a biting well-read Afrocentric intelligence. It seemed to me that while most products of the post-soul generation weren't focused on political thought in any systematic way, Lisa was different.

Majoring in American history and African studies at Rutgers University, Lisa had been very active in the national antiapartheid movement, the one true unifying political cause for African-American college students during the largely apathetic '80s. Lisa struck me as a throwback to the era of highly literate, deeply committed stalwarts of the civil rights movement.

Her philosophy wasn't integrationist, however, but informed by commonsense black nationalism. "I believed," she later wrote, "that we should organize where we lived. That we needed to dedicate our skills and devote our resources and attention to the African youth in the communities we lived in. It seemed obvious to me that you helped your own first and foremost."

Whatever parallels I may have found between Lisa and her ancestors in activism, Lisa was very much a product of her times. She was raised in a broken home by her mother, first in the Bronx and then in various New Jersey towns. She didn't have much use for the elders in the black church and loved rap music. "Rap music," she has said, "could make me feel overtly sexual and controlled by the drum beat. Or it could bring to mind the urgency of the poor condition of black people in this country." After college Lisa got a job offer from Reverend Ben Chavis at the United Church of Christ's Commission for Racial Justice. She was initially skeptical of working for a minister, but Chavis's proposal that Lisa begin working on building a network of youth activists around the country appealed to her.

Chavis was no ordinary establishment preacher. Aside from working in the civil rights movement he'd been jailed for 4½ years as a member of the Wilmington Eight, a group of civil rights figures implicated in a North Carolina racial incident. Most thought the charges were trumped up. Chavis's recognition of Lisa's leadership qualities at various student events belied a progressive quality that would later lead him to the presidency of the NAACP where he did outreach with black youth gangs (before being fired for financial mismanagement) and that in 1997 would lead him to renounce Christianity and join the Nation of Islam as a deputy to Louis Farrakhan.

At the Commission for Racial Justice Lisa spent most of her time communicating with other young activists, marshaling forces for various conferences and events in the black community. However, it was a chance meeting with a child living at one of New York's then notorious welfare hotels that would change her life. In building a relationship with the child and other youngsters living in these squalid city-subsidized domiciles, Lisa became obsessed with the idea of somehow redirecting their lives.

It turned out that the Church of Christ owned an abandoned black college campus in North Carolina with a pool, dorms, and classrooms. Lisa believed "that if I could take about one hundred kids for the summer months to this facility—removing them from the intense pressure of their inner city lives—we could make some progress" in teaching traditional curriculum as well as everything from black history to personal hygiene.

Lisa made her first real music business contact when she met Bill Stephney, then Def Jam vice-president. She proposed a rap concert that would raise money to fund her camp, utilizing rap to directly aid at-risk black youth. The 1990 Apollo Theater event showcased an all-star lineup of New York rap—Public Enemy, L.L. Cool J, Heavy D., Big Daddy Kane, Stetsasonic, and MC Lyte—and raised $60,000 to open Lisa's African Youth Survival Camp. It was a triumph for the young organizer and impressed many in the rap community. Her fiery oratory and commitment drew her to Public Enemy's members and vise versa. She grew close to producer Hank Shocklee and Chuck D—so much so that in the wake of Professor Griff's dismissal in 1989 over his alleged anti-Semitism, Lisa Williamson was recruited to be the new minster of information. Chuck D renamed her Sister Souljah and began positioning her as Public Enemy's female counterpart.

In contrast to the unglamorous, behind-the-scenes work Lisa did bringing people together, Sister Souljah was conceived from the start as a pop icon with consciousness and public presence. With Public Enemy's endorsement Lisa was primed to go from potential leader to marketable commodity. Sister Souljah was signed to Epic Records in 1992 and her debut, *360 Degrees of Power*, plus its provocative single "Slavery's Still in Effect," hit stores in the heat of that summer's presidential campaign. For all its good intentions the album was imitation P.E. and Sister Souljah's rhyme skills were minimal. It probably would have been just another unsuccessful attempt to mimic P.E.'s success if the ex-governor of Arkansas hadn't been made aware of a May 13 interview Lisa had done with the *Washington Post*.

In an address on race, Bill Clinton charged that Sister Souljah was "calling on blacks to kill whites" and challenged Reverend Jesse Jackson and his Rainbow Coalition to condemn her. Someone in Clinton's camp must have mistaken Sister Souljah for a major rap star—though in truth she wasn't the real target of the speech. The man who would be president was reaching out to the white Americans who thought the Democratic party would always cater to its highly visible gadfly, Jesse Jackson, and the "special interest group"—black folks—he represented. Clinton's words were tailored to put Jackson on the defensive as well as take the moral high ground against black "racism." This might have been a worthy endeavor if Clinton's aides hadn't ripped her statement out of context.

Commenting on that year's Los Angeles riots Sister Souljah told the *Post*, "This government and that Mayor were all well aware of the fact that black people were dying everyday in L.A. under gang violence. So if you're a gang member and you would normally be killing somebody, why not kill a white person? Do you think that somebody thinks that white people are better or above dying, when they would normally be killing their own kind?"

The GOP has often attacked pop culture when politically convenient, and the "new" centrist Democrats of Clinton's generation were not new to scapegoating hip hop either. The Parents Music Resource Center, the group that would force the record industry to sticker its records with ratings for obscenity, was inaugurated by Al Gore's wife, Tipper, in 1984. Clinton, who has become so brilliant at preaching public morality and remains so slippery in handling his private affairs, successfully used Sister Souljah as a pawn in his game. Among white voters it made Clinton seem unafraid of the black man whose constituency Democrats had traditionally cartered to and been intimidated by. It also exploited mainstream ignorance of who Sister Souljah was and what her comments really meant, playing on the general discomfort with hip hop's growing prominence in American society. As a result, Sister Souljah had more than her fifteen minutes of fame. Op-ed pieces abounded. So did sound-bite interviews. *Newsweek* put her on the cover. She did a *Playboy* interview. Despite all this attention her album only sold under 50,000 units.

For a less resourceful or interesting personality this could have signaled the end of her public career. Instead, Sister Souljah, with the aid of Times Books, reinvented herself as an author. Just as black nationalism had burned through hip hop as a worthwhile fad, fiction and nonfiction tomes about black relationships by African-American women have become one of publishing's hottest genres. Sister Souljah's *No Disrespect* hit the stores in 1996. It was a highly explicit memoir of her romantic life that used her political activities as a distant backdrop for her own observations on love among Generation X. The book was commercially successful, while managing to make no mention of her run-in with President Clinton, the subsequent controversy, or the effect of this national notoriety on her mental state, much less her love life. Ironically, Souljah's anecdotes about dating drug dealers, sexual growth, and romantic dos and don'ts were reminiscent of the lyrics of hip hop-R&B hits by SWV, TLC, and Changing Faces.

Lisa Williamson has since married and had a child and is now working for Puffy Combs, running his Daddy's House charities, including a summer camp much like the one that originally brought her in contact with the music industry. Her journey from antiapartheid activist to angry nationalist rapper to relationship expert back to do-gooder suggests how the pendulum has swung in this most hyperactive culture, where the most important thing being sold is not entrenched idealism, commitment to a cause, or even a melody. The most consistent element of hip hop has been a captivating, yet ever mutating, sense of self.

chapter 13
too live

I WAS SPEAKING ON A PANEL AT ATLANTA'S SPELMAN COLLEGE IN 1989. I don't remember the exact topic, but I'm sure it dealt with hip hop since at that point every panel I spoke on was about hip hop: Why did it exist? What did it mean? Would it last? These were the questions most asked ten years into its recorded history. Since I was at a woman's college in the South and the 2 Live Crew's raunchy rhymes were already becoming a topic of national debate, I weighed in with an attack on Luther "Luke" Campbell and company, focusing on what I viewed as their lyrical violence toward women (which I saw as an ugly compensation for their absence of rhyme skills). Spelman seemed the perfect venue for just such a talk.

I was wrong. While the front of the room was filled with Spelman women and faculty, in the back were students from all-male Morehouse College across the street. As I assailed the 2 Live Crew, catcalls emanated from the back of the hall. Brothers from Miami were trying to shout me down, claiming "Luke knows those girls!" and he's "just rapping about freaks he knows in Liberty City!" Even more striking was that several Spelman students in the crowd spoke in Luke's defense. They asserted that Luke's personal experience with "skeezers" gave validity to every nasty word he said. No matter how ill Luther's views were on women, a number of Spelman's female students had no problem with "Give Me Some Pussy" or "Throw the Dick" as long as they were about hoes Luke knew. To my Morehouse attackers and Spelman apologists Luther Campbell was not a pornographer on wax—in fact, he was actually kind of a cultural hero. To the keep-it-real mentality of many that night, I was wrong for speaking poorly of a man putting street reality on record. The larger issues raised by the 2 Live Crew's mass market sexism was, in their minds, immaterial.

After the panel, a female professor at Spelman put the evening in perspective for me. Sexual harassment and assault on Spelmen women by male students from Morehouse and the other neighboring black colleges in the Atlanta University Center was on the rise. Spelman had recently instituted counseling for its students on how to deal with male harassment, including date rape; meanwhile, at the time, the male-dominated colleges nearby had not.

I found the attitudes of both male and female students frighteningly old-fashioned. If a girl was labeled a hoe, a skeezer, or a freak by other students, no one seemed willing to defend her. If a male student went too far, would her reputed promiscuity justify everything that happened to her? That Victorian rigidity was doubly disturbing since the young people in question weren't living in some beat-down, poverty-scarred public housing project but on the campuses of two prestigious well-heeled African-American universities.

I sat in my hotel that night thinking about the 2 Live Crew and black misogyny. At a very basic level, there was something I clearly hadn't gotten. Part of it was the music. It wasn't New York beats or Compton funk samples, it was Miami pumping bass, a kinetic, dance-happy sound that owed its rhythmic underpinning to electrofunk like the Soul Sonic Force's "Planet Rock."

It was the music of frenzied Liberty City house parties, of white frat boys in Broward County, and, ultimately, the soundtrack for strip clubs worldwide. For college kids on Spring Break, be it the black Freaknik in Atlanta or the white hedonism of Daytona Beach, the 2 Live Crew was the unofficial soundtrack of wet T-shirt contests and other uplifting collegiate pursuits. So, to the degree that I denigrated Campbell's music, I was coming from a place of cultural ignorance.

It was that claim of "reality," as the students used it, that nagged me all night. It struck me then, and still does, that many folks raised on hip hop have bought into a very limited view of life, one that deems that truth is defined by street dogma or, at least, their perception, not necessarily experience, of that dogma. Sadly, there is often no larger vision at work. The social ramifications of the 2 Live Crew's music—that it was black men saying some pretty horrific things about women—didn't make a dent that night. Nor did the argument that the 2 Live Crew was, perhaps, the latest salvo in a subterranean battle of the sexes.

CULTURE WARS

An indirect yet high-intensity cultural war between the African-American sexes has spanned the post-soul era. It is a war in which the shots have been fired with words, with books, magazines, and poets on one side, and MCs and movies on the other. The opening shot, as far as I see it, was fired by Ntozake Shange in the bicentennial year. The weapon was her theatrical choral poem *for colored girls who have considered suicide/when the rainbow is enuf*. Speaking dialogue written with a poet's ear for language and in a spirit of female communion, its seven characters evocatively tell tales of life, love, and the evil done to them by the men they loved. The chilling centerpiece of *for colored girls* is the story "a nite with beau willie brown" related by the Lady in Red. Willie Brown, a charismatic, crazed, drug-addicted Vietnam veteran, abuses his girlfriend and, in a spasm of murderous anger, tosses their small children out a window. It is a show-stopping piece of theater, one that captures years of black female frustration, confusion, and pain in one indelible image.

The second round of fire was Michelle Wallace's *Black Macho and the Myth of the Super-Woman*, published to much fanfare in 1978. Feminists were deep in their "the black man is the boogeyman" phase, during which African-American males were regularly depicted as rapists, muggers, and all-purpose predators, as if we all lived in D. W. Griffith's *Birth of a Nation*. Part confessional, part cultural history, Wallace's book points out how exploitive of women black men often were during both the civil rights movement and the black nationalist era. The work highlights the sense of sexual entitlement that went along with visionary rhetoric and leadership— a dirty secret that enraged feminists and sent black spokespeople into spasms of denial. Though not a perfect book, it shed light on the un-comfortable truth about machismo among the African-American political leadership and altered views of the struggle for equality in ways some found traitorous.

Shange and Wallace, of course, were not alone in creating a vibrant, contentious new chapter in black literary history. Starting in 1970, a variety of black novelists, influenced by feminism and inspired by the details of their lives, produced some remarkable and groundbreaking literature. Gayle Jones's *Corregidora*, Alice Walker's *The Third Life of Grange Copeland*, and the early work of Toni Morrison's Nobel Prize–winning career (*The Bluest Eye, Sula*) all evolved out of the same desire: to give a voice to the long-suppressed experience of African-American women, a voice that inherently led to a critique of white racism and the pains inflicted upon African-American women by the men in their lives.

Through the efforts of novelist Walker and scholar Mary Helen Washington, Zora Neale Hurston—once restricted to black literary anthologies in which she was dubbed a minor player in the Harlem Renaissance—was anointed a patron saint of black womanhood. Hurston's motherwit, use of Southern ritual, and eye for characterization influenced works as diverse as Walker's *The Color Purple* and Terry McMillan's *Disappearing Acts*. In a canon of African-American literature that, as traditionally chronicled, had been dominated by men, Hurston's revival put her alongside Ralph Ellison and Richard Wright atop the pedestal, announcing that black women were rethinking the past and writing themselves into the narrative.

This effort had nothing to do with nostalgia. For the growing African-American female middle class it was a conscious effort to create a role model for the present. Just as b-boys were an emerging post-soul force, so was a national community of college-educated, upwardly mobile, socially conscious, somewhat politicized black women. They were college professors, social workers, magazine editors, local news anchors, owners of small boutiques, administrative assistants, film development executives, and working mothers of all descriptions. The black woman's monthly *Essence*, launched in 1971, became the popular forum for empowering images, practical advise, and praise songs to sisterhood. (In contrast, the last three decades have produced no black male–oriented periodical of equal class or impact.)

Male resentment of this new assertiveness among black women coa-
lesced in the early '80s around *The Color Purple*—both Walker's novel and
the subsequent Steven Spielberg movie. Much of the criticism aimed at
the work harked back to the barbs aimed at Shange and Wallace (Why
air dirty laundry in public?). Deeper still was black male disgust at how
"pop," as in popular, womencentric views of the black community were
proving to be. The implication was that Walker had put black male
misogyny on equal footing with white racism, and many found that parallel offensive. As a young writer, I attended many conferences where
the race loyalty, or lack of same, displayed by prominent black woman
writers was the cause of name-calling, shouting, and general disrespect
by men.

HIP HOP'S WILLIE HORTON

That night at Spelman caused me to recall those writers' conferences, especially when I thought that many of the women students in that room
were likely reading Wallace, Shange, Morrison, etc., in class or for the
pleasurable sense of self-empowerment their books could give young
women. Yet, in the wonderfully contradictory manner of human nature,
these young women could both defend and party to the sexist chants of
the 2 Live Crew.

Black folks have always walked both sides of the tracks—on one
praising the Lord, on the other sweating happily with the Devil. The attacks I leveled at Campbell were, I realized later and with some embarrassment, not very different from those that "proper" Negroes used
against the blues and jazz years before. That was a sadly sobering
thought.

The Color Purple and the 2 Live Crew are artistically miles apart, but
both are products of the sometimes mean battle of the sexes found
throughout the South, each reflections of country chauvinism—just
from radically different points of view.

Again I tried to understand how people could defend Campbell's dia-
tribes. If you called Luther Campbell a cultural drug dealer who sold
quick hits of danceable misogyny, his young defenders would counter

that Luther Campbell was just trying to get paid—which meant that getting paid justified everything. On some level they were arguing that his music's content had no meaning outside of whether it made money.

For many Southerners in particular, Luther was a financial role model. He owned a building in Miami's worst 'hood, Liberty City, and employed many community residents. He owned clubs in Miami. He composed and produced a song, "Janet Reno," that praised the Dade County State's Attorney (and future attorney general) for forcing fathers to pay child support, an activity that won him the enduring enmity of her GOP opponent Jack Thompson. Most important from a record business viewpoint was that at the height of his success Luke's recordings were distributed by independents. No Sony, Warner Bros., or PolyGram got a cut of his cash.

Unlike the more celebrated and respectable Uptown or Def Jam, Luther's label was not dependent on any multinational corporation for backing, which made it, ironically, more in the traditional of Motown than any of the corporate-financed hip hop record companies. Luke, then, was not just a social rebel but a business one as well. Even rap connoisseurs who hated his music respected his independence. But don't mistake commitment for genius. He started his company under the name Luke Skyywalker Records, something George Lucas did not appreciate. After some correspondence from Lucas's lawyers, Skyywalker Records disappeared and Luke Records took its place.

Not long after my Spelman talk, debating the 2 Live Crew's merits became a national pastime. In his quest for the family values vote, Florida's GOP governor Bob Martinez began attacking the group. He started with a fax campaign aimed at politicians and police around the state, making them aware of Campbell's lewd material. Later he requested that the state prosecutor investigate. All if it created a hostile legal environment for Campbell within the state.

It seemed all the anger aimed Luther's way would be capped by a federal judge in Florida declaring *Nasty as They Wanna Be* obscene, making the 2 Live Crew the first U.S. recording group to have sales to minors banned on the grounds of indecency. At the trial an amazing array of folks would stand up for the 2 Live Crew—from Harvard's black academic powerbroker Henry Louis Gates, Jr., to the American Civil Liberties

Union. According to the testimony this wasn't simply a nasty rap group but an example of the long tradition of African-American humor and satire. The band survived that flap—in fact it boosted sales nationally—but wasn't out of the line of fire yet.

In 1990 a Fort Lauderdale retailer was arrested for selling *Nasty as They Wanna Be* after the judge had ruled it obscene. Soon after, another Florida clerk was caught selling the album to a minor. Later in 1990 the anti–2 Live Crew movement finally caught up to Campbell himself when the whole group was arrested in Broward County for obscenity while performing at a college frat party. In the resulting media frenzy, Luther Campbell and the case against him made the gap-toothed mogul the poster boy for rap raunchiness and the fight against censorship.

In 1991 the 2 Live Crew's parody of Roy Orbison's "Pretty Woman" was attacked by the song's publishers, Acuff-Rose, a power in country music who felt they were protecting a valuable copyright tainted by the group's interpretation. Ironically, the 2 Live Crew's take on "Pretty Woman" was one of its rare truly amusing efforts. A high-minded debate over this low-down group ended with the Supreme Court ruling that, as a parody, the 2 Live Crew's "Pretty Woman" was protected under the fair-use provisions of the copyright law.

Despite that impressive victory, things were never the same for Luther's empire. 2 Live Crew members DJ Mr. Mixx and Brother Marquis left in a dispute over money. In 1994, MC Shy-D, a former Luke Records artist signee, filed a suit for back royalties and won a judgment of almost $700,000. Between other judgments found against him, the overhead costs of his label, and the legal bills he ran up defending himself nonstop for several years, Luther Campbell declared bankruptcy in 1996. Just as Campbell's career declined, the Miami pumping-bass sound that he'd introduced to the country began flourishing nationally as several (relatively) clean dance hits—Tag Team's "Whoomp! (There It Is)," the 69 Boyz's "Tootsie Roll," the Quad City DJ's "Ride the Train," the Ghost Town DJ's "My Boo," B-Rock & the Bizz's "My Baby Daddy"—exploded out of the scene's Atlanta/Miami axis.

In 1997, Campbell landed a new record deal with Island, and though the 2 Live Crew is no more, his performances continue to be known for their highly sexual content. At his shows, female fans are regularly brought on stage to dance, strip, and, if they wish (as one woman did in Japan), engage Campbell in oral sex. As a natural extension of his records, Campbell, who took on the nickname "Captain Dick," published a black men's magazine and hosts an X-rated pay-per-view talk show.

Luther Campbell's days as hip hop's Willie Horton have passed, yet my memories of that verbal beat down in Atlanta have not. I recalled it when African-Americans, including several ministers, blindly took the side of Mike Tyson against the black female beauty contestant in his Indiana rape case. I recalled it when hip hop fans unhesitatingly took the side of Tupac Shakur in his New York hotel room rape case. I recalled it when blacks dismissed O.J.'s pattern of domestic violence toward Nicole Simpson. There is an intense knee-jerk defense of black male privilege loose in the African-American community that can be irrational and destructive. Usually the stance is supported by paranoia that this particular black man—be he Campbell, Tupac, or Tyson—is being targeted by white people because of his public profile. Often they are right. There are many whites who love to pull black icons off whatever pedestal they've climbed upon. But not all brothers have that excuse. That paranoia often makes folks blind to the facts of a case. They see everything as a plot by white people to destroy black men when, the truth is, some of these brothers have seriously fucked up and deserve both the censure from our community and jail time.

In truth, both explanations can be true—white plotting and black male foolishness often create one big mess. In the 2 Live Crew's case, their lyrics pushed as hard at the boundaries of decency toward women as Larry Flint does in *Hustler*. Campbell definitely dared the Goddess upstairs to come after him.

It is also true that Jack Thompson, the man Luther Campbell helped defeat for Miami D.A., made it his priority to get Campbell arrested. This was no undercover conspiracy. Thompson shouted into the microphone of any journalist who cared to tape him that the 2 Live Crew was obscene—a campaign that influenced Governor Martinez and officials across the state of Florida, including the Broward County D.A.

Perhaps Luke Campbell, the man who popularized the big-butt-black-girl video as a vehicle for selling records and celebrated multiple-partner sex in the age of AIDS, wasn't the villain I'd said he was. But neither was he the hero his Morehouse and Spelman defenders shouted that night a decade ago.

OF QUEENS AND CHICKENHEADS

Hip hop has produced no Bessie Smith, no Billie Holiday, no Aretha Franklin. You could make an argument that Queen Latifah has, as a symbol of female empowerment, filled Aretha's shoes for rap, though for artistic impact Latifah doesn't compare to the Queen of Soul. Similarly, you can make a case that Salt-N-Pepa's four platinum albums and clean-cut sexuality mirror the Supremes pop appeal, though neither of the two MCs or their beautiful DJ Spinderella is ever gonna be Diana Ross.

In the twenty plus years of hip hop history on record, a period that has produced black vocalists Chaka Khan, Whitney Houston, Anita Baker, Tracy Chapman, Mary J. Blige, and Erykah Badu, there are no women who have contributed profoundly to rap's artistic growth. Aside from Latifah and Salt-N-Pepa, MC Lyte has recorded for over a decade and Yo-Yo has garnered some respect. So has longtime spinner and mix tape star DJ Jazzy Joyce. In the late '90s Foxy Brown and Lil' Kim have proven that raw language and sex sells, but no one is mistaking them for innovators. Old-school MCs like Sugar Hill's female trio Sequence and Sha-Rock of the Funky Four + I made a mark. (Missy "Misdemeanor" Elliott, a rapper, singer, and writer from Virginia, has emerged in the late '90s as the multifaceted female in the form and is becoming a seminal creative force.) Yet I would argue that if none of these female artists had ever made a record, hip hop's development would have been no different.

In contrast to soul music, which evolved out of the black church where a female sensibility is an essential part of the environment, rap's sensibility was molded in the street where macho values have always dominated. The competitive nature of hip hop has, with few exceptions, excluded women. The 1985 Rap Battle for World Supremacy where Roxanne Shanté ripped both Stetsasonic's Fruitkwan and old-school hero Busy Bee—and almost won the belt as MC of the year—sticks in memory precisely because it is so rare to see a woman in hip hop allowed to compete on equal footing. There is an adolescent quality to hip hop culture that makes it clear that most of its expressions are aimed to please teenage boys, and this usually excludes women from the dialogue. The dynamics of *adult* relationships are the backbone of blues and soul music, in which both women and men tell stories of love, hate, infidelity, and lust. Hip hop's typical narrator is a young, angry, horny male who is often disdainful of or, at least, uninterested in commitments of any kind.

For much of hip hop's history, it has been a truism that the male rap consumer, white and black, simply won't accept female rappers. Early in their careers, Latifah and Lyte, the genre's most lyrically significant females, seemed to be trying to compete with men in terms of toughness. Lyte, who cut her first single in 1988, didn't enjoy her first gold record until 1993's single, "RuffNeck." Latifah, who debuted in 1989, got her first gold album only after four years. "RuffNeck" was a woman's celebration of young black maleness backed by a great rhythm track and video, while Latifah's sales were accelerated by her rise to sitcom stardom on Fox's *Living Single*.

That Lyte broke through using sex (and has since beautified her image) is not surprising; Salt-N-Pepa have been mining that terrain for years. Hip hop's most commercially successful female group (and one of rap's best-selling acts of any gender) began as slightly chubby b-girls who have evolved into taut glamour girls, and they have been consistent in talking about sex since 1986, under the close supervision of their producer-mentor Hurby Luv Bug (Hurby Azor).

Foxy Brown and Lil' Kim took Salt-N-Pepa's formula, made it more explicit, dropped in designer references (Foxy favors Dolce & Gabbana, Kim sports Versace), and sold themselves as aggressive objects of desire. Whether they present themselves as sex kittens or demanding lovers, the truth is neither of these MCs has truly explored in her music the complexity of being a young black woman in the '90s—certainly not with the nuance or insight the subject demands.

To be fair, these MCs work within the constraints of the young black women's troubled role in everyday urban life. Around the middle of the '80s an intense focus on ghetto life as the nexus of African-American life seemed to overwhelm the community. This ghettocentric view was harsh, unsentimental, and antiwoman in ways that made softness, grace, and maternal instincts seem unnecessary. It was a time when calling a woman a bitch became weirdly respectable. A lot of this had to do with crack, a drug that devastated women as profoundly as it did men, mothers as it did fathers.

Hip hop style spurred women to wear the same clothes as men, curse with the same intonation, and adopt, not just a b-boy viewpoint on life but a harsh mentality that didn't place much value on their feminine instincts. Adornments like big dangling ear rings were feminine symbols within hip hop culture. Being an "around the way girl" was praised: An active sex life was certainly encouraged, judging by the rate of out-of-wedlock births in the African-American community. Still, there was an androgynous power in '80s hip hop culture that made more substantive traditional feminine values—softness, nurturing, faithfulness, intimacy—seem unnecessary, irrelevant, and even dangerous. There was, and remains, a homoerotic quality to hip hop culture, one nurtured in gangs and jails, that makes women seem, aside from sex, often nonessential.

Since the mid-'90s, the pendulum has swung the other way. Tight clothing, extravagant hairstyles, long, elaborately designed fingernails, and bare midriffs have turned the tide on androgyny, as if the culture is aggressively compensating for the '80s. Perhaps this is due to a communal exhaustion with "hardness" as the be-all and end-all of urban cool, and a slight return to earlier, sexy visions of style. The '70s nostalgia that has pervaded '90s movies, commercials, music, and fashion is one source of this glammed-up sensuality. Now the $150 Nike warm-up has been replaced by the desire for Versace sunglasses. The proliferation of glittery, designer-garbed female vocal groups, a traditional ignited by En Vogue in 1990, is the most obvious projection of this new hyped-up femininity.

Ultimately, however, the clothes haven't altered the dysfunctional vision of black women still in place. Rap made slang aimed at women like "skeezer," "hootchie," "chickhead," and the ubiquitous "bitch" (or, as they say on the West Coast, "bee-yatch!") staples of the African-American lexicon. They've become so commonplace that many young women use them freely to attack other women and, even more alarming, to describe themselves. It is one thing to be sexually assertive; it is another to buy into men's negative language about yourself. Whereas hip hop has spiritually and financially empowered African-American males, it has boxed young women into stereotypes and weakened their sense of worth. It was this landscape that made the 2 Live Crew profitable.

Such misogynistic rap records were not, of course, a direct male response to womanist literature or to female African-Americans' movement into the educated middle class in the '80s. Most of hip hop culture's leaders were ignorant of this literary warfare. A good percentage of them were functionally illiterate. Yet as rap developed, its records articulated the general assumption that black males were under attack by white racism and, to a great degree, by black women. The perception of women as gold diggers has been rife within hip hop since Kool Moe Dee's "They Want Money" in 1989, which was one of the first popular singles to make women as financial predator its subject, and Doug E. Fresh and Slick Rick's "La-Di-Da-Di" back in 1984, which was cited by the *Source* as the first rap record to refer to a woman as a "bitch."

Public Enemy's "Sophisticated Bitch" from *Yo, Bum Rush the Show* in 1987 was a benchmark, in that the critique wasn't about money alone but the class differences between an upwardly mobile woman and a working-class man. On the track, Chuck D attacks an uppity black woman for ignoring him at a party and looking down on him: "Now she wants a sucker but with an attache / And if you ain't got it—she'll turn you away." The song's message is basically "she thinks she's better than me so fuck her." As a depiction of the prickly relationship between working-class black men and black professional women, the song relates an uncomfortable truth. P.E. was criticized as women-hating for "Sophisticated Bitch" (as well as "She Watch Channel Zero?!" on *It Takes a Nation of Millions*) and, if rap is black CNN—as Chuck D once suggested—then this broadcast was surely spreading the news.

The sexual and class tensions that P.E.'s lyric outlined would be played out in hip hop's relationship to black women. Many MCs made a living portraying middle-class sisters as the enemy, and many of these women returned the favor by viewing the culture as a force of evil in the black community. While several gifted young women built careers writing about hip hop (Joan Morgan, dream hampton, Sheena Lester, Danyel Smith), other women, especially older women who grew up on soul and gospel, couldn't relate to the music, its subject matter, or audience. In fact, these women found much in hip hop that was an affront to all they held dear. "Had Dr. King given his life," they asked, "so that young men could grab their privates and call women bitches?" In this context, the emergence of someone like C. Dolores Tucker was inevitable.

LADY IN A TURBAN

Washington, D.C., is a terrible place to be caught in a snowstorm. Its city services, notoriously shoddy, have nearly collapsed in the '90s owing to mismanagement and brutal budget cuts mandated by the GOP-dominated Congress. So, on February 11, 1994, I should have been making plans to hop an Amtrack home at Union Station. Instead, I was being driven past snow piles by an Ethiopian cabdriver on the way to the Capitol where I was to speak before (take a deep breath) the Committee on Energy and Commerce's subcommittee on Commerce, Competitiveness, and Consumer Protection. The subject was "gangsta rap."

This hearing was tangible evidence of the impact a sixtyish black woman was having on the national dialogue on hip hop. When I arrived at the hearing room the first thing I saw was a blowup of the inner sleeve of Snoop Doggy Dogg's *Doggystyle* CD, which had enraged many women with its salacious cartoon of a randy dog and his long tail. C. Dolores Tucker was already sitting in the high-ceilinged, wood-paneled chamber looking queenly in her trademark turban—this one purple—surrounded by a coterie of black female retainers. These women weren't just political aides. Several female vets of the recording industry, most over thirty, were advising her on record industry politics and using her to voice not just their feelings about rap but about being powerless in the industry. Singers Dionne Warwick and Melba Moore were visible supporters of Tucker's, but they were just the tip of the iceberg. Behind the scenes was a collective of women who resented the power hip hop culture had granted younger African-American males. It wasn't just the music that irritated them—they were motivated by a sense of unfairness that rap had been a vehicle for a new, unworthy generation of entrepreneurs to push past them.

To the conspiracy theorist among them it seemed like gangsta rap was taking over black culture. Dr. Dre's *The Chronic* had sold four million for

Interscope—Death Row and Snoop's *Doggystyle* CD was on its way to five million. Twangy West Coast rappers seemed to be everywhere, and their party-oriented videos ruled BET and MTV. With this as a catalyst, Tucker had gone after Death Row's distributor, Time-Warner—at that time the only American-owned multinational entertainment conglomerate. One of the women from the industry introduced me to Mrs. Tucker, who greeted me with that same glassy-eyed, grim-faced visage I'd often seen on *Nightline*. I know older people who disliked rap but had affection for young black people, but I found C. Dolores as chilly as the sidewalk outside. According to her, since I was speaking on behalf of gangsta rap, I must be, by definition, a dupe of the white men who controlled it.

A veteran of the civil rights movement (she'd marched with Dr. King) and a longtime liberal activist and civil servant (she'd served as Pennsylvania's Secretary of State from 1971 to 1977), Tucker had certainly paid her dues in the struggle. Her stated goal to persuade rappers to "clean up" their lyrics was an understandable culmination of adult black women's longstanding discomfort with rap. However, instead of emerging as a credible voice against rap's lyrical excesses, Tucker came off as your out-of-touch grandma, or worse, a naive opportunist. Fundamentally, her argument was that rap, at least the rap she and her advisors disliked, was not popular on its own merits because white corporations sold it.

She told reporter Erika Blount:

> Gangsta rap symbolizes a form of genocidal prose, which has been encouraged and distributed by those in the industry who are driven by drugs, greed and racism. Rap in its purest form was an artform of prose and poetry which expressed life in the same sense that the spirituals did. Gangsta rap is a perverted form which has been encouraged by those who have always used the entertainment industry to exploit and project the negative stereotypical images to demean and depict African-Americans as subhuman, which is the antithesis of what we as African-American people are.

I too disdain rap that is hateful toward women. But Tucker was either misinformed or plain old ignorant of the music's history. The 2 Live

Crew, Niggaz with Attitude, the Geto Boys—three of the bands that played crucial roles in creating rap's rep for misogyny—were all composed by black males, signed by black entrepreneurs and independently distributed. This material was not the vision of white men in suits. Its words and music, plus the ghettocentric marketing zeal that put it on the national agenda, were pungent products of the black male imagination. Even in the case of Death Row, which in 1994 was still distributed by Interscope through Time-Warner, the engine behind the music and the images were Suge Knight, Dr. Dre, Snoop Doggy Dogg, and the posse of friends that influenced their worldview. You see, the insulting and ultimately self-defeating view that underlined Tucker's position was that these black creators had no agency in their lives, that without white corporate intervention this music wouldn't exist, be distributed, or have an audience.

Out of a kind of condescending race loyalty that put a white face behind everything evil among black Americans, Tucker was unwilling to take on the artists and black executives directly. This was also how, later, Tucker found herself duped by Knight and company. In private conversations with Tucker he blamed Time-Warner for his musical direction and asked her to help him gain his freedom (and potential millions in the buyout). Knight told Tucker that as soon as he was free of Time-Warner's corrupting influence, he'd make sure his label went in a new direction.

At one point, as a sign of good faith, Knight offered to obtain Tucker and her industry aides the rights to Melba Moore's version of the "Lift Every Voice and Sing," James Weldon Johnson's Negro national anthem from Capitol Records. Subsequently Tucker, along with her female industry advisors, offered to set up a meeting between then Time-Warner music division head Michael Fuchs and Suge Knight in hopes of freeing Death Row from their existing distributor deals, with an eye toward having an entertainment industry entity funded by either Knight or Fuchs. Tucker's advisors had grandiose dreams of leveraging the power that working with the activist could win them. Representatives from both sides spoke to me about serving as a go-between. I declined the role.

The meeting was arranged at Dionne Warwick's house between Knight and Fuchs, behind the back of Interscope. Knight never came. A legal letter did. It announced a lawsuit against Tucker from Interscope for "tampering." Tucker's people believed that Interscope had found out about the meeting and pressured Knight. I think it was all a setup, that Knight and Interscope just saw Tucker as another bit of leverage to be used in negotiation against Time-Warner.

If Tucker's condescending attitude and innocence of industry politics wasn't enough, her alliance with William Bennett and the self-righteous, self-serving moralists of the GOP Right was worse. Her explanation was that without their support she was a voice in the wilderness. In making this alliance Tucker joined hands with the people who are enemies of black America: Bennett, whose tenure as coordinator of this nation's antidrug efforts coincided with the incredible growth of crack into the inner city, and the Republican Party, whose cutbacks in social spending worsened the conditions that had inspired hard-core rap in the first place. Most profoundly, Tucker committed the same hypocrisy that she accused the hip hop community of—making a deal with the white power structure to further your own selfish ends. Whatever Tucker's justification for bonding with Bennett, it lessened her moral authority and made her blunders seem more like botched power plays than innocent mistakes.

Nothing of great note happened that snowy 1994 morning in D.C. *Soul Train* founder Don Cornelius attacked rap in a most dignified manner. Tucker showed her Snoop Doggy Dogg album sleeve. Hip hop defenders—rapper Yo-Yo, Def Jam president David Hareleston, and I—read prepared statements. Unexpectedly, Congresswoman Maxine Waters, who represents South Central L.A., stopped in the chamber to make a very eloquent defense of rap, particularly its incendiary Cali branch. Of course it didn't hurt her enthusiasm that Knight, Ice Cube, and other hip hop figures had contributed funds to an antipoverty program she was developing in Watts. Tucker's acolytes were dismissive of Waters, claiming she'd taken "blood money," as if their liaison with the GOP gave them the moral authority to judge. Nothing came of these hearings save a bunch of press clippings.

In 1997, Tucker made a return engagement to a Time-Warner stockholders meeting to attack the conglomerate for releasing Lil' Kim's nasty *Hard Core* album. Tucker still got some ink, but few seemed to care. Death Row was now distributed by Interscope through Universal Records. Her buddy Suge Knight was in jail for violating his parole. (At the mogul's final hearing Tucker had sat next to his mother, offering moral support and giving an unspoken endorsement of his character.) Snoop Doggy Dogg, after beating a murder rap, had come out of it more subdued and less popular. Two rappers who would have guaranteed headlines, Tupac Shakur and Biggie Smallz, were dead.

But Tucker is a determined lady who wasn't going to let death stand in her way of warning the general populace. In August 1997, she sued Tupac's estate for damages, alleging that two negative references to her on Tupac's *All Eyez on Me* had harmed her marriage, resulting in the inability of her and her husband to have sex for two years—a charge as gross and exploitative as anything Luther Campbell ever recorded.

chapter 14
skills to pay the bills

YOU'RE A FIVE DOLLAR BOY AND I'M A MILLION DOLLAR MAN
YOU'RE A SUCKER MC AND YOU'RE MY FAN

— RUN-D.M.C.,
   "SUCKER MCs"

AN AIRPORT IN ZURICH, SWITZERLAND. NOVEMBER 1995. METHOD
Man, Wu-Tang Clan member, platinum solo artist, and current hip hop
icon, stands with DJ Lovebug Starski, pioneering old-school DJ and rapper. The pair, along with Russell Simmons and a motley crew of musicians and roadies are touring Europe to celebrate Def Jam's tenth
anniversary. In each city Method Man performs tracks from his Def Jam
solo project, *Tical* while Starski, on the turntables, gives European heads
old-school New York flavor prior to Meth's sets.

Starski, who is talking incessantly about making a comeback as a MC,
pulls out a boom box and plays a new track he has been working on. He
begins rhyming over the beat. It's not an embarrassing display—Starski's
got a real flow and he'll die with one. It's just an old flow, a relic from the
fondly remembered '70s when he emerged as an uptown legend.

Then Meth jumped on the beat and blew up the spot. With the com-
mand and rhythmic eloquence that is his hallmark, the young MC came
off the head with clever rhymes and tricky syncopation. Everything
about Meth's performance spoke to how fruitless Starski's efforts were to
attempt a comeback as a MC. As a DJ, Starski was still fine. By staying up
on the latest records and continuing his mastery of old-school jams,
Starski would always find work, but not as a MC.

The cadences, much less the words, of what constitutes contemporary hip hop shifts gears as rapidly as an Indy 500 driver. As much as the subject matter—from party chants to boasts, to politics, to gangsterism, back to party chants again—the speed, syncopation, and tone of rap has evolved time and again. Almost all the greats—Melle Mel, Run, Rakim, Chuck D, Snoop Doggy Dogg, the Notorious B.I.G.—are as notable for their flow, their individual rhythm, as for what they said. Melle Mel declaimed. Run and Chuck D shouted. Rakim insinuated. Snoop and Biggie employed laid-back conversational deliveries thick with the accents of Cali and Brooklyn.

L.L. Cool J has enjoyed the longest, commercially viable career as a MC precisely because he had proven remarkably versatile. Over ten years as an recording artist L.L. has shouted convincingly ("Rock the Bells," "Mama Said Knock You Out"), seduced ("Jingling Baby," "Hey Lover"), used a conversational flow ("I'm That Type of Guy," "Goin' Back to Cali"), and variations of them all. He has had definite moments of failure—much of *14 Shots to the Dome* in 1993—and suffered his embarrassment: He was booed at a Harlem rally for slain youth Yusef Hawkins in 1989. Yet he always bounces back. He's a hip hop chameleon, able to sound current and authentic whatever the mode. As L.L. said of himself in a 1997 effort (later the title of his autobiography), "I make my own rules."

Against such competition, the Starski's of this world don't have a bad rhyme's chance of a comeback. While the youth-driven hip hop audience may be nostalgic about beats and old-school names, it has little desire to purchase new records by old stars. With the exception of Run-D.M.C.'s "Down with the King" single in 1993, once a rap star falls he or she usually lands in the basement and can't be raised back up.

CLASS IS OUT

When writers first started trying to get a handle on hip hop's history, they generally went along with the conventional wisdom that DJ Hollywood was the first "rapping DJ." I myself wrote this as if it were fact on several occasions. But now it is clear that the style's origins and evolution wasn't that clear. The late Cowboy of the Furious Five, as well as Kidd

Creole and Melle Mel, helped create a lot of the contemporary rap vocabulary. Coke La Rock, who pumped the crowds for Kool Herc, is cited by some as a crucial creator of the style. There are other precursors, party jocks like Pete "DJ" Jones, whom old schoolers mention with reverence.

What can't be disputed is that Hollywood was one of the biggest stars of the prerecorded era of MCing, that he made his rep working in disco and after-hours clubs in Harlem and the Bronx, and that he created many of hip hop's signature phrases. In 1977, when I was a college student in New York, he was a legend. Ten years later, in terms of records, he was a has-been or, to be more accurate, he was a never-was.

My memories of Hollywood as a performer are magical, but for the growing mid-'80s rap audience he was a name without a face or a sound. In summer 1986 he released a 12-inch on an uptown indie label. To say it was unremarkable is an extreme understatement. Instead of mimicking the shouting style of Run-D.M.C. or the boasting of L.L., Hollywood tapped an old country toast ("Poon tang, poon tang, I don't want it, slept all night with my hands on it, gimme some of that yum yum yum before I go to bed") that had nothing to do with the current direction of hip hop. Such a record usually would have ended up a short item in my *Billboard* column if I hadn't been contributing at the moment to a nationally syndicated TV show called *The Rock & Roll Evening News*. I was no Bryant Gumbel but I did work as a correspondent on the show, and when I received Hollywood's record, I pitched a look at the original hip hop MC. The producers went for it, so we arranged to interview Hollywood at a Lenox Avenue playground. I hadn't seen Hollywood since the '70s when he was a chunky, funky, happy-go-lucky ghetto star. The man who showed up that day had lost some thirty to forty pounds. His answers were guarded and his eyes were hollow. Something sad had certainly happened. After the Q&A we moved over to the Roof Top, a roller disco–nightclub that was then one of rap's reigning temples. I had arranged for Dr. Jeckyll and Mr. Hyde to back Hollywood, both to spice up the B-roll footage and give my friends—who as an act where verging on hip hop obsolescence themselves—a little publicity.

After that 12-inch, Hollywood disappeared from sight. But then why should we (or he) expect anything else? It's cool and PC to decry the fact that an artist who helped create a style, be it in blues or jazz or rap, didn't benefit as much as artists who came later. To this day, people often con-trast the careers of the Starskis and Hollywoods with rappers who came later, some of whom were deemed unworthy successors to the old school. Because Run-D.M.C.'s members were from soft-as-butter Queens, they were once castigated as being somehow inferior to the Bronx originators. Similarly, New Yorker's used to ridicule rappers from the West Coast and the South for their accent and lack of skills, as if the only valid crite-ria for rap was what New Yorkers said it was.

The truth is that in art no one actually owes anyone anything. Yes, older artists influence younger ones. But "influence" is likely the wrong word—I would suggest that worthy younger artists build on what older artists started, constructing their own thing atop what already exists. Run-D.M.C., KRS-One, and Snoop Doggy Dogg all benefitted from the energy of Hollywood, but their own personality and perspectives made them stars.

There is an aspect of the American psyche, one forged in this nation's overheated furnace of racism and stoked by liberal guilt, that tempts us to romanticize the often obscure—and not necessarily genius—pioneers of African-American musical culture. Yet in hip hop this impulse is often turned against new stars who are attacked either for biting the styles of their elders or, perversely, for moving too far from hip hop's roots. In truth, Starski, Hollywood, and their peers laid the ground for hip hop, but they couldn't compete as the scene moved from playgrounds to vinyl. It isn't a tragedy; it is the survival of the fittest—a concept inte-gral to hip hop's competitive nature.

The real tragedy occurs when the old schoolers can't move gracefully into the next phase of their lives. We're not talking about elderly blues men who had been making music for decades; these were men and women in their thirties with a lifetime ahead of them. The Cold Crush Brothers come to mind—back in the day, this Bronx quintet was one of rap's most powerful performing ensembles. Its members prowled the stage shouting into mikes and moving with swaggering intensity. They were true underground legends and their major label shot, *Punk Rock Rap*, made noise around New York, but it didn't travel well. Their leader, Grandmaster Caz, has argued over the years that the Sugar Hill Gang got most their lyrics for "Rapper's Delight" from him. Apparently Big Bank Hank of the group had been a bouncer at several parties where Caz performed and simply used the Bronx MC's words instead of introducing him to the Robinsons. So Caz, perhaps rightly, has always felt hostile to the record industry.

Yet, like Starski and Hollywood, Caz was reluctant to give up his dream of blowing up nationwide, and he cultivated resentment toward the newer crews who had. I remember a 1989 Beastie Boys concert at the Factory, a barnlike space in the Twenties off Sixth Avenue. Cypress Hill, just beginning their careers, opened to the predominantly white male crowd and were quickly followed by the Beasties, who were touring to support *Paul's Boutique*—the weird, witty album that marked the band's transition from obnoxious teens to mature raconteurs. Moreover, this was the Beastie Boy's first New York gig since they'd moved to Cali, so the crowd was really hyped.

Midway through a spectacular set, the Beasties introduced Grandmaster Caz, the Cold Crush Brothers' leader, to the crowd. Though known to the crowd more as a legendary name than a well-remembered act, Caz received an enthusiastic welcome. He responded by getting on a mike and refusing to let go. One song would have been cool, but the old schooler didn't want to get off, haranguing the crowd to respect him and boasting about his old-school credentials instead of just dropping science.

There's an old hip hop adage that goes back to battles in the park: Once given a mike, a MC won't voluntarily relinquish it until he has rocked the crowd. Clearly the Beasties were naive to give up control, especially since class and tact have never been synonymous with hip hop. An argument can be made that, in fact, hip hop exists in opposition to such tidy notions of decorum, that tact and hip hop's in-your-face attitude is as different as Luther Vandross is from Flavor Flav. Yet there are some old-school giants who have bowed out gracefully. For example, Kool Moe Dee (Mohandas Dewese).

The first time I heard Kool Moe Dee's name was on Mr. Magic's overnight WHBI radio show, circa 1980. As a member of the Treacherous Three, Moe Dee was on the air talking about their Enjoy Records 12-inch *The New Rap Language*, along with posse members Special K, L.A. Sunshine, and DJ Easy Lee. In 1982, Enjoy owner Bobby Robinson sold the group to Sugar Hill where they cut some solid material ("Feel the Heartbeat," "Yes We Can Can") but never enjoyed success to equal their talent. The Treacherous Three disbanded but Kool Moe Dee, who had been the trio's chief lyricist and lead vocalist, reinvented himself. By 1986, Moe Dee had gone solo, releasing his self-titled debut featuring "Go See the Doctor" on Harlem's Rooftop Records. It was a jokey ditty about getting a sexually transmitted disease in one of the last years in which that topic could be funny. Jive scooped it up and "Doctor," because of its light tone and humorous lyrics (much like Kurtis Blow's "The Breaks") became a minor pop hit. As a Treacherous Three member Moe Dee wore color-coordinated Kangols, shirts, pants and loafers. As a solo act he embraced blocky blue wraparound shades and two-piece leather ensembles (often by Pelle) with matching boots and leather caps that made him appear futuristic.

However, Moe Dee didn't truly jump-start his career until he tapped into that essential hip hop energy source—the desire to battle. From the days of dueling break-dance crews to rival graffiti artists tagging over the work of others to rappers challenging each other in the park, hip hop has had at its core a quest for the ultimate in one-upmanship. Moe Dee took as his target the brash L.L. Cool J. It was old school versus new school; Harlem versus Queens; Moe Dee's stern, crisp delivery versus L.L.'s early yelling style.

On *How Ya Like Me Now*, Moe Dee's 1987 signature album, he accused the Def Jam star of biting his rap style and other crimes against nature. He even went so far as to pose on the album cover with a Jeep crushing L.L.'s then trademark Kangol. In short, Moe Dee dissed L.L. before the term even existed and, in so doing, set the stage for L.L.'s "Jack the Ripper" answer record and Moe Dee's comeback, "Let's Go," which featured derogatory interpretations of L.L.'s initials (lousy lover, etc.). There was even talk of a pay-per-view boxing match. The beauty of this battle was that it never came close to being physical and was in fact handled in the spirit of healthy competition by both men. But, over the long run, Moe Dee's career has been more than L.L. bashing. Usually in collaboration with new jack swing innovator Teddy Riley, Moe Dee had a string of danceable hits ("They Want Money," "Wild Wild West," "I Go to Work") that mixed boasts of his sexual prowess and rap ability. His appeal was enhanced by a lively, tightly choreographed stage show.

In the late '80s, when rap was still struggling for airplay on black radio, Moe Dee's output helped break through many prejudices. In his way, Moe Dee, along with Heavy D. and his rival L.L., were crucial in making rap palatable to African-American adults and closing the gap between hip hop and R&B audiences. And though not as associated with socially conscious rap as Public Enemy or KRS-One, Moe Dee took a turn toward the positive with his *Knowledge Is King* album. And the single-best rhyme of his career wasn't a dis of anyone but a sharp one-liner on the Stop the Violence Movement's antiviolence all-star jam *Self-Destruction*: "I never ran from the Ku Klux Klan / so I shouldn't have to run from a black man."

That was in 1989. After that, like most other New York stars, Moe Dee was eclipsed by the '90s West Coast explosion led by Ice-T and N.W.A. Moe Dee released two albums in this decade, one on Jive and one distributed by Atlanta indie Ichaban, each to diminishing sales. Like a great many other rappers, folks who had gotten used to playing larger-than-life characters, Moe Dee made a lateral move into acting, doing a nice job as a gunrunner in Forest Whitaker's HBO directing debut, *Strapped*, and later in Tupac Shakur's last film *Gang Related*. To his credit, Moe Dee took the acting instinct a step further. He moved to L.A. and became a screenwriter, selling some pieces and dancing the Hollywood shuffle. In 1996, in partnership with director Matty Rich, Moe Dee sold himself to Disney as a talk show host. The project never made it to the pilot stage but the idea of a rapper as a TV host is a natural one, due to the verbal dexterity and street-smart philosophizing the genre requires. (Geto Boy Willie D hosted a Houston call-in show, Ice-T had a TV gabfest in the U.K. and hosts a syndicated radio broadcast in the States, and Chuck D does political commentary for Fox News in New York.)

Moe Dee hasn't exactly emerged as a star in his new vocations but, nearly a decade removed from his hip hop glory, he has refashioned his life in a way that builds on his past yet gives him hope for the future. Not that Moe Dee, like some itchy ex-fighter, hasn't felt the lure of the ring. In the summer of 1996 L.L. released the 12-inch *I Shot Ya*, an old-fashioned yet crisply executed boastfest featuring guest appearances from Fat Joe and Foxy Brown, among others. During L.L.'s final salvo he proclaimed, "I took out Hammer, Moe Dee, and Ice-T's curl." In listing Moe Dee among his conquests, L.L. relit the retired rapper's competitive fire. Using his own money, Moe Dee went into the studio and cut an answer record that he planned to issue himself.

However, when the Notorious B.I.G. was murdered in L.A., Moe Dee pulled the plug on his record, feeling this was no time for rappers to battle, even playfully on record. Moreover, he joined forces with a new generation of rap industry figures in working to mount a well-meaning, though aborted Stop the Violence II record and campaign. Though no longer a star himself, Moe Dee is still committed to both the music and its audience. Far from bitter or unrealistic, Moe Dee has actually lived through hip hop and come out the other side.

chapter 15
funk the world

I FOUND THAT STRANGE, HOW BLACKS WHO HAD TALENT AND COULDN'T GET RECOGNI-TION IN THE UNITED STATES WOULD GO OVER TO EUROPE AND IMMEDIATELY BE APPRE-CIATED AND BECOME BIG CELEBRITIES.

—DIZZY GILLESPIE, 1979

IT IS 1995 AND I AM IN A BIG BARN OF A NIGHTCLUB IN ZURICH, Switzerland. The place is jammed with teenagers and young adults in drooping pants, T-shirts, sneakers, Stussy and Kangol caps. The scent of high-grade marijuana hovers. The crowd is, surprisingly, not all white but sprinkled with multiethnic children various shades of light brown and yellow. The music is all old school and East Coast as the Theme from *SWAT* segues into the Poor Righteous Teachers' "Rock Dis Funky Joint." The New York underground jam "The East Is in the House" by Blazhay Blazhay is received like a blessing by the crowd.

Pale, skinny girls sway their slim hips and bare bellies with the enthusiasm—not the heft—of sisters in Brooklyn. It is a late-night tribal moment in one of the world's most expensive cities, a place better known for money laundering than dancing. Yet hip hop has, literally, made its mark as old-school-style graffiti can be found on walls all over town.

A day later I'm in Paris at the Bain Douche (the Bathtub), a dark, inti-mate two-level club, dancing with a short Iranian debutante and a tall, absolutely gorgeous African girl to the sound of hip hop made in Mar-seilles. The flow and cadence of the music is as intense as anything back in the States, but it has a sensuality unlike anything from back home. A young black French record executive explains to me that hip hop in southern France is heavily influenced by African and Arab culture, while the words are specific to France's uneasy ethnic mix. He points across the room to where France's biggest rap star, MC Solaar, is holding court. Solaar, a lean, rather slight black man in his late twenties, turns out to be very pleasant to speak with, a welcome surprise since French b-boys seem to have chips on their shoulder larger than their Carhart jackets.

A few hours later, at a larger club in the more tawdry, working-class part of town known as Pigalle, I dance too close to a frizzy-haired French black girl for the comfort of an integrated posse of roughnecks. The homies step to me in pidgin English. Home girl extricates me from what would surely have caught a critical beat down. For all its beauty, there is an undercurrent of hostility in the City of Light, and in France overall, which may be why it produces the best hip hop in Europe.

Then it's over to Amsterdam, where I watch a Benetton ad come to life. A rainbow of chilled-out kids inhale huge quantities of legal herb, smiling and talking in total buddah bliss. I'm approached by a black kid in a New York Rangers jersey who recognizes me because he subscribes to American music magazines. As the large crowd listens to East Coast beats overlaid with some beautiful mixing by local DJs, I indulge in some of the medicinal herbs that flow freely in Amsterdam, feeling in the perfect mood to savor Q-Tip's conversational tone as it floats through the gray crowd just above my head.

Next, I'm in a high-ceilinged club in central London, where members of the local Fruit of Islam are being pushed and prodded by rude boys determined to squeeze in to see Method Man. The energy inside is mean and chaotic in that seething manner unique to drunken young males. Tim Westwood, the longtime radio announcer and England's most important hip hop gatekeeper, once or twice tries to calm the crowd but there is a taste for teen rebellion in the air that words aren't going to quell. When Method Man performs the crowd moves in waves, as if at a soccer match. At one point Meth dives into the crowd where some enterprising Londoner pulls a sneaker off his foot and, later, tosses it at the MC's head. It is the most passionate, wild interplay between rapper and audience I've seen since the '80s.

Hip hop has, to paraphrase Craig Mack, truly funked the world. Since the mid-'80s, hip hop and its culture has been embraced by young people as a conduit for information and attitude that irritates the C. Dolores Tuckers of every country. And each country has, in turn, embraced the culture differently. In some, hip hop's very Americanness is central to its appeal, making it seem larger than life and dangerous. In other countries, it has been molded to fit the language and needs of the indigenous culture. In general, it speaks to a sense of fun and a romance of the exotic, much as it does to its American suburban consumers. Because hip hop has so many elements—music, clothing, dance, attitude—its essential mutability makes it adaptable worldwide.

COUNTRY CODES

In France, MCs flow in their own language, while MCs from countries such as Denmark and Sweden usually rhyme in English because the sentence structure of their native tongues doesn't work well for rap. Since many European groups are composed of kids from mixed cultural backgrounds, they often employ English as a universal language. Sweden's ADL, for example, is from a Swedish-Trinidadian heritage, while Denmark's bootfunk is composed of three MCs—one from Denmark, the others from the United States and Nigeria.

Non-Americans have actually shown more loyalty to certain aspects of hip hop than their American counterparts. In the big cities of Spain graffiti is alive and well; subways and streets are heavily tagged in the tradition of New York in the '70s. A local spray can company named Montana has so profited from graffiti that it has local artists consult on the quality of its paint and spray caps. Across the border in Italy graffiti tags adorn trains and walls around Rome and Milan.

DJing, not as an accompaniment to rapping but as an art in itself, is much more respected overseas than here. Old-school MCs such as Grandmaster Flash, Eddie Cheeba, and Lovebug Starski still perform lucrative gigs in Japan, France, Germany, and the Netherlands where their pedigree and skills are celebrated in a manner reminiscent of how venerable jazzmen found respect in Europe. Similarly, young non-American DJs have helped popularize the phrase "turntablists" to describe the current generation of DJs who have brought an artist's pretension to mixing and scratchin'. The turntablist's goal is not to accompany dancers but to create sonic tapestries for listeners, showcasing the DJ's dexterity and library. Inherent in this is an elitist disdain for "commercial hip hop." If their techniques sounds a lot like what Herc, Bam, and Flash did back in the day, the emphasis is more on a self-conscious display of artistry than rocking parties.

U.S. rhyme cadences and sample techniques are heard throughout South America, both because of the shared African underpinnings in music from both Americas and the cultural interplay between U.S. immigrants and the folks back home. From Puerto Rico down to Brazil, Latin culture has taken bits and pieces of American hip hop, using it to support salsa, merenge, and samba, just as reggae has been adapted to local music throughout the Americas.

Some of the world's most heavily coded lyrics come from Ireland where Irish brogues and local slang can make it as difficult for Americans to decipher as Jamaican patois. Hip hop abroad can be really bad, as in Germany where the language's harsh, guttural pronunciation works against a smooth lyrical flow. Germany's biggest mid-'80s group, die fantastischen vier, adopted a pop style analogous to Jazzy Jeff & the Fresh Prince to overcome this cultural problem.

In Japan, some rap has been inventive, but ultimately hip hop culture there is more interesting for style than musical content. Young Japanese hip hop kids have become fixtures in New York, wearing the latest gear from Mecca and Phat Farm and are up on the latest grassroots developments in the music. Generally, the Japanese have shown little tolerance for softer or more pop-oriented rap, preferring rawer, noncrossover acts like the Alkaholiks and the Large Professor, which they feel are closer to hip hop's essence. Over in Tokyo this fascination has been labeled the "new blackism"—a phrase not always used affectionately. Some young Japanese fans have gone as far as to frequent tanning salons in seriously misguided efforts to get darker.

Surprisingly, England has never produced a real powerful hip hop MC (if you don't count the U.S.-reared but U.K.-born Slick Rick). Many U.K. acts have tried, such as MC Derek B in the '80s. Female MCs the Wee Papa Rappers and Monie Love made a little noise in the mid-'80s. Monie collaborated with Queen Latifah and was signed to Warner Bros., but since her minor hit single, "Monie in the Middle" on her *Down to Earth* debut, she's settled into a career as a New York radio announcer.

One of the reasons for the absence of a great U.K. MC is the presence of a vibrant dance hall culture there. If you are of Caribbean-Brit stock and have skills on the microphone, the tendency has been to gravitate to Jamaican dance hall music, calypso, soca, or any of the other Caribbean musical forms that parallel American MCing. For example, a Shabba Ranks or Super Cat, both of whom have built American audiences, are true to their particular game and, usually, are at their weakest when they bend over too far to accommodate hip hop tastes. Similarly, dance hall is so dominant in Jamaica that indigenous hip hop groups on the island have little chance to blossom.

Perhaps the most important U.K. artist influenced by hip hop is Tricky, a demonic, brilliant, and brooding Caribbean-Brit from Bristol. By blending hip hop's sampling and drum programming with his own idiosyncratic use of guitars, keyboards, and voices, Tricky has helped define a moody, seductive U.K. style labeled "trip-hop." Along with Portishead, Morcheeba, and others, Tricky has created a sound in which hip hop is imbedded in the texture but the music is not a slave to its clichés. Often, despite Tricky's respect for hip hop, he actually subverts the genre. His cover of Public Enemy's "Black Steel in the Hour of Chaos," which features the voice of his female collaborator, Martika, reconstructs that macho, militant masterpiece in an energetic sonic landscape that makes the familiar rhymes sound more mysterious and gender-bending than Chuck D ever intended.

The legacy of rap's socially conscious period when Public Enemy used the music to raise political issues is still visible around the world. In Italy, a place where extremes of political thought mesh with a passionate nature, there are many groups that have gravitated toward the culture for its ability to articulate anger. Articolo 31's *Legge Del Taglione*, which translates in English into "an eye for eye," is a prime example of this use of hip hop.

In France, the culture's political aspect has been a vehicle of protest for music- and filmmakers. The right-wing Front National, led by the fascistic Jean-Marie Le Pen, rose to electoral power in the '90s by attacking immigration with slogans like "France for the French" and "Immigration equals unemployment." This xenophobic approach has worked in crystalizing white fear of Africans and Arabs, particularly Algerians, and resulted in racial strife throughout the nation.

In 1995, a FN member, Jean-Marie Le Chevallier, was elected mayor of Toulon, a city in southern France. NTM (which stands for "nique ta mere" or, in English, "fuck your mother"), a hard-core rap group inspired by the toughness of P.E. and KRS-One, hosted a concert in July of that year to protest Le Chevallier's election. The band's MCs, Kool Shen (Bruno Lopez) and Joey Star (Didier Morville), shouted "fuck the police," "fuck Le Pen," and "fuck all the FN members" and NTM was immediately arrested. Subsequently, members of the group received one-year jail sentences and were banned from performing for six months.

Another forum for French youth anger in 1995 was the film *La Haine* (*Hate*) that won its young auteur, Mathieu Kassovitz, the best director award at that spring's Cannes Film Festival. Kassovitz's previous film, *Cafe Au Lait*, inspired by Spike Lee's *She's Gotta Have It* and featuring a bicycle-driving, hip hop–loving white French b-boy, set the stage for the raw, black-and-white *La Haine*.

Drawing upon *Do the Right Thing* and *Boyz N the Hood*, Kassovitz depicted twenty-four hours in the life of three male residents of Paris's suburban projects. The boys—one black, one Arab, one white and Jewish—suffer through riots, poverty, and police brutality, casting France's internal problems through a harsh American-styled eye. All the hip hop arts—MCing, DJing, graffiti, and breaking—are featured in *La Haine*, giving a graphic illustration of how powerful an impact hip hop has had on France's youth culture. Much like its American inspirations, *La Haine* has a sad, violent end that suggests a society at the breaking point. The film was a phenomenon in France, becoming the highest grossing domestic film of the year and inspiring a new wave of French filmmakers. From a hip hop viewpoint, the reverence paid by the filmmaker to the culture and its ability to resonate so profoundly across the Atlantic again testifies to its vitality.

From Vancouver and Toronto in Canada, to Dakar in Senegal, to Holland, to Cuba's Havana, to every place satellites beam music videos and CDs are sold (or bootlegged or counterfeited), hip hop has made an impression. Ironically, according to foreign fans and businesspeople, the penetration would be stronger if American performers were more adventurous. Concert promoters and record companies throughout Europe, the Caribbean, and South America complain that hip hop acts either regularly cancel dates or perform unprofessionally when they do appear.

In Jamaica, for example, a 1994 appearance by Kriss Kross and a 1996 date by a wheelchair-bound Notorious B.I.G. are legendary for their ineptitude, since both occurred at one of the island's biggest music festivals. And, in 1998, many Europeans are pissed that Puff Daddy canceled a major tour.

There is a reluctance on the part of many hip hop–generation performers to leave the USA—a manifestation of some weird extension of the ghettocentricity that informs the culture. Its sound juvenile (and it is) but many rap stars are reluctant to leave their hotel rooms or tour buses when overseas, complaining about the food, weather, etc., instead of enjoying the chance to explore other cultures. For every Chuck D, who loves touring and built a strong international base for Public Enemy because of his enthusiasm, it is a disgrace how many MCs, old and new school, blow off or curtail overseas concerts. In contrast to jazz and soul era performers who created loving fans wherever they went, hip hop's recording stars have too often dropped the ball. The same lack of focus that hampers live shows in the States manifests itself overseas as well. Yes, hip hop has a worldwide following, but to date its own narrow-mindedness has limited its international clout.

chapter 16
"da joint!" and beyond

As for the future of rapping, I think it will become a prerequisite for all black club jocks (and many whites) to be fluent in some form of the language.

—Nelson George,
Musician magazine, 1980

I REMEMBER WHEN ATTRACTIVE WOMEN WERE SIMPLY "FLY" AND GREAT records were "da joint." Then everything, from laceless sneakers to baseball caps worn sideways, was "fresh." For a while things got "stoopid" and even "stoopid fresh," which could also be "def" when it wasn't "dope." Sometimes, when you really wanted people to believe what you said, "on the strength" certified your commitment, though "word is bond" and, ultimately, "word" could work when you wished to be succinct. "Word" was once a powerful affirmation that you were "droppin' science." When you were "in effect" you were truly "large." A woman or a record always "got me open" but at the moment I write this they both better be "jiggy" if I'm supposed to pay attention.

The language of hip hop, a particularly active subset of the African-American linguistic tradition, marks moments lived and gone. The words go with outdated clothes, closed clubs, and careers startling in their brevity. The distance traveled from the Funky + Plus One's "That's the Joint" to Will Smith's "Gettin' Jiggy with It" spans the history of rap on record and the rapid journey of this culture from cult item to entertainment commodity. That so many of those words and phrases sound ancient and even quaint show we've entered a new era in hip hop, one that embraces cutting-edge and nostalgic artifacts.

On New York radio, Grandmaster Flash and Kool DJ Red Alert host midday old-school radio shows, while in Los Angeles Kurtis Blow has a late-night show and has compiled a three-CD history of rap. As a producer on Chris Rock's HBO comedy show in 1997, I recruited Flash to serve as the musical director and was pleased to see the love Flash received when introduced to the studio crowd. *Wild Style*, both the home video and the CD of the music, were reissued by the archival experts at Rhino, testament to a growing fascination with hip hop's past.

After twenty years of defining the edge, hip hop dances, art, and music are being used as shortcut references to set a mood of the past and to jog memories. "Rapper's Delight," performed by an elderly white woman, is a comic set piece in *The Wedding Singer*, a 1998 film set in 1986. Three-stripe Adidas have become cool fashion statements for off-duty models, and breakers have begun working again in the music videos of Mariah Carey, KRS-One and others, as signs of solidarity with hip hop's roots. Of course, Puff Daddy's magnificent mid-90s hit-making run was based on many riffs taken from earlier hip hop eras, a kind of slightly submerged nostalgia dressed as new music.

Yet hip hop still resists becoming a museum piece as jazz and '60s soul have. Like flesh, it keeps regenerating itself and with each new generation becomes more rooted and builds new alliances. For example, the social schism between buppies and b-boys has been completely smoothed over by the thirst for profit. Sylvia Rhone, product of Pennsylvania's Wharton business school, longtime record biz veteran, and, as president of Elektra, the highest ranking African-American executive in the industry, enjoyed one of her best years in 1997 by aggressively signing and promoting the hip hop–R&B of Missy "Misdemeanor" Elliott. Unlike the previous generation of black executives who missed the boat on hip hop, Rhone has backed this Virginia-based talent with the full commitment of her company, confident that her off-kilter, clean records, lightly spiced with U.K. jungle beats, have as much right to be the sound of young America as fading rock bands and country balladeers.

The buppie–b-boy connection is apparent in other areas as well. Although Quincy Jones conceived *Vibe*, it is Keith Clinkscale, a black Harvard business school grad, who runs the operation on a daily basis. Publishing a hip hop magazine is not exactly what black folks expected from black MBAs when they moved into the business school in the '60s but Clinkscale, who had published his own buppish *Urban Profile* mag before joining *Vibe*, is symbolic of the synergy between African-American street culture and the black upwardly mobile class throughout the industry and the country. There's probably not a college campus in the country in which some of its African-American students are not involved in various entrepreneurial-cultural ventures tied to hip hop.

But, as always, innovations in the culture come straight from the street. Master P (Percy Miller), ex–New Orleans street hustler and University of Houston dropout turned country MC and rap mogul, has been selling hundreds of thousands of records since opening his No Limit operation in 1990. His self-promoted and financed *Ice Cream Man* sold 300,000 copies with no visibility outside the South. He has had similar regional success with his signees Mia X, TRU, and Mr. Serv-On, controlling all aspects of their marketing and promotion, and has a distribution deal with that longtime supporter of non–New York rap, Priority.

Master P, who had already made his mark the old-fashioned hip hop way, then made a bold futuristic move. He wanted to make a movie but received nothing but skepticism from the film industry. Working with his protégé, director-writer Moon Jones, Master P created *I Bout It*, a raw tale of the drug life in New Orleans, augmented on a home videotape by a few music videos and some X-rated action. The tape never made it to theaters, but it was the home video phenomenon of summer 1997. It topped the music video sales chart and challenged Hollywood products like *Jerry Maguire* for the top spot on *Billboard*'s Video Scan chart. While Hollywood blacks moaned about lack of distribution, Master P showed that a gutsy, aggressive black businessman could reach his audience outside the regular distribution channels. Cinematically, *I Bout It* is extremely crude. He's no Spielberg or Scorsese, yet Master P has shown himself to be an-up-by-his-bootstraps Booker T. Washington disciple, which, in this era of corporate control, makes him both a throwback and a visionary.

The crack epidemic that overwhelmed America has abated. Aggressive policing and a major change in how it's sold (clocking on curbs has been replaced by indoor trafficking) have brought crime down all over the country. In response, the tenor of hip hop culture has softened. Rap records with R&B choruses, female vocalists performing over hip hop beats, and dance-oriented records abound. Times are still tough for most black folk during Bill Clinton's second term, yet there is a yearning for a more humanistic, less nihilistic, but still acquisitive future reflected in the current music.

Though hip hop dancers haven't returned to spinning on their heads, movement is again central to the culture with dancers, nasty and otherwise, appearing in videos and stage shows, adding energy and sex appeal. People are sweating in designer clothes (or well-done knockoffs) as dressing down to go out has faded. Where Nike warm-ups once ruled, Dolce & Gabbana T-shirts can now be found. Once high-top fades and, later, bald heads were the official garb of basketball players. Now Allen Iverson's elaborate '70s throwback cornrow hair is the new cutting edge of athletic hair care. Young brothers contemplate whether to follow his lead, while old schoolers wonder, "Where there are men with braided hair, can Afros be far behind?" Out in Cali, young Kobe Bryant is already there with an Afro as fresh (in the old hip hop sense) as his game.

In music, Iverson's stylistic peer is D'Angelo, the soulful crooner who sports cornrows while displaying a falsetto and keyboard touch that recalls uncut soul music. Many feel this singer, who, like Iverson, was born and raised in Virginia, is the future of black music. (Between Iverson, D'Angelo, Timbaland, Missy Elliott, and recent resident Teddy Riley, Virginia, of all places, is looking like the new cutting edge.) While D'Angelo's promise remains to be fulfilled, the anticipation surrounding his career speaks to a quietly insistent question: What will come after hip hop? Since the '60s, musical and cultural trends have risen and burned with blazing speed.

Yet hip hop endures. Despite the vaguely liberal rhetoric of the Clinton presidency, poverty has not receded, the schools have deteriorated, drug addiction has changed—from crack to marijuana and heroin—but hasn't abated, and the class schisms in the country are naked.

This is all terrible for the social fabric of the nation, but it is prime fodder for the makers and consumers of edgy, aggressive culture. The truth is that hip hop—in its many guises—has reflected (and internalized) our society's woes so evocatively that it has grown from minority expression to mainstream appreciation. Our nation's clothes, our language, our standards for entertainment, our sexuality, and our role models are just a few items that have been affected by hip hop's existence. This thing labeled hip hop has simply been in the middle of much, and nothing at

the turn of the century has changed that. The allegiance of its true believers is deep and looks to be lifelong. The mainstream—that majority
of Americans of all colors for whom culture is a commodity and not a
calling—seems far from exhausted by it.

The long-term direction of America, and hip hop's role in it, will be
decided by two very different factors. First, the state of America's soul.
Will a commitment to social justice, to nonpolarizing politics and old-
fashioned community resurface? If so, such a humanist movement would
certainly alter the culture, perhaps spawning a musical movement as optimistic as the golden days of Motown. Don't hold your breath.

The second unknowable factor is the taste of twenty-first-century
teens. They will find hip hop artifacts everywhere—videos, CDs, Web
sites—and what will they think of them? At some point they will likely
react as teens have always ultimately reacted to the passions of their
elders—they'll shout, "It's boring!" and move on.

One day in the year 2005, 2010, 2020, all this fun and fury will seem
as antiquated as spats and big bands do to us. The next generation may
reject hip hop for the next sweeping cultural trend. And, by the logic of
pop culture, they are actually supposed to.

But, whether they like it or not, they'll know there once was a hip hop
America.

Word.

sources / further reading

PUBLICATIONS

In terms of magazines, I looked at all the obvious suspects (*Vibe, Source, Rap Pages, Rolling Stone, Musician, Billboard*) as well as plenty of respectable mainstream publications (*New York Times, Daily News, Los Angeles Times, Time, Newsweek*) and that font of eternal wisdom, the *Village Voice*.

Off the main track, *Premiere, Amsterdam News, Black Enterprise, Essence,* and the United Kingdom's *Melody Maker* and *New Music Express* aided the process.

BOOKS

I dipped back into all my books (even those not still in print) and quite a few others.

Adler, B. *Tougher Than Leather: The Authorized Biography of Run-D.M.C.* New York: Signet, 1987.

Adler, William M. *Land of Opportunity: One Family's Quest for the American Dream in the Age of Crack.* New York: Atlantic Monthly Press, 1995.

Beadle, Jeremy J. *Will Pop Eat Itself?* London: Faber and Faber, 1993.

Benjamin, Daniel K. and Roger Leroy Miller. *Undoing Drugs.* New York: Basic Books, 1991.

Block, Fred, ed., *The Mean Season: The Attack on the Welfare State.* New York: Pantheon, 1987.

Campbell, Luther, and John R. Miller. *As Nasty As They Wanna Be: The Uncensored Story of Luther Campbell of the 2 Live Crew.* New York: Barricade Books, 1992.

Christgau, Bob. *Christgau's Record Guide: The '80s.* New York: Pantheon, 1990.

Cross, Brian. *It's Not About a Salary: Rap, Race + Resistance in Los Angeles.* New York: Verso, 1993.

Gillespie, Dizzy. *To Be or Not . . . To Bop.* New York: Doubleday, 1979.

Goff, Stanley, and Robert Sanders with Clark Smith. *Brothers: Black Soldiers in the Nam.* Novato, CA: Presidio Press, 1982.

Goodman, Fred. *The Mansion on the Hill.* New York: Times Books, 1997.

Hager, Steven. *Hip Hop: The Illustrated History of Break Dancing, Rap Music, and Graffiti.* New York: St. Martin's, 1984.

Ianni, Francis. *Black Mafia: Ethnic Succession in Organized Crime.* New York: Simon & Schuster, 1974.

Katz, Jack. *Seductions of Crime.* New York: Basic Books, 1988.

Lapham, Lewis H. *Money and Class in America.* New York: Ballantine, 1989.

Lusane, Clarence. *Pipe Dream Blues: Racism and the War on Drugs.* Boston: South End Press, 1991.

Murray, Albert. *Stomping the Blues.* New York: McGraw-Hill, 1976.

Peck, Abe, ed., *Dancing Madness.* New York: Rolling Stone/Anchor, 1976.

Perkins, William Eric, ed., *Droppin' Science: Critical Essays on Rap Music and Hip Hop Culture.* Philadelphia: Temple University Press, 1996.

Rose, Tricia. *Black Noise: Rap Music and Black Culture in Contemporary America.* Hanover, NH: University Press of New England, 1994.

Sister Souljah. *No Disrespect.* New York: Times Books, 1994; Vintage, 1996.

Tate, Greg. *Flyboy in the Buttermilk: Essays on Contemporary America.* New York: Fireside, 1992.

Toop, David. *The Rap Attack: African Jive to New York Hip Hop.* Boston: South End Press, 1984.

Williams, Terry. *Crackhouse: Notes from the End of the Line.* Reading, MA: Addison Wesley, 1992.

MEMORIES

My primary resources for *Hip Hop America* were the clippings and interviews I've collected over the years, a potential bonfire of papers in the den. I looked back on interviews I did during my *Billboard* tenure and my old column there, "The Rhythm & the Blues." I also looked at a lot of music videos from the '70s to remind me of the gear and the style of a particular pop moment.

Mostly this is a book of memory. Recalling an incident or a person would jog my mind and send it flowing into thoughts of the past and how that affected the future. This was a difficult book to write—because of my personal involvement with some of the events and people, it was sometimes hard to get the distance to understand their contribution (or lack thereof). I had to stop writing about music full-time to be able to write *Hip Hop America*—strange but true.

Also, time had to pass. When I began to seriously write this book the gangsta phase was receding, which made me happy. I hoped that twenty years after it had debuted on record that hip hop's logical conclusion wouldn't be gory depictions of self-genocide. That would have saddened me. Not that everything is "mop & glow" right now, but every new age creates new possibilities and I feel we're at the verge of some fresh (in the old hip hop sense) energy.

acknowledgments

I want to thank my many music editors over the years: Radcliff Joe, Roman Kozack, and Adam White at *Billboard;* Peter Keepnews at *Record World;* Barbara Nellis at *Playboy;* Doug Simmons, Joe Levy, Bob "the Dean" Christgau at the *Village Voice.*

Peace to my favorite colleagues Lisa Jones, Barry Michael Cooper, Greg Tate, Carol Cooper, and others I kicked it with in the reading room on Thirteenth and Broadway.

To the new jacks—Kevin Powell, Toure, and Joan Morgan—keep on doin' what cha doin'.

Much love to Russell Simmons, Chris Rock, Sean Daniel, Bill Stephney, Lee Davis, Ann Carli, Mtume and Reggie Hudlin for enduring friendships filled with insights and arguments.

To everyone I've ever dissed in a review, let it be known I always tried to be fair.

To Stephen Barnes, Brian Siberell, Scott Gilden, and Sarah Lazin, thanks for keeping my business tight.

Love to my girls—Arizona, Ebonee, Amber, Jade, and Andrea too!

This is my fifth book with Wendy Wolf and it just keeps getting better.

The best of health to Robert "Rocky" Ford who first put me in this unpredictable game.

And to the scores who've put up with me while I was writing, sorry for being short on the phone but, hey, I'm through now!

index

freebase, 39–40
Fresh, Doug E., 187
Fresh, Hip Hop Don't Stop (Flinker), 157
Fresh Fest, 131
Fresh Prince (Will Smith), 54, 61, 73, 82, 109, 111, 119, 131, 208
Friday Night Videos, 98
Front National (FN), 205–6
Fuchs, Michael, 190
"Fuck Compton," 136
Furious Five, 19–20, 40, 60, 106, 194

G, Warren, 82
Gamble, Kenny, 7, 125
gangs, 18, 160
gangsta rap (reality rap), 44–49, 136, 138, 143, 168, 188–90
  crack and, 42–43, 49
  hearing on, 188–89
  incarceration and, 44
  LaRock and, 45–46
  narrative strategies in, 46–47
"Gangsta's Paradise," 64
George, Nelson, 208
Germany, 204
Geto Boys, 136, 190
ghetto glamour, 119, 121, 122
GhettOriginals, 14
Gibson, Pam, 100
Gillespie, Dizzy, 201
"Gin & Juice," 64
Glover, Melvin (Melle Mel), 19, 20, 40, 46, 61, 98, 194, 195
Glover, Nathanial (Kidd Creole), 19, 20, 194–95
Goines, Donald, 36–37
"Good Times," 93
Gordy, Berry, xi, xii, 81–82, 83, 125
graffiti, 11–14, 20, 33, 99, 203
Grammy Awards, 8–9
Grandmaster Caz, 196–97
Grandmaster Dee, 73
Grandmaster Flash, xiii, 16, 17, 19–20, 26, 40, 52, 57, 60, 106, 107, 209
Grand Puba, 67, 69, 161–62, 170
Grand Wizard Theodore, 17, 19
Grier, Pam, 104
Griff, Professor (William Griffen), 58, 173
Griffin, Gene, 115–16, 118
Gums, Willie, 27–28
guns, 42

Guru, MC, 40
Guy, 117, 118, 127

Haine, La (*Hate*), 206
hairstyles, 211
Hall, Aaron, 117, 118
Hammer, MC, 54, 62, 95, 111, 113, 119
Hancock, Herbie, 61
Harrell, Andre, 73, 84, 114–15, 118–20, 123–24, 126–27, 141
Harris, Michael, 142–43
HE (Harrell Entertainment), 127
Heavy D., 118, 119, 120, 121, 122, 173, 198
Heller, Jerry, 135, 139
Herc, Kool, xiii, 16, 17, 18, 19, 20, 25–27, 57, 107, 195
heroin, 34–35, 36–38, 41, 42
Hilfiger, Andy, 162
Hilfiger, Tommy, 85, 161–62
Himes, Chester, 168
Hinojosa, Jorge, 135
hip hop:
  bubblegum, 65
  old school of, xv, 20–21, 29, 196–97, 203
  origins of, xiii, 7, 57, 194–95
"Hip Hop Hooray," 63
Hirogifics Posse, 74
Holloway House novels, 36
Hollywood, DJ, 24, 194, 195–96
Holyfield, Evander, 54–55
homosexuality, 44
Hoop Dreams, 108–9
House of Pain, 63
House Party I, 110
"How Ya Like Me Now," 116
How Ya Like Me Now, 198
Hudlin, Reggie and Warrington, 100, 110
Huff, Leon, 7
Hughes, Allen and Albert, 34, 74
Hughes, Langston, 130
Human Beat Box (Darren "Buffy" Robinson), 56, 57
"Humpty Dance," 62
Hunter, Paul, 100
Hurston, Zora Neale, 179
Hutchins, Jalil, 72–73
Hutson, Rolando, 100

"I," 51, 52
I Bout It, 210
Iceberg Slim, 36, 167, 168